The Past in the Present

The Past in the Present brings together, for the first time, contemporary ideas from both the psychoanalytic and humanistic therapy traditions, looking at how trauma and enactments affect therapeutic practice.

Enactments are often experienced as a crisis in therapy and are understood as symbolic interactions between the client and therapist, where personal issues of both parties become unconsciously entwined. This is arguably especially true if the client has undergone some form of trauma. This trauma becomes enacted in the therapy and becomes a turning point that significantly influences the course of therapy, sometimes with creative or even destructive effect.

Using a wealth of clinical material throughout, the contributors show how therapists from different therapeutic orientations are thinking about and working with enactments in therapy, how trauma enactment can affect the therapeutic relationship and how both therapist and client can use it to positive effect.

The Past in the Present will be invaluable to practitioners and students of analytic and humanistic psychotherapy, psychoanalysis, analytic psychology and counselling.

David Mann is a consultant psychotherapist for an NHS Trust in Tunbridge Wells and also works in private practice as a psychoanalytic psychotherapist and supervisor. His previous books include: *Psychotherapy: An Erotic Relationship* (1997), *Erotic Transference and Countertransference* (1999) and *Love and Hate: Psychoanalytic Perspectives* (2002).

Valerie Cunningham works in private practice as a qualified art psychotherapist and transactional analysis psychotherapist and supervisor in Tunbridge Wells. She has 12 years' experience as a core tutor on both humanistic counselling and psychotherapy courses and is registered with the HPC, UKCP and the BACP.

The Past in the Present

Therapy enactments and the return of trauma

**Edited by David Mann and
Valerie Cunningham**

Routledge
Taylor & Francis Group

LONDON AND NEW YORK

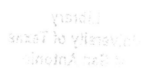

First published 2009
by Routledge
27 Church Road, Hove, East Sussex BN3 2FA

Simultaneously published in the USA and Canada
by Routledge
270 Madison Avenue, New York, NY 10016

*Routledge is an imprint of the Taylor & Francis Group, an informa
business*

Typeset in Times by Garfield Morgan, Mumbles, Swansea
Printed and bound in Great Britain by TJ International Ltd, Padstow,
Cornwall
Paperback cover image: "Moonstruck" by Jim Dales, in the collection
of the artist
Paperback cover design by Design Deluxe

This publication has been produced with paper manufactured to strict
environmental standards and with pulp derived from sustainable
forests.

British Library Cataloguing in Publication Data
A catalogue record for this book is available from the British Library

Library of Congress Cataloging-in-Publication Data
The past in the present : therapy enactments and the return of trauma
/ edited by David Mann & Valerie Cunningham.
    p. ; cm.
  ISBN 978-0-415-43369-3 (hardback) – ISBN 978-0-415-43370-9
(pbk.) 1. Psychotherapist and patient. 2. Acting out (Psychology) 3.
Psychic trauma. 4. Psychoanalysis. 5. Humanistic psychotherapy. I.
Mann, David, 1954– II. Cunningham, Valerie, 1943–
  [DNLM: 1. Role Playing. 2. Stress Disorders, Traumatic—therapy.
WM 172 P291 2008]
  RC480.8.P35 2008
  616.89'14—dc22
                                                        2008008128

ISBN 978-0-415-43369-3 (hbk)
ISBN 978-0-415-43370-9 (pbk)

From David to Michelle, Mark and Peter with much love

Love from Valerie to Dylan, Echo and Lindsay, friends and family

Contents

List of Contributors

Marie Adams is an integrative psychotherapist, trainer and supervisor with a private practice in London. She is currently conducting doctoral research into the influence of the therapist's process on the psychotherapeutic dyad.

Caroline Case is a child psychotherapist (SIHR) working in a Child and Family Mental Health Service in the NHS in Bristol. She is also an analytical art therapist working in private practive. She has published widely on art psychotherapy, including *The Handbook of Art Therapy* (Routledge, 1992, 2nd ed. 2006) and *Art Therapy with Children: From Infancy to Adolescence* (Routledge, 2008), both with Tessa Dalley; *Imagining Animals: Art, Psychotherapy and Primitive States of Mind* (Routledge, 2005); and with Joy Schaverien, *Supervision of Art Psychotherapy: a Theoretical and Practical Handbook* (Routledge, 2007).

William F. Cornell maintains an independent private practice of therapy, consultation and training in Pittsburgh, PA. He studied behavioral psychology at Reed College in Portland, Oregon, and phenomenological psychology at Duquesne University in Pittsburgh, PA, following his graduate studies with training in transactional analysis and body-centered psychotherapy. Bill has published numerous journal articles and book chapters, many exploring the interface between TA, body-centered and psychoanalytic modalities. He is editor of the ITAA *Script* newsletter and co-editor of the *Transactional Analysis Journal*. He edited *The Healer's Bent: Solitude and Dialogue in the Clinical Encounter*, a collection of the psychoanalytic writings of James McLaughlin, and is co-editor and author, with Helena Hargaden, of *From Transactions to Relations: The Emergence of Relational Paradigms in Transactional Analysis* (Haddon Press). He is the author of the forthcoming *Explorations in Transactional Analysis* and *The Impassioned Body*. He often leads training groups in Europe. E-mail: bcornell@nauticom.net

Valerie Cunningham is a counsellor and trainer who graduated from the RA Schools for Fine Art before studying art psychotherapy and transactional analysis psychotherapy and supervision. She is an experienced tutor on both humanistic counselling and psychotherapy courses. She has published in counselling and psychotherapy periodicals and has designed and presented courses and workshops in the UK and at international conferences. E-mail: valcunningham@talktalk.net

Louise Embleton Tudor trained at the Minster Centre for Analytic and Humanistic Psychotherapy, London. She taught humanistic psychology at the Minster Centre for three years and co-founded Temenos in Sheffield where she is a director, course tutor on its diploma course and facilitator of the human development module on its postgraduate/MSc course. She is the author of a number of articles and chapters in the field of mental health and psychotherapy and a co-author (with others associated with Temenos) of *The Person-Centred Approach: A Contemporary Introduction* (Palgrave, 2004). She has her own clinical practice offering counselling, psychotherapy and supervision. She is particularly interested in infant and child development, politics in general and specifically the politics of therapy.

Celia Harding is a psychoanalytic psychotherapist in private practice in East London. She trained with the Westminster Pastoral Foundation, and she is a member and Training Therapist of the Foundation for Psychotherapy and Counselling (FPC). She organised ten post-qualification courses for FPC members on the basis of which she edited two selections of papers: *Sexuality: Psychoanalytic Perspectives* (Brunner-Routledge, 2001) and *Aggression and Destructiveness: Psychoanalytic Perspectives* (Routledge, 2006). She is a founder member of the Association for Psychotherapy in East London.

Raymond Kenward is a UKCP-registered existential psychotherapist and consultant chartered counselling psychologist. He manages a large NHS Primary Care Psychology and Counselling Service in his native Kent. In addition he maintains a small private psychotherapy practice. He is the co-author, with Emmy van Deurzen, of the *Dictionary of Existential Psychotherapy and Counselling* (Sage, 2005). He lives in the remote countryside with his wife Daniela.

Alison Knight-Evans is a principal adult psychotherapist, St George's Eating Disorders Service, London and in private practice. She is a psychoanalytic member of the British Association of Psychotherapists.

David Mann is a consultant psychotherapist for an NHS Trust in Kent and also works in private practice in Tunbridge Wells. He is a psychoanalytic psychotherapist and supervisor and a member of the London Centre for Psychotherapy, registered with both the BPC and the UKCP, as well as a Registered Art Therapist. He has published extensively in psychotherapy journals and has run a workshop on 'Working with the erotic transference' around Europe. His previous books include: *Psychotherapy: An Erotic Relationship, Transference and Countertransference Passions* (1997), also published in German (Klett-Cotta Press, 1999). He edited *Erotic Transference and Countertransference: Clinical Practice in Psychotherapy* (1999) and *Love and Hate: Psychoanalytic Perspectives* (2002), all published by Brunner-Routledge. In his spare time he is lead singer and guitarist with the Freudian Slips. Website: www.counsellingtherapy southeast.co.uk.

Patricia Marsden is a consultant adult psychotherapist and Head of Psychology and Psychotherapies, St George's Eating Disorders Service, London. She is a psychoanalytic psychotherapy member of the Foundation for Psychotherapy and Counselling, and has published a number of articles on eating disorders.

Janet McDermott is an Asian woman writer, trainer and counsellor from Sheffield, who currently works as a counsellor for refugees and asylum seekers and as a young women's therapist. Her professional background is in teaching and black women's self-help organisations, and her skills and experience lie in working with identity and difference, and creating new representations of contemporary experience. Her first novel, *Yasmin*, was a commission from Mantra Publishers published in 1992.

Keith Tudor is a qualified social worker and psychotherapist. He has a small private/independent practice in Sheffield offering therapy, supervision and consultancy and, in addition to being a director of Temenos, is a proprietor of the Sheffield Natural Health Centre. He is a widely published author in the fields of mental health, psychotherapy and counselling, including five books: *Mental Health Promotion* (Routledge, 1996); *Group Counselling* (Sage, 1999); with Tony Merry, the *Dictionary of Person-Centred Psychology* (Whurr, 2002); with others associated with Temenos, *The Person-Centred Approach: A Contemporary Introduction* (Palgrave, 2004); and, with Mike Worrall, *Person-Centred Therapy: A Clinical Philosophy* (Routledge, 2006). He has edited two books: *Transactional Approaches to Brief Therapy* (Sage, 2002); and (with Mike Worrall) *Freedom to Practise: Person-Centred Approaches to Supervision* (PCCS Books, 2004); and is the series editor of Advancing Theory in Therapy (published by Routledge).

Penny Webster is a psychotherapist in private practice in Benoni, South Africa. She qualified as a clinical psychologist at the University of Johannesburg, South Africa in 1989, received her PhD from Rhodes University in Grahamstown, South Africa in 2004 and received a diploma in integrative psychotherapy from the Sherwood Institute, UK in 2006. She is a member of The Psychological Society of South Africa, the South African Psychoanalysis Initiative and the Johannesburg Psychoanalytic Psychotherapy Study Groups.

Christina Wieland is a psychoanalytic psychotherapist in private practice and a visiting fellow of the Centre for Psychoanalytic Studies, University of Essex. Her book, *The Undead Mother: Psychoanalytic Explorations of Masculinity, Femininity and Matricide*, was published by Karnac in 2002.

Acknowledgements

David Mann would like first and foremost to express his thanks to his clients who have helped him understand the complexities of the therapeutic relationship better. In addition he would like to thank Michelle MacGrath who has contributed so much in so many different ways to this book.

Valerie Cunningham gives her unreserved appreciation and gratitude to all her clients past and present. Also, she would like to thank Elizabeth Imlay especially for her unstinting patience, guidance and encouragement.

We would also both like to thank Senior Editor Joanne Forshaw and all the staff at Routledge who have helped prepare this book.

1   Introduction

David Mann and Valerie Cunningham

Prologue: 'The Murder of Gonzago'

The pivotal scene in Shakespeare's *Hamlet* is the play-within-a-play, 'The Murder of Gonzago'. Up until this point the tension between the protagonists has been mounting but has not spilt over into action. Hamlet's father has died, his ghost has returned to say he was killed by his brother, Claudius, who has then married the Queen and Hamlet's mother, Gertrude, thereby denying Hamlet the right to succeed as king. The chance arrival of a group of actors gives Hamlet the opportunity to set a trap to 'catch the conscience of the king'. He gets the players to act a play which reproduces the murder of a king by his brother, followed by the seduction of the queen. Hamlet's plan works, but he unleashes in himself and others more than he bargained for. After watching 'The Murder of Gonzago', all the characters are moved to express their emotions in action and thus the tragedy unfolds. Hamlet, less bothered about the death of his father and missing out on the crown, now confronts his mother with the issue that has really been bothering him: his mother's sexual relationship to his uncle; his unconscious intention had been to 'catch the conscience' of the queen. This leads to the murder of the king's Lord Chamberlain, Polonius, whose daughter then goes mad and commits suicide. Her brother wants to kill Hamlet, and Claudius himself now knows how dangerous Hamlet is and sets about to plot his death. None of this works out as expected which results in the deaths of all the leading protagonists: Hamlet, Gertrude and Claudius.

As psychologically insightful into human nature as Shakespeare was, we are not suggesting he discovered the psychoanalytic idea of enactment. What the play-within-a-play does illustrate, however, is a viable description of how enactments work. If, as editors, we take a little artistic licence, we could suggest that Hamlet, like the psychotherapist, sets in motion procedures over which he has some understanding and influence; Claudius and Gertrude, as patients, have no idea what is coming. Enactments have the qualities of a play-within-a-play in as much as they release the unexpected and unconscious into action, which decisively alters events in the therapy which may then have either a benign or malign effect on the therapy. Enactments, just like the play-within-a-play, push unconscious processes into expression, initiate actions, and alter the course of the therapy. We might also add that watching 'The Murder of Gonzago' revisits or reawakens the trauma that all the protagonists have experienced. The important difference, however, is that it is not the original event itself, but rather a symbolic representation, a trigger that sets off associations as in Post Traumatic Stress Syndrome. An enactment occupies a similar status: a symbolic representation that seems close enough to the original trauma, which then envelopes both the therapist and the patient. In *Hamlet*, 'The Murder of Gonzago' reveals just how unaware all the protagonists have actually been; enactments in psychotherapy demonstrate just how unaware the patient and the therapist have been. The therapist, like Hamlet, might have knowledge of the unconscious processes that therapy is likely to activate – for example, transference and countertransference – and might even anticipate enactments, but will never be entirely conscious of how this will unfold in any particular relationship. Even if therapists anticipate an enactment, they can never know when and how it will happen or what form it will take. They might be able to foresee something of how the patient's trauma may open up, but they cannot know their own unconscious involvement beforehand. Like Hamlet, the therapist experiences a mixture of the expected and the unexpected; and like Hamlet, the therapist's blind spots and unconscious processes play a significant part in how the enactment develops and resolves. We would like to stress, though, that *Hamlet* deals with enactments as a tragedy which leads to disaster for the leading protagonists. It is our view that enactments, unlike Shakespeare's play, do not always mean a tragic result, but can indeed, have a powerful therapeutic effect.

The psychoanalytic and the humanistic psychotherapy traditions

It was after a particularly taxing, though stimulating, clinical discussion, that Valerie Cunningham spontaneously remarked: 'I wish I knew how other psychotherapists think and feel about times of enactment with clients, let alone how they manage them.' Out of this chance remark came the idea for this book. In brief, we thought we would invite psychotherapists, who used a broad variety of models, to contribute their ideas on the subjects of enactment and trauma and present them in book form. We were interested in both the theoretical underpinning to the therapists' understanding of the process of enactment, and in all the questions which enactments raise. Also, we hoped to gain insight from sharing with our contributors the way they hold their psyches intact, and metaphorically hold their clients' psyches too, in order to maintain the focus and purpose of their work.

One of our starting points was that enactments seem to occur in all kinds of therapies regardless of the therapist's theoretical orientation. We therefore decided to opt for a range of therapeutic perspectives covering a range of therapies currently being practised in both the psychoanalytic and humanistic traditions. As editors, we ourselves represent these therapeutic trends. Though both of us had previously trained as art therapists our development differed after that.

David Mann had a background in Jungian analytic psychology before going on to train in British Object Relations ideas in psychoanalysis. Becoming particularly interested in the transference and countertransference led slowly to a more Freudian perspective influenced by the Intersubjective ideas coming from America. The evolution of these ideas can be followed in his various publications about Eros in the therapeutic relationship (see Mann, 1994, 1997, 1999, 2001, 2002).

Valerie Cunningham's background is in the creative arts, transactional analysis, and Jungian analytic psychology. In her training as an art psychotherapist, the unconscious components underlying communications, as evidenced by transference and countertransference reactions, were no less central than they were in her analytic psychotherapy experience. In her early experience of being in a transactional analysis group, the therapist focused on an interactive style which emphasised open communication with group members. Central TA concepts: the tripartite ego state model of Parent, Adult and Child, transaction games and script theory provided further perspectives towards understanding both the interpersonal and the intrapsychic dynamics of relationships.

Both the psychoanalytic and the humanistic traditions, separately and independently from each other, had been evolving towards the contemplation of similar material. For example, surprisingly to us now, Freud worked in fact in an openly relational style. He socialised with his clients in a way that would be frowned on today by most reputable trainers, and was similarly responsive to clients in clinical settings. His writings on analytic technique, however, contradicted his actions. We suspect that he had already mastered the analytic techniques so well that he became more confident about being spontaneous himself. He thought he could do whatever he wanted, whereas he preferred that others did what he taught. However, Lipton (1997, 1983) believed that Freud's followers in America, in order to gain acceptance of the model, electively practised Freud's techniques in a more restrained manner with the aim of avoiding any criticism about possible sexual activity between client and analyst.

An important additional perspective which challenged accepted analytical theories focused on the early development of parent-child relationships. The work of Bowlby (1969, 1973, 1979, 1980) and Ainsworth et al. (1978) culminated in the theory of Attachment and Loss following the study of the effects on children when they became reluctantly separated from their caregivers. This direct observation of the non-verbal, behavioural interactions between infants and parents provides considerable reinforcement for the theory of attachment.

In the 1940s the Humanistic movement became established, some of its main exponents being Carl Rogers, Fritz and Laura Perls and Eric Berne.

Each challenged orthodox methods by developing personal theories and techniques, and each of them did so after studying classical models. Often, socialising with clients and inappropriate sexual activity were mixed up in the new wave of therapies. Current trends suggest that inter-linking circles have formed among proponents of the analytic and humanistic schools. One circle is formed by some analysts who, determined to break with tradition, have insisted on working in an intersubjective way with their clients. They believe that the work cannot be authentic if analysts hold back from owning their side of the relationship dynamics; instead, they openly explore their internal experiences with their clients (Lipton, 1977, 1983; McLaughlin, 1987; Ghent, 1995).

Some TA psychotherapists are returning to the Freudian roots of the model's founder, Berne, and working with unconscious processes as revealed by mutually emanating transferences (Moiso, 1985; Novellino, 1984). Others have immersed themselves in analytical psychotherapies in such a way as to experience transference directly. They are also risking new ways to be with their clients. They rely on the genuineness of the therapeutic relationship as being the most important curative factor (Cornell and Bonds-White, 2001; Hargaden and Sills, 2002; Summers and Tudor, 2000). This is self-disclosure not for the purposes of personal gratification but as a means of honouring, at all levels, the two-sided nature of the undertaking (Cornell and Hargaden, 2005). We consider this approach worthwhile, though fraught with risks and requiring considerable restraint, discipline and personal self-knowledge, so that boundaries can be ethically and therapeutically maintained. It is essential that the therapist should take the major responsibility for any failure in using this collaborative approach, if untrained clients are involved, as they often have little or no experience for what lies ahead. In the case of both parties being trained in therapy, it is reasonable that each should bear some responsibility.

Definitions about enactments in analytic circles appear diverse, but without exception all are based in the transferential-countertransferential domain. In the 1980s, a plethora of analysts based in the USA wrote a series of papers which explored the meaning of this term by reconsidering the differences between 'acting out' and 'enactment'. Analysts who were most interested in examining the results of unconscious communication between both analyst and patient include courageous self-disclosing public accounts of their work. We are beholden to all our contributors who researched this subject and especially to Cornell (2007) for his American analytic investigations, who cites McLaughlin as being at the forefront in writing comprehensively about enactments (1987, 1991, 1994, 2005).

The importance of enactments

The relatively recent discussion about enactments in the last 15 years opens up a much more interactive way of viewing the relationship between therapist and patient. Enactments are a bridge between the patient's transference and the therapist's countertransference. By understanding the processes of enactments better we begin to understand how the subtle relationship between transference and countertransference works in clinical practice. The concept of enactments provides a framework for comprehending the unconscious processes in therapy which affect both the participants. Having a greater awareness of how enactments work can only enhance our clinical practice about how the patient's material becomes wound up and tangled with the therapist's own issues and vice versa. While there will clearly be times when it is useful to continue to think in terms of transference and countertransference and thereby make a distinction between the client and therapist's unconscious, the concept of enactments sign-posts our attention in the direction of how the unconscious 'other' may resonate between two people.

Upon reading these chapters we find that repeatedly the therapist's unconscious process leads to a break in aspects of the therapeutic frame: missed sessions, changing times, disclosure for lectures or publishing and so forth. Of course the most obvious way to avoid enactment would be for therapists to become more perfect and faultless in their practice! This would indeed be possible if the therapist's own unconscious processes could be taken out of therapeutic practice. However, in reality this is neither possible nor indeed desirable.

If the practice of psychotherapy is going to be 'good enough', rather than ideal, then understanding enactments lets us see more carefully how the client and therapist impact each other. This is why the thinking about enactments is both so useful and timely to understand unconscious mechanisms better. Our understanding from Winnicott (1958) is that it is developmentally helpful if an infant or a patient experiences some degree of parental or therapeutic failure as a way of putting omnipotent fantasies into perspective. We believe this is true. But not all patients or infants are able to deal with such failings. This is especially true if the client or the therapist has a history of trauma. Such therapeutic failings are experienced as cataclysmic and annihilatory. It should not be thought that we are recommending that enactments are always a good thing. Actually they can affect the therapy in negative and destructive ways. The point about enactments is that at some point they may need to be considered because they are common enough in clinical practice.

In conclusion we recognise the courage of our contributors in writing about enactments in their clinical practice. It remains the case that psychotherapists of all theoretical orientations find it easier to write about their clients than to write about their own difficulties with the work. A passage from Bunyan's *The Pilgrim's Progress* comes to mind:

Hobgoblin nor foul fiend
Can daunt his spirit:

He knows he at the end
Shall life inherit.
Then, fancies, flee away!
I'll fear not what men say,
I'll labour night and day
To be a pilgrim.

In essence the therapist is faced with a similar struggle to that of Bunyan's pilgrim Mr Valient-for-truth: it takes a lot of courage to fight demons, especially the internal kind that harbour doubts.

References

Ainsworth, M., Blehar, M., Waters, E. and Wall, S. (1978) *Patterns of Attachment: Assessed in the Strange Situation and at Home*. Hillsdale, NJ: Lawrence Erlbaum.

Bowlby, J. (1969) *Attachment and Loss*, vol. 1, *Attachment*. London: Hogarth Press.

Bowlby, J. (1973) *Attachment and Loss*, vol. 2, *Separation: Anxiety and Anger*. London: Hogarth Press.

Bowlby, J. (1979) *The Making and Breaking of Affectional Bonds*. London: Tavistock Publications.

Bowlby, J. (1980) *Attachment and Loss*, vol. 3, *Loss: Sadness and Depression*. London: Hogarth Press.

Bunyan, J. (1966) *The Pilgrim's Progress from This World to That Which Is to Come*, 1678 ed. Keeble, NH: World's Classics, OUP.

Cornell, W. F. & Bonds-White, F. (2001) Therapeutic relatedness: the truth of love or the love of truth. *Transactional Analysis Journal*, 31: 71–83.

Cornell, W. and Hargaden, H. (2005) *From Transactions to Relations: The Emergence of a Relational Tradition in Transactional Analysis*. Chadlington, UK: Haddon Press.

Cornell, W. F. (in press) *The Past in the Present: Therapy Enactments and the Return of Trauma*. Hove, UK: Brunner-Routledge.

Ghent, E. (1995) Interaction in the psychoanalytic situation. *Psychoanalytic Dialogues*, 5: 479–492.

Hargaden, H. and Sills, C. (2002) *Transactional Analysis: A Relational Perspective*. Hove, UK: Brunner-Routledge.

Lipton, S. (1977) The advantages of Freud's technique as shown in his analysis of The Rat Man. *International Journal of Psychoanalysis*, 58: 255–274.

Lipton, S. (1983) A critique of the so-called standard psycho-analytic technique. *Contemporary Psychoanalysis*, 19: 35–45.

Mann, D. (1994) The psychotherapist's erotic subjectivity. *British Journal of Psychotherapy*, 10(3): 344–354.

Mann, D. (1997) *Psychotherapy: An Erotic Relationship, Transference and Countertransference Passions*. London: Routledge.

Mann, D. (1999) *Erotic Transference and Countertransference: Clinical Practice in Psychotherapy*. London: Routledge.

Mann, D. (2001) Erotics and ethics: the passionate dilemmas of the therapeutic couple. In Barnes, F.P. and Murdin, L. (eds), *Values and Ethics in the Practice of Psychotherapy and Counselling*. Buckingham, UK: Open University Press.

Mann, D. (2002) *Love and Hate: Psychoanalytic Perspectives*. London: Routledge.

McLaughlin, J. T. (1987) The play of transference: some reflections on enactment in the psychoanalytic situation. *Journal of the American Psychoanalytic Association*, 39: 557–582.

McLaughlin, J. T. (1991) Clinical and theoretical aspects of enactment. *Journal of the American Psychoanalytic Association*, 39: 595–614.

McLaughlin, J. T. (1994) Analytic impasse: the interplay of dyadic transferences. Paper presented to The Karen Horney Psychoanalytic Institute and Center & The Association for the Advancement of Psychoanalysis, 5 March.

McLaughlin, J. T. (2005) *The Healer's Bent: Solitude and Dialogue in the Clinical Encounter*. Hillsdale, NJ: The Analytic Press.

Moiso, C. (1985) Ego states and transference. *Transactional Analysis Journal*, 15(3): 194.

Novellino, M. (1984) The analysis of countertransference. *Transactional Analysis Journal*, 14: 63–67.

Summers, G. and Tudor, K. (2000) Co-creative Transactional Analysis. *Transactional Analysis Journal*, 30: 23–40.

Winnicott, D. W. (1958) The capacity to be alone. In *The Maturational Processes and the Facilitating Environment*. London: The Hogarth Press, 1987.

1 Enactments and trauma

The therapist's vulnerability as the theatre for the patient's trauma

David Mann

Enactments are often experienced as a crisis in the therapeutic relationship. I use the word 'theatre' in my subtitle to place emphasis on how both the client and the therapist may participate as characters in scenes authored by the other and themselves, in effect become characters from the split-off aspects of the self. I will describe how enactments are particularly likely if the patient presents with a history of trauma. Enactments are most appropriately viewed as aspects of the erotic transference where the passions of the therapeutic relationship are in the full throes of love and hate.

Current thinking in the Intersubjectivity and Relational Schools of thought is that there is a considerable amount of unconscious interaction that happens in therapy that the therapist is not at first aware of. This unconscious relationship operates in the transference and countertransference. Amongst the many implications of this is that the patient's material finds a place in the therapist's blind spots. A review of the literature will suggest that the patient's problem comes into play with difficulties that the therapist is experiencing either temporarily or chronically in his or her own life. The result is an enactment whereby both the patient and therapist unconsciously find expression in the other for their own difficulties. Enactments are therefore joint creations of the therapist and the patient; unconsciously communicated feelings become 'unwitting participation' (Hirsch, 1993). Regarding trauma specifically, it will be suggested that patients often repeat their trauma in the transference. This is widely understood clinical experience. The expression of trauma in the patient's transference might encounter therapeutic difficulties if the patient also comes to represent something significant in the therapist's countertransference. The collision between the patient's trauma and the therapist's trauma can lead to a traumatic crisis in the therapy: the enactment. This might either advance treatment or prevent the therapy from developing.

Enactments and unconscious process

The term 'enactment' entered psychoanalytic theory with Jacobs (1986) closely followed by McLaughlin (1987) referring to non-verbal interaction between analyst and patient. The concept of enactment is especially useful in focusing on the interactional aspects of the analytic relationship.

Some authors like McLaughlin (1987) focus on the less conspicuous elements of enactment, for example, the 'kinesic level of communication' (p. 557) in both verbal and non-verbal data. Jacobs (2001) considers that not only do we register more information about our surroundings than we realise, we also communicate to others far more than we realise. These communications in both directions are at a nonverbal, subliminal level outside conscious awareness. He describes 'covert enactments', as opposed to the more overt which are easily recognised by both participants. 'Covert enactments' are easily overlooked or missed as they might be expressed subtly in tone or slight shifts in body posture and minor alterations of the frame, though they can influence the course and outcome of an analysis. Jacobs writes:

> Operating silently outside of the awareness of the patient and analyst, not uncommonly, they contribute to the development of difficulties in treatment. And when, as often happen, these forces go unrecognized, they can neither be understood nor, like their more recognizable brethren, made part of the analytic work. In such instances, they constitute invisible, but dangerous, shoals in the waters of analysis, perilous areas that can disrupt the analytic journey and can contribute to blocks, impasses, and failures in treatment.
>
> (p. 8)

In a similar vein, Cassorla (2001) suggests that enactments relate to either repressed early trauma or threatening unconscious fantasies that would cause too much suffering if perceived. Chused (1991) defines enactments as 'symbolic interactions between analyst and patient which have unconscious meanings to *both*' (p. 615, italics in original). That is to say, they occur during regression to experiences beyond words, either from preverbal life or from traumatic experience that cannot be symbolised and processed. When the patient has been stimulated to a significant regression, they may at that stage attempt to actualise the transference through enactment. In this way enactments bridge the past and the present, not in a like-for-like repetition, but close enough to the original experience to appear identical to the participants. Whereas the past is largely reported through the verbal content of the session, enactments change the time frame to 'now' in the session. In this sense, the term 'enactment' accurately evokes the dramatic quality of the interaction. The difference from the past is that the other participant is re-experiencing their own past and not that of the other. In other words, though both are recreating something of their past, by coming together in the chemistry of this particular relationship, it is not an exact replica for either. In that sense, the enactment is a joint creation, something new to them both, but each experiences it as familiar from their respective pasts. Conscious communication is not part of this process; both patient and therapist are caught in archaic, primitive unconscious experience dramatising real or fantasised hopes and fears. The point is that neither participant is conscious of what is really going on at the time. A common understanding concerning enactments is that they are not under the therapist's conscious control; therefore no matter how careful the analyst might be, the unconscious processes cannot be known beforehand, only after they have occurred. They cannot be guarded against, but the analyst at least has the foreknowledge to know something unconscious is likely to be enacted. In effect: expect the unexpected!

McLaughlin (1991) proposes that both patient and therapist are:

> vulnerable to falling back on behaviours that actualize their intentions ... reflecting transference hopes, fears and compromises shaped in their developmental past. Specifically, enactments can then be defined as those regressive (defensive) interactions between the pair experienced by either as a consequence of the behaviour of the other.
>
> (p. 595)

Friedman and Natterson (1999) describe something similar and see an added benefit of enactments being to provide the opportunity for the analyst to wonder, 'What are my wishes and hopes, what values am I communicating, how am I conveying them, am I reacting only to the patient or am I presenting a separate agenda of my own?' (p. 243). This encourages the analyst to reflect upon the continuous involvement of their subjective life in the therapy.

Analysis is a profound two-person experience and cannot always be captured by an exclusive focus on the patient's inner world. In that sense, enactments serve as a humbling reminder that transference ghosts from the past are not resolved once and for all. New relationships may revive forgotten conflicts. Enactments facilitate the two-sidedness of the therapeutic relationship.

In the American literature there is some common ground about definitions (e.g. Chused, 1991; McLaughlin, 1991). Enactments result from the interplay of unconscious processes that involve the analyst at an affective and behavioural level resulting from the patient trying to create an interactional representation of an object relationship. Put another way: enactments have to do with the specifics of the unconscious of both the patient and the analyst. As Chused writes: '*Enactments occur when an attempt to actualize a transference fantasy elicits a countertransference reaction*' (author's italics, p. 629). If, once they are aware of being caught in an enactment, the therapist can subject themselves to rigorous self-analysis, they will often have new information available that was not understood or known when they were less involved or engaged.

There is another aspect to enactment that I think is worth noting. An enactment is generally thought of as an event followed by analytic working through in the aftermath. While it seems clear that enactments, or working through them (or not) are significant factors, I believe they need to be considered in the context of the therapy as a whole. A number of psychological transactions may have taken place before a significant enactment arises in the therapy. There is widespread agreement that it is not the enactment but what happens afterwards that influences the therapy. However, it could also be said that what happens before the enactment is also important: that is to say, the patient and therapist have already built some sort of relationship; some of this would be unconscious as well as what we might think of as the ordinary therapeutic alliance. It is quite possible that the patient needs to feel fairly secure and safe before a traumatic enactment can occur which might permit an unconscious trauma to repeat itself.

Definitions and distinctions

Any definition of enactment is difficult. As one panellist discussing the subject put it: 'The definition of enactment is bound to be blurry at the edge' (1992, p. 84). This is partly because, like all other psychoanalytic terms, it gets used in an idiosyncratic fashion by different analysts. One distinction is to be made between acting out and enactment. For example, acting out is often considered as a motor action, embedded in drive theory and one-person psychology: acting out is something the patient or the therapist might do, but either way it is derived from one participant's issues. Enactment has developed out of two-person psychology and the inevitability of the analyst's intersubjective participation. Clearly these concepts were not to be thought of as mutually exclusive, but they are distinctive. There is also a distinction to be made with projective identification. The Panel discussion (1992) suggests projective identification carries the idea of 'a single theme view. The patient is "out there" instead of being viewed as an interactive pattern' (p. 836). Crude descriptions of projective identification, e.g. Bion (1959), depict the analyst as a container of the patient's projections. More sophisticated descriptions of projective identification, e.g. Ogden (1979) identify the inciting fantasies and behaviour of patients as eliciting a mirrored response in the analyst: these have the therapist's own, not projected, feelings and result from the impact of a different personality system. Ogden falls short of seeing the analyst's feelings as originating from the analyst's own wishes, feelings and object representations. While projective identification might recognise the analyst's responsiveness to the patient, it does not acknowledge the therapist's contribution to the analytic experience which is a function of the therapist's own psychology. Enactment emphasises the conjoint process of attempted mutual influence and invites exploration of both the patient and the analyst.

It is worth noting that some Kleinian writers, e.g. Weiss (2002) and Cassorla (2001, 2005) describe enactments in terms of 'crossed projective identifications'. In so doing, they follow the object relations tradition rather than the intersubjective model: the concentration on the patient's internal world that the therapist is caught up in. In my opinion, this does not constitute true enactments as it does not account for the contribution of the analyst's own subjectivity. I would suggest that the confusion arises in Kleinian thinking as it fails to distinguish and indeed muddles up 'role responsiveness' and enactment. Sandler (1976) introduces the idea of 'role responsiveness' to describe how both participants seek to impose on the other an intrapsychic object relationship whereby the analyst might find themselves accepting the role imposed on them by the patient and thereby colluding with the patient's acting out.

Enactments and trauma

I would suggest that trauma is particularly prone to expression through enactment. Freud (1916–17) had described the 'function of a protective shield' which might be overwhelmed when the mind experiences a stimulus too powerful to be dealt with in the normal way, thus leading to a disturbance in mental operations. Dorpat (quoted in Roughton, 1993) proposes a 'cognitive-arrest' theory to explain memory gaps in those who suffered childhood trauma: denial at the time of trauma prevents the formation of representation memory of the event, which is not easily recovered verbally. Roughton suggests perceptual defences and denial block the encoding of representational memory, though this may be organised in a 'sensory motor mode' and accessible only through 'enactive memory' (p. 454). Hartke (2005) proposes that in analysis a traumatic situation provokes emotions that exceed the capacity for containment in the therapy couple. This excess can originate from either participant. Hartke describes how this 'excess' can bring about a period of 'dementalisation' sufficient to disturb the analytic relationship in either a positive or negative manner. 'Dementalisation' refers to the failure in the mental function to transform sensory impressions and raw emotions into 'mental experience'. He notes that greatly traumatised people not only tend to carry such experiences into the analytic encounter but are also more likely to enter a new trauma as a result of any circumstantial or specific limitations in the therapeutic capacity for containment. Hartke formulates these ideas in the concepts of Klein and Bion. In more general psychoanalytic terms, this can be transcribed to suggest that experiences that cannot be formulated symbolically into words are more likely to find expression through the unconscious. This suggests the greater the trauma the more likely the unconscious disturbance. The difficulty or incapacity to transmute trauma into symbolic thinking processes means trauma is most likely to be expressed through the only outlet available, which is through action. Trauma, I would add, is therefore likely to be a consistent feature in enactments precisely because the overwhelming unconscious experience compels action rather than words and is not easily contained by the ordinary analytic functions of the patient and the therapist.

Like everybody else, therapists might be blown about by events in their own lives whether this is in relation to current circumstances or the reactivation of old issues. The analyst is not an invulnerable participant-observer. Each therapist brings a full set of hopes, needs and fears to their work. Both the analytic training and a more or less strong ego serve the therapist well much of the time. However, this is vulnerable to disruption and regression to less evolved states both from the work itself and from the pressures of everyday. A number of writers indicate that the patient's material at the time found a resonance in what was happening in their, the therapist's life. For example, Jacobs (2001) recounts that his father was very ill after a stroke which left him with cognitive and expressive defects; at this time, Jacobs began to make mistakes with bills, appointments and breaks, his identifications with his father's symptoms finding a place in his patient's material even though he was quite unaware of his own symptomatic behaviour. Bemesderfer (2000) traces the trauma of having her son diagnosed with cancer and how such tragedies profoundly influence what we do and how we do it. Reviewing some of the literature where analysts have written about personal illness, or of deaths of family members, she refers to 'self disclosure and countertransference enactments, both of which appear to be inevitable consequences of the analyst's traumatic experiences' (pp. 1522–1523). She notes that patients sense changes in us even though they do not understand the causes.

The therapist enacts their own inner conflicts but in so doing also creates a situation that involves the patient having to come face-to-face with a situation they are avoiding. The mutual resistance blocks progress in the analysis and life as well. When caught in an enactment the therapist's observations are clouded.

Clinical vignettes

I will give three instances of enactment in therapy. I am mindful of the slant that the therapist always brings to material either in the consulting room or publication. In all three examples I wish to describe, I am making a selection of thoughts that may give a distortion to the work with these patients as a whole. For example, I could cite the same three patients to describe other aspects of the therapeutic process, such as the erotic transference and countertransference or the function of regression in therapeutic process. Since I am describing enactments what I write will not be representative of the complete therapy.

In the following examples I will describe three enactments: in one where I think it helped the therapy, the second where it wrecked the therapy altogether and a third which illustrates enactment processes that did not significantly impact on the therapy. My purpose is to indicate how power-fully unconscious processes can take a grip during an enactment, the fact that the therapist's contribution is made through their vulnerabilities and how this can decisively influence therapeutic development for better or for worse.

Enactment 1

I have had, from quite a young age, a poor reaction to the sight of blood. When I was 12 I witnessed at close hand a stabbing incident in my school, and even as I write this I can vividly recall the sight of blood oozing from the victim's neck. My reaction at the time was to come over all weak, I needed to sit down, felt faint, broke out into a cold sweat and got spots before my eyes. After this specific incident, this reaction became generalised, in true Pavlovian style, to the sight of blood on any occasion in any context. My professional development took me at one time to work as a residential therapist in a crisis centre. Here I had ample opportunity to compound my feeble reaction to the sight of blood: many of the patients self-harmed. Two in particular stay in my mind: the patient who slashed her arm with a razor blade in front of me, a situation from which I had to walk away because I could not deal with it; on another occasion mopping up a large pool of blood after another patient had used a meat cleaver on his wrist. Frankly, I am feeling a bit queasy just recalling this and writing it down! I still have the same physical reactions as I did as a child, which can momentarily over-power and incapacitate me. My personal analysis, so helpful and trans-formative in many ways, did nothing to change this reaction to the sight of blood. And sometimes it is not even the sight of blood that leads me to collapse. Possessing, as I do, a vivid imagination, at times even the thought of it can create realistic scenes in my mind. The only thing that has given me a more adaptive response is fatherhood. Only great love has enabled me to override such a neurotic reaction to the sight of blood; only with my children can I avoid collapsing because they need to be looked after and comforted. When my squeamish reaction to the sight of blood comes up in conversation, as it does from time to time, I sometimes make a joke: I can cope with most forms of madness, pathology or mental distress, so I am okay as a psycho-therapist but I could never have been a doctor or nurse.

This preamble about my vulnerability to the sight of blood provides the context for the enactment I wish to describe. Mr V was in his mid-thirties and had a medical background. He had sought therapy for a variety of reasons amongst which were issues concerning his mother's death and what he considered to be his difficulty in getting close to people and drifting through life. Early on in his therapy he wondered if he would have to regress to a 'messy heap' in order to allow his defences to diminish. His mother had not liked mess. As a baby he had suffered from constipation for the first year and mother had taken this as a sign he was a clean baby. He felt a deadness inside and wondered if he would ever feel fully alive. He was worried therapy would not change this and that I would not understand him or be able to connect with him.

His mother had died when he was in his early adolescence. The experience was traumatic: she was suddenly taken ill when they were alone in the house. Mr V recalled how he had tried and failed to resuscitate her. The medical authorities had assured him that no matter what he had done he would not have been able to save his mother's life; this reassurance had never assuaged his guilt that he had failed to keep her alive. Mother's death heralded a period of depression and suicidal thoughts. When older he did a medical training, in part to gain mastery of how to save life.

In the transference I was experienced as the good, reparative father. He called me his 'sugar daddy' but was quick to deny any erotic implications contained in the phrase. Death and intimacy could be linked as he felt he might die if somebody got close to him; in the therapy it might be either one of us who might die, but especially me.

The session I wish to describe occurred after about three years of therapy. He began by saying that his wife had fainted the previous night owing to her low blood pressure. He was upset because he worries about her having a heart attack and how he might have to resuscitate her. He connected this to his mother dying in front of him and how he still blames himself for her death even though his mother would not have survived no matter what he had done. He said, as he had told me before, that this had led him to working as a professional in acute medicine. Then, unlike on previous occasions when talking about his mother's death and his work in medicine, he began to give detailed examples from his professional life. In particular, he vividly described one man bleeding to death. His imagery was graphic and his account was detailed. As the gruesome and gory account developed I felt myself starting to feel sick and queasy; I was aware that all my usual reactions to blood had taken hold of my imagination and I was unable to get a grip. I recall I deliberately started looking at the floor to break eye contact in the hope that this would help me disconnect and snap out of the situation. The next thing I knew Mr V was leaning half out of his chair looking very concerned and repeatedly saying to me, 'Are you all right?!' In between the last memory of looking at the floor and him saying this I had apparently fainted for no more than a few seconds. I recall that, as I came to, I did in fact say I was allergic to the sight of blood and had found his account rather graphic. He said that for a few seconds I looked white and appeared asleep and the look in my eyes was 'withdrawn from listening, very interior'. When I had recovered my senses and some composure we were able to discuss what had happened: he was worried he had damaged me, touched a raw nerve and that his mother had died like that. He needed to know that something had happened to me and that it was not just his imagination. I said that I could not tell him the details but acknowledged that yes, indeed, something had happened to me. At the end of the session I noticed that he lingered long enough to see that I could get out of my chair, so he was clearly still keeping a medical eye on me.

Over the next few weeks we kept returning to this incident. It became quite striking how our thoughts about what happened ran parallel or diverged. He blamed his mother's heart problems on her smoking, and blamed me for not telling him about my squeamishness. He wondered about his power to induce this reaction in me. He said he was concerned it might happen again, and as in his mother's house, he did not know where my telephone was. For my part, I felt terribly bothered and embarrassed that I had fainted. I shared his concerns that it might happen again. In addition, I had some of my own: I felt that by fainting like this in front of Mr V I had inadvertently recreated a similar situation as the one he had experienced with his mother and had thus re-traumatised him. I felt my professional attitude had badly slipped with this patient. I expressed my concern that my reaction would make him hesitant to say whatever was on his mind in case I fainted again and that his concern for me would be the therapeutic role reversal of him looking after me rather than the other way round. The difficulty as I saw it was that he might have doubts about my capacity to offer containment for his thoughts and feelings. Privately I wondered if the therapy would ever really recover fearing that, rather than providing a therapeutic opportunity, this therapy might have the more iatrogenic effect of doing him harm.

By way of a contrast, Mr V began describing a different reaction. In addition to the concerns he had already expressed, he thought my fainting and his reaction had also been about making a genuine connection with me; in a way he was pleased that I was not just a composed and detached therapist but that I had real feelings in the session. In that sense, it made me more human and showed he could affect me. His mother's depression had been experienced as her being lost in her own internal world, detached and unavailable to him. I wondered whether this was something similar to what he saw in my expression before I had fainted, that I had looked as internally preoccupied as his mother had. We came to realise that my 'therapeutic blank screen' had been experienced by him as his uninvolved, detached and depressed mother. Some time after the occasion when I fainted, the issue of whether he could hear emotion in my voice was often more important to him than the things I said. Knowing I had feelings meant I was affected by him so he could believe we could be connected.

He also thought it gave him a chance to show his genuine concern for me. This was a mixed reaction. He was aware that he often felt chaotic and that trauma could put him in touch with the essence of being alive. Trauma had the capacity to give him a sense of identity. In that context, he said that his mother would often call him by his brother's name and his brother by his name, as though they were both 'interchangeable' with no separate identity. My fainting had felt confirming in that I did indeed perceive him as a separate identity.

What began to emerge more fully in the material was his rescuing fantasies, beginning with his trying to rescue me; but he soon realised how much it had previously defined his life. He could see this side of him operating in all his relationships past and present. As he realised the extent of his rescue fantasies he became preoccupied with the thought of being boring, that he bored me and that this showed how dislikeable he was. The only thing he could use to prove to others that he was good was to save them from something. Without a trauma he was dull and empty. Deeper issues emerged about not letting anybody enter what he called his 'mental space', partly in case they would be aggressive, but mostly from the fear of their indifference. This touched on his mother's early reaction of not taking his infantile constipation seriously. What he feared more than love or hate was lack of interest and concern saying, 'At least if somebody is angry with me I know something I've done matters to them.' His rescuing of others was also connected to making people have a reaction to him rather than ignoring him. His fear of being boring was thus a symptom of his mother's neglect because he experienced this as though he was not important to her.

Towards the end of his therapy, some two years after I had fainted, he had a dream: He goes to a hair dresser to have his hair dyed but the colouring does not work and his hair starts to fall out. He goes to another hairdresser who is ugly but kind and who puts it right. The associations about the dream began with the interchangeable word play between 'dyed' and 'died'. He thought the first hairdresser was his mother who had died and caused something to die in him. The second hairdresser was myself, 'ugly' because when I fainted this was something horrible that scared him, but 'kind' because rather than dying I had stayed with him to talk about it. That put something right for him.

What I think happened in this therapy is that the enactment clearly came from the joint creation of an event from the patient's past: Mr V's mother dying in front of him collided with a personal issue of my own about reactions to the sight of blood that have made me faint in the past. The enactment was how each of us for our own very separate and distinct reasons experienced something in the analytic environment that took us both back to an earlier trauma. The enactment had the potential to derail the therapy and make it unsafe for both of us but especially for Mr V. I believe that our discussions after this event were helpful not just because they clarified things in themselves but probably more importantly because they demonstrated to each other that we could survive. In this instance, I am thinking of Winnicott's (1971) paper on 'The Use of the Object' in which aggression is spent but the object is able to come through and still engage in a relationship and neither be totally destroyed nor retaliate. In that sense, though my fainting was traumatic for Mr V I did not die like his mother, or indeed the man who bled to death, the recounting of which event had led me to faint in the first place. Unlike both of the people who died in front of Mr V, I survived and we could talk about what had happened. Clinically, this enactment significantly moved Mr V's material on: not only issues about his mother's death but also his life style as a rescuer became much more significant than previously in this therapy; it enabled him to have an experience that somebody could be affected by him and that I was not simply indifferent to him: in that sense, although it was traumatic, at least I had not neglected him. Also, by bringing the issues about his mother into such a sharp perspective the enactment also brought up issues about his mother and early infantile experience which had hitherto been difficult to access during the therapy.

It would seem to me that the breakthrough in the patient's material was the enactment. The enactment itself occurred not solely from the patient repeating something from his past but it found a foothold in the here-and-now experience of the analytic setting. That foothold was precisely an area of vulnerability in myself which allowed for the possibility of Mr V and me re-creating something that became a joint creation between us. While I am not suggesting fainting as a therapeutic technique, I would want to stress the mechanism of enactment. Enactments engage the therapist and the patient at a deeply unconscious level and require both participants to make a contribution. I would emphasise what has been described in the literature: that the therapist is a participant and not just an observer in the analytic situation. What makes enactments particularly powerful is the extent to which they involve the therapist's unconscious in the patient's world.

Enactment 2

I wish to describe the case of Mr E with a view to demonstrating that enactments do not always lead to a successful outcome for therapy. This is a point that needs to be emphasised. In much of the literature on enactments the clinical cases described tend to illustrate a successful therapeutic outcome, that the enactment was successfully utilised to bring a significant advance in the therapy. I have come to think of enactments as turning points in a therapy, and quite clearly a turning point does not always have a happy ending. I have come to the view that many of the therapies that fail due to a breakdown in the therapeutic alliance, often described as acting out of a negative transference, are in fact enactments. Every therapist has the experience of a therapy ending badly. I am currently of the view that most, if not all, therapies that end badly are best understood as enactments in which the therapist makes a significant contribution to the therapeutic failure.

The therapy I wish to describe ended badly for the patient. For that I am deeply sorry. Balbernie (1988), reflecting on writing about a mishandled, failed therapy, wryly comments on the lack of such reports in the literature, saying: 'Failure is important but usually unpublicised' (p. 149). In writing up this account I think I am certainly trying to resolve something for myself and possibly, I would hope, make some reparation to the patient. Again to quote Balbernie, 'it can only be retrieved here: a reparative fantasy' (p. 149).

Mr E came to therapy following an acrimonious divorce and custody battle with his ex-wife. He began his therapy with the expressed worry that therapy would cause a 'breakdown'. He was now in his late thirties. He was an only child of average abilities. His parents were high achievers both academically and in the business world. Even though Mr E always tried to win approval by becoming the comedian in the family he felt sure his father was disappointed in his meagre talents. There was a much less clear picture of his mother. She was experienced as lacking in empathy and had not understood the patient when he was a child. There was an early trauma when at about six months old his mother went back to work and he was looked after by a maternal grandmother who was very strict.

The early transference was to expect my disappointment and disapproval if he under-performed regarding my expectations of what a good patient should be like. He expected to be judged and humiliated by me as I came to embody some 'combined parent' in his mind, uniting all the worst aspects of his parents in one. Running parallel with this anxiety was the hope that I would be the 'good father' who would appreciate him as he was. During those moments he could feel very contained; on other occasions, when he felt very understood and accepted by me, I became a 'good mother'.

At other times, he became the critic: sometimes he felt I was moving too fast in my understanding and leaving him behind; at other times I was too slow on the uptake, not knowing what he needed. A lack of 'kindness' was experienced by him as akin to neglect, which he felt happened when his grandmother looked after him once his mother had gone back to work, which felt like a terrible rejection of him. In the transference, he was looking for the kindly mother who could cope with her own and the baby's bad feelings, would never be rejecting and would always be available. Each session would start with him in a state of high anxiety which usually diminished as the session went on, only to be rekindled again between sessions or sometimes later in the same session. If I did not smile during a session he assumed I must be disapproving of him. At other times he thought I must be bored listening to him 'whine' or I would be 'angry at his self obsessed egotism'. While in this anxious state, his speech would pour out: he would talk rapidly, going from one idea to the next, the subject being either his or sometimes my shortcomings. He would be overwhelmed by feelings and was afraid he would overwhelm me with them. At other times he felt like a 'sponge' soaking up other people's feelings. He knew he played this role with his mother who would pass her anxiety on to him, leaving her feeling great and him highly agitated.

At this stage in the therapy I would say my countertransference did not resemble what he feared: I was neither bored nor disapproving of him. I had noticed early on in the treatment that he would slowly calm down as the session progressed; over the course of several months his active distress was very much less. He was now very much more contained. Altogether I would have said that things were progressing well enough.

Two events changed all that. The first was that, owing to my other work commitments, I had to change the time of our weekly appointments from early to late in the day. This non-negotiable disruption caused Mr E much distress. Part of his growing containment rested on the regularity of our meetings. Of course, in an ideal world most therapists understand the necessity of keeping regular slots which helps keep the therapeutic frame reliable. I have noticed, however, that other professional demands, not to mention domestic concerns, do occasionally make changes necessary. Such a drastic change left Mr E feeling very unsafe. His response was to become very anxious again, which he tried to deal with by becoming rigid in an attempt to impose order on both his inner chaos and what he experienced as a disintegration of the therapeutic frame; in retrospect, I also think his rigidity was an attempt at trying to get my chaos in order. His rigidity took the form of attacking the therapy, pointing out what I was not doing correctly. His attitude was that if only I were to do it by the book all would be well. He made it clear he had not wanted to change the time, that it was poor practice to mess him around in such a way. He also felt more aggrieved about how I worked, the use of silence, what I did not say about myself, failures in my empathy: all these points demonstrated the failings of this kind of therapy in general and my personal limitations in particular.

The second event that posed a problem for this therapy was related to events elsewhere in my life: at this time elsewhere in my career and work as a psychotherapist I was experiencing a serious low point. This change had left me very upset and extremely angry to the point where I would have relished a bare-knuckle fight with my then manager! This is an image that indicates just how much of an emotionally primitive state I was in. I knew at the time that this felt like a struggle to contain my own emotions. Feeling so despondent and powerless, I took refuge in my clinical work, thinking I could still do it well and that it was worth concentrating on. It was at this point that Mr E began his criticisms of the therapy and of me as a therapist. If this had been any other emergence of the negative transference I feel in my bones that I would have handled the situation differently and better. However, given what was going on with me, his criticisms, whether justified or not, were not well received. After listening to another tirade during a session I eventually, and I would add uncharacteristically, replied with a trace of annoyance, that if he did not like the way I worked he could always go and find another therapist. That was it, the therapy never recovered from this and two months later he terminated.

I understand the enactment in the following way. I think Mr E and I understood what my rejection meant to him. Telling him he could go and find another therapist was a rejection with historical significance for him. Simultaneously I represented the critical, disappointed father and the mother with no empathy. There was also the re-enactment of the critical event from his childhood. This related to being handed over at six months old to his maternal grandmother, but in this instance it was me as the rejecting parent. I think both he and I went as far as understanding that he might even have been trying to induce anger in me or perhaps to set up a situation where I would reject him. In that respect, the 'breakdown' that he worried about from the first session had indeed been created, which drew attention to his own destructive capacities. The sticking point for him was that I had so evidently been annoyed: if I had not contained his provocative behaviour, why could I not do so? Even while we talked I knew there was no point in denying my annoyance. But it was obvious to him that I was not owning something or not understanding something. That 'something' only dawned upon me some months after this therapy abruptly ended. I kept on thinking about this case and what had gone wrong. Frankly, I was not having any great insights and my thoughts seemed quite circular. It was only after some while I realised I had an abiding mental image of him. As he arrived for the fateful session he picked up the cushion and then said something to the effect of: 'I think therapists should be taught to fluff up cushions so that the entering client doesn't have to see evidence of the previous person sitting in the chair before them!' He then 'fluffed up' the cushion and sat down. At the time neither of us came back to this opening move, which became submerged in a deluge of negative transference, and by then, negative countertransference. But this scene was the one that I kept recalling until I realised it came to represent or signify or become emblematic of why this therapy went badly. My late understanding in itself suggested the extent I had been unconsciously caught up. I had little insight or understanding of myself, much less of him, to be helpful to the therapy. In fact, the professional blow had affected me much more that I had allowed myself to imagine. I had convinced myself that I could at least take sanctuary in doing good clinical work, that somehow the clinical work could be protected or immune from my state of mind! By compartmentalising my mind in this way it meant I did not have 'linking' ability, so clearly described by Bion (1967). Mr E's criticisms hurt, not simply because he might have been right (or just provocative or evacuating) but because I was feeling vulnerable. At another time in my life I think I would have kept things in perspective, but unsettled as I was in my own primitive fantasies of violence and rejection, I was more fired up to retaliate rather than to contain attacks on my therapeutic practice. The real problem was not that he was angry at me, or even that I might have been irritated with him: what got in the way was my own unconsciousness of just how annoyed I was and why; nor had I seen the link with my manager; nor had I referenced this back to some other occasions from childhood of feeling unjustly wiped out.

This was an enactment, and not just a negative transference, because of the therapist's participation at an unconscious level: if I had become his rejecting mother, he similarly turned into a bad object for me. Between us we created a repetition, different yet feeling the same as the past. Because the therapist will always have areas of vulnerability, whether fleeting as with my example of Mr E, or chronic as with Mr V, there will always be the possibility of enactments. I find it difficult to imagine a therapist so detached or well analysed that they no longer have unconscious processes that might make them vulnerable to an enactment with some patients.

Enactment 3

I now want to give a third example of an enactment. The following vignette illustrates very well how the mechanisms of enactments happen.

Mr S, now in his late fifties, had been a convicted paedophile. He voluntarily brought this information and a prison social worker's report to our first meeting. He had wanted therapy while in prison but it was unavailable. He was looking for therapy now because, as he stated, he wanted to learn how to sublimate his sexual feeling into a more appropriate setting. Specifically he wanted therapeutic help to allow him to enter the gay community with more confidence so he could channel his sexual desire into adult relationships with men. He had been sent to prison after being convicted of sexually abusing three boys aged about 11 years. As he told me this I recalled that statistically the average paedophile sexually abuses about 200 children over the course of a lifetime. I was left to wonder whether he was being honest or just owning up to the three he had been caught for. He told me he had not abused any children since he left prison some 18 months earlier. I set up a contract with him that if he abused children while in therapy, or if it was brought to my attention he had been abusing children while in therapy, the therapy would be instantly terminated.

Over the following sessions we explored his history. As a child he recalled never fitting into his family. He believed his parents favoured his more talented and able brother. He grew up feeling isolated and in this brother's shadow; he was shy, lacking in confidence, socially awkward with his peers and with low self-esteem. He had few friends: his parents discouraged bringing anyone home, so he spent most of his childhood in his own company. When he was ten the family moved home, which was particularly difficult, and he felt even more handicapped at making friends. He considered the influence from his childhood left him lacking in confidence and with few social skills. He felt uncomfortable in the company of adults and more at ease one-to-one with a child. It was my impression that this sense of neglect, whether actual or imagined, had left him isolated and vulnerable as a child, probably an easy target for a paedophilic seduction. At 11, a paedophile scout-master took an interest in him and began to 'abuse' him. I place the word abuse in inverted commas because Mr S did not consider it abuse either at the time or now. Instead, his view was that nothing terrible had transpired, he had not seen himself as a vulnerable child and he had benefited by being given sweets and, more importantly, he had been noticed and given attention. Since he had felt so isolated and neglected, the attentions of the scout-master were described by him as much appreciated.

Shortly after being introduced to sexual practice he began his own career of seduction. He had sought out another boy and, in the view of Mr S, there was sexual interest so he did not consider it exploitative. As an adult, he had been convicted of abusing three boys aged about 11. He reported he preferred the company of males to females. He was uncomfortable with adults and, as he hated football, he felt he had nothing to talk about. Instead, he would feel intimidated by men's company and referred to the mass of people as 'being like sheep' and never interested in him as a person. At the same time as holding other adult men in contempt, he felt they made him feel inferior in their company. Not surprisingly, he experienced himself as an outsider to ordinary human relations and discourse. He only felt truly comfortable, to be his own person, when with boys with whom he could offer nurturance and guidance. Rather like the scout-master who had abused him at 11, Mr S used a seduction technique, I suspect, that involved adopting the role of mentor to gain trust. I had already come to such a conclusion when the enactment occurred.

Now, there are many things in this world I do not know or understand. For example, I know nothing of the historical development of the nation state of Luxembourg, nor do I know anything about twelfth-century Islamic theology. I have, however, a mild curiosity and interest so that if the information came my way in an easily accessible form I would be curious enough to find out more. But generally speaking, I neither experience an imperative to learn nor a lack of confidence because I am ignorant of these things; I neither experience a sense of lack that affects my self-esteem nor any anguish at the 'not-knowing'. I do, however, feel very self-conscious about the fact I know little about computers and do not really cope well with modern technology. The Luddite in me tries to say, 'Why should I care?' but actually I do care and for many years have been rather embarrassed about my lack of technological skill. If Mr S did not know how to talk about football with other men, I certainly do not know how to talk about computers with them. I am very self-conscious about not understanding computer technology and terminology.

It was an ordinary session with Mr S. Often the therapy felt like supportive counselling that only occasionally dipped into psychoanalysis. With a view to accessing the gay scene through the internet he was describing setting up his own website. He asked me: 'Do you know anything about setting up e-mail addresses?' I said, 'No, not really'. He then proceeded to explain to me how it was done. Now, if I had been in the frame of mind to be attentive to his explanation I might have learned something about e-mails. As it was I was suddenly felt disorientated and ill at ease, experiencing considerable discomfort. I was instantly bothered: why had I answered his question so quickly, honestly and directly? My sensations lasted for the rest of the session. It was only many hours later at home that it suddenly occurred to me that I had been part of his seduction method. Had Mr S asked me what I knew about the history of Luxembourg or twelfth-century Islamic theology, or any other number of subjects of which I know little or nothing I would have responded differently; if I had not felt diffident about my lack of computer knowledge I would have responded differently. But that was not how it was. Mr S was unconsciously playing out his own seductive method as mentor and also that of the scout-master who had seduced him at 11. He could still have acted this out without my personal involvement. For example, he could have asked the question and still attempted to give me the explanation, and had I not got unconsciously involved I would have made the appropriate analytic interpretation at the time. Alternatively, if we thought of this in terms of projective identification we might wonder if he was projecting his own confusion and vulnerability into me, giving me the experience of what it was like to be him as a confused and vulnerable child. However, what made this an enactment was not only that I had been caught in the seduction but, just as importantly, *why* I had become caught up. Looking back on this incident I believe it unfolded the way it did because Mr S had located a vulnerability in me. I was pulled off analytic balance by his question, and from then on I could not function analytically for the rest of the session but went along with what he was doing. Given his career as a paedophile, I would expect that he was particularly good at both consciously and unconsciously being able to scan The Other for their vulnerabilities on which he could then capitalise by becoming the mentor, thereby enabling the sexual seduction of the vulnerable child. In his finding my vulnerability, I was then caught in my own unconscious process so that I could not find a way out while the seduction was in process. He had asked me a question on a subject I am sensitive about and was able to seduce me while at the same time giving the illusion that this was good for him and me. In that sense I must confess the seduction worked precisely because he had accurately located an area of vulnerability in me.

Though I do not believe this enactment had a big impact for better or worse in this therapy with Mr S, I cite it because I think that it illustrates rather well how the therapist's vulnerability may intermesh with the patient and that enactments are a two-person process and not just a matter of the patient's projection into the therapist. It is through the therapist's vulnerabilities that their unconscious participation can be so receptive.

Discussion

Post-enactment benefits and the need for the therapist's involvement

Is it possible for the analyst to rise above their unconscious processes? Phrased differently: is there ever a moment that the analyst is not unconscious? To a greater or lesser extent, the analyst is always going to be unconscious of aspects of both themselves and the patient. We might realistically aspire to the best possible outcome, namely that the analyst will eventually become aware of at least some of the most significant aspects of the unconscious process in themselves and the patient, but will never be so detached, or observant, or outside the process to be totally aware.

Analysis works not by avoiding enactments, indeed they seem unavoidable, but by analysing them in an interactional relationship. Often the significant part of the analysis is post-enactment. Awareness of the enactment initiates both patient and therapist in a search to find a way out of the patient's transference. The analyst is actively included in the patient's neurosis. This risks a loss of analytic perspective, but by avoiding such risks the analyst has little chance of effectively reaching the patient. The therapist is able to be more powerfully effective when their subjectivity is seen as an integral part of the therapeutic experience. A number of writers (Gill, 1982; Jacobs, 1986; Eagle, 1993) make the point that, to an extent, transference and countertransference are an interplay of each participant's (both therapist and patient) reaction to the cues communicated by the other. Chused (1991) notes that when actions are forbidden their impulses can also be forbidden. This can be problematic in analytic work where the ego ideal of most analysts is to contain impulses and examine them. The analyst runs the danger of being so constricted as to never become stimulated, or so defended that they are not aware of their own behaviour. Instead, Chused suggests that 'at times it may be more useful for an analyst to act on an impulse, catch himself, and thereby learn about the impulse and its stimulus' (p. 616). In this regard, she makes a distinction with Alexander (1950) who would recommend a consciously manipulated experience for his patients as part of a 'corrective emotional experience'. Chused argues strongly that the real therapeutic value is not in conscious manipulation but in the fact that the analyst does something *unconsciously*. The value of enactments lies not in itself but in the post-enactment analysis of observation, description and understanding of transferential meaning. Put another way: the therapist is not consciously choosing to enact; since the processes are unconscious, the therapist enacts. Ideally, after the enactment the therapist then begins to question why they said or did what they did. As one panellist (Panel, 1992) put it: 'The analyst always works at the edge of darkness' (p. 837), which clearly means there are times when the therapist is in the dark. If there is a therapeutic effect it is in the period of reflection after the enactment. The concept of enactment enables us to comprehend communication from one person's unconscious to that of another. The unconscious motivations will be different for patient and analyst. In that sense, the repetition is not an exact facsimile, though the psychic conflicts may be similar enough for the similarities and differences to emerge in the post-enactment analysis.

Not all writers agree that insight and verbal understanding are necessary for a therapeutic effect from an enactment. Eagle (1993) describes a case where the beneficial effects of the therapy were understood by neither party at the time, but a successful working through had occurred after the enactment by virtue of the therapist not fulfilling the expected role. In this he links therapeutic effect to Alexander's (1950) idea of a 'corrective emotional experience'. Roughton (1993) also wishes to rehabilitate Alexander's term, though he does so free from the conscious manipulation suggested by Alexander.

Enactments and negative therapeutic reaction

In the literature it is often suggested that enactments are a crisis in the therapy that provides the impetus and opportunity to take the therapy forward in significant ways for the patient's benefit. For example, the following view is typical of the analytic literature on enactments: 'Enactments that are recognized and defined become valuable dramatizing moments that have condensing, clarifying and intensifying effect upon consciousness' (Friedman and Natterson, 1999). This seems to me to be an instance of accurate description colliding with misplaced optimism. It is possible to accept that enactments are useful once understood. The severe problem posed by enactments, though, is this: will the therapist be astute, reliable and consistent enough to bring their own unconscious process into conscious awareness? Will the unconscious issues behind the enactment always come to light and be understood? While I would believe most analysts make the attempt to understand the unconscious process it is frankly doubtful to assume they will always grasp its meaning. Can therapists always be conscious of the unconscious? Is there ever an analytic moment when there is no unconscious process in the analyst? The answer to both questions must surely be 'No'. Despite the therapist's best efforts the unconscious can never be entirely known. So in any therapy there will always be unanalysed or even unanalysable unconscious processes in both the patient and the therapist. *Negative therapeutic effects have the appearance of representing a huge gulf between the patient and the therapist. I would suggest, though, that they represent intense unconscious communication and connection.* I would stress this becomes particularly problematic if the patient (or the therapist) has a history of serious trauma. If the original trauma overwhelmed the symbolic thinking process the repetition of trauma in an enactment will encounter a similar unconscious resistance to the symbolising process of thought and language. I have become doubtful about these fairytale endings. There is evidence to suggest that enactments might indeed help the therapy progress but they might also be the reason it might end very badly (Jacobs, 1997). I would suggest that many negative therapeutic reactions and therapy failures might be understood as enactments in therapy that were not properly analysed by the therapist.

In addition, what must also be considered in this process is the fact that, even if the therapist is able to recover and understand their unconscious process after the enactment, the therapy might not always recover. This is particularly an issue when the patient has a history of trauma. Even if the therapist comes to understand the enactment, the enactment may have so severely damaged the therapeutic alliance that the therapy might not be repaired. In this situation, the patient might experience the enactment as such a close repetition of their original trauma that any attempt to find a working through becomes impossible. As stated earlier, trauma often has not found its way to be mentally symbolised into language. That might still be the case after the enactment so that, even then, the re-emergence of trauma cannot be thought about successfully.

Enactments and the erotic transference

Another way of thinking about negative therapeutic reaction is to locate it in the more global experience of erotic transference/countertransference. As Freud described, the erotic transference, Eros, propels us to unity and greater complexity. Unfortunately Freud (1920) then sought to explain disunity via the death instinct, Thanatos. I have discussed elsewhere the problems encountered by introducing a misleading idea of the death instinct (see Mann, 2002).

Disunity is better understood as an aspect of Eros itself, and not as a different and opposing force. Green (Green and Kohon, 2006) links Eros to Eris, defined as the concepts of love and dissent that are bound together. In Green's view, Eris is what Freud was writing about when he described the unbinding action of destruction as manifestations of the death instinct. In love relationships, Eris is present as the possibility of betrayal, as the possibility that the love object cannot be trusted or that the lover (not the beloved) might not deserve to be loved. Eris is present as idealised love that becomes extinct as it changes perception: 'the experience of love teaches us that it is linked to illusion – and is eventually capable of turning into delusion' (p. 16). I would think 'Dis-illusion' would probably have been a more accurate term here. Anyway, the implication is that this transforma-tion can change from the happiest to the most destructive of consequences. 'Love is synonymous to reunion therefore separation may seem unbearable' (p. 16). We might put this differently: both love (especially the early stage of romantic love) and hate contain strong degrees of illusion and pro-jection. Eros and Eris might, therefore, be more appropriately described as the process of the illusions of love turning into the illusions of hate. Put another way, enactments of negative therapeutic reaction could be described as 'Dark Eros' or Eros with poisoned arrows. Not a separate force opposed to Eros but the ambivalence and conflicting wishes within the same desire.

The concept of Eris becomes particularly useful when describing enact-ments and especially those ending with a negative therapeutic reaction. Eris unbinds, creates disunity and dissent. The link with betrayal is particularly important. Amongst all its meanings, enactments leading to negative therapeutic outcomes also represent a mutual disillusionment between the analytic couple. The patient's disillusionment in the therapist is the most conspicuous. But Eris is a two-way process. Therapists can be disillusioned in so many ways about their patients (see Mann, 1997, pp. 81–82, on why therapists may hate some patients). The time is ripe for an enactment to occur when a negative transference elicits a negative countertransference in the 'law of talion' (Racker, 1968) which happens at an unconscious level. This is all the more likely if the patient is presenting with a history of trauma and with anxiety at being re-traumatised. This is especially so if such a patient begins the therapy with an omnipotently grandiose expectation of how therapy might help. Idealisation easily slips into denigration when expectations are betrayed and unfulfilled. The enactment might be experienced as Eris: a betrayal of love and of the expectations of therapeutic fulfilment, growth, change and transformation. The negative therapeutic enactment might transform the therapeutic encounter from an act of love into an act of hate, disillusionment and aggression. Whatever else might be said about enactments, their most striking feature is the degree of feeling and passion they arouse in both participants. Though sometimes these feelings might be pleasurable, mostly they are felt as uncomfortable, whether a negative therapeutic reaction or not. The intensity of the feeling hints at the unconscious importance of what is being enacted. For this reason alone I would suggest enactments need to be viewed as part of the erotic transference.

Conclusion

There is no unified agreement in psychoanalysis about the definition of an enactment. One panel (1989) discussion, however, did find common ground around the idea that enactments occur in most analytic situations, some more than others; that they derive from the unconscious resistances in both the therapist and the patient; and that the patient's transference resistance interacts with the analyst's resistance. The ensuing enactment situation is the observable presentation of unconscious meaning residing in both the analyst and patient. Analysis of enactments offers a road to unconscious mental life which otherwise could be left untraversed by a tacit unconscious agreement between patient and analyst. Failure to comprehend an enactment, especially the contribution made by the therapist, may be the main reason behind therapies that end badly. While I agree with the prevailing analytic assumptions that enactments occur in most therapies, it is my experience that they are most likely with patients who have a history of trauma. If there is a personal vulnerability in the therapist, then an enactment is also more likely. I have sought to suggest that enactments are most appropriately viewed as a passionate collision between the unconscious of the therapist and that of the patient, which heightens the feelings of love or hate and has a decisive effect on the course of the therapy. Finally, I suggest that a negative therapeutic outcome might be understood as a negative enactment in which both participants, including the therapist, are largely unconscious at the time and afterwards.

References

Alexander, F. (1950) Analysis of the therapeutic factors in psychoanalytic treatment. *Psychoanalytic Quarterly*, 19: 482–500.

Balbernie, R. (1988) Failing to connect – failing to contain. *British Journal of Psychotherapy*, 5(2): 149–158.

Bemesderfer, S. (2000) Countertransference enactments informed by cancer in an analyst's child. *Journal of the American Psychoanalytic Association*, 48(4) 1521–1539.

Bion, W. R. (1967) *Second Thoughts: Selected Papers on Psychoanalysis*. London: Maresfield Library, 1987.

Cassorla, R. M. S. (2001) Acute enactment as a 'resource' in disclosing a collusion between the analytical dyad. *International Journal of Psychoanalysis*, 82: 1155–1170.

Cassorla, R. M. S. (2005) From bastion to enactment: the 'non-dream' in the theatre of analysis. *International Journal of Psychoanalysis*, 86: 699–719.

Chused, J. F. (1991) The evocative power of enactments. *Journal of the American Psychoanalytic Association*, 39: 615–640.

Eagle, M. (1993) Enactments, transference, and symptomatic cure: a case history. *Psychoanalytic Dialogues*, 3(1): 93–110.

Freud, S. (1916–17) *Introductory Lectures on Psychoanalysis*, Standard Edition, Vols 15–16. London: Hogarth Press.

Freud, S. (1920) Beyond the pleasure principle. In *On Metapsychology: The Theory of Psychoanalysis*. Harmondsworth, UK: Penguin, 1985.

Friedman, R. and Natterson, J. (1999) Enactments: an intersubjective perspective. *Psychoanalytic Quarterly*, 68: 220–247.

Gill, M. (1982) *Analysis of the Transference*. Madison, CT: International Universities Press.

Green, A. and Kohon, G. (2006) *Love and its Vicissitudes*. London and New York: Routledge.

Hartke, R. (2005) The basic traumatic situation in the analytical relationship. *International Journal of Psychoanalysis*, 86: 267–290.

Hirsch, I. (1993) Countertransference enactments and some issues related to external factors in the analyst's life. *Psychoanalytic Dialogues*, 3(3): 343–366.

Jacobs, T. I. (1986) On countertransference enactments. *Journal of the American Psychoanalytic Association*, 34: 289–307.

Jacobs, T. J. (1997) In search of the mind of the analyst: a progress report. *Journal of the American Psychoanalytic Association*, 45: 1035–1060.

Jacobs, T. J. (2001) On unconscious communications and covert enactments: some reflections on their role the analytic situation. *Psychoanalytic Inquiry*, 21: 4–23.

Mann, D. (1997) *Psychotherapy: An Erotic Relationship – Transference and Countertransference Passions*. London: Routledge.

Mann, D. (2002) *Love and Hate: Psychoanalytic Perspectives*. London: Routledge.

McLaughlin, J. (1987) The play of transference: some reflections on enactment in the psychoanalytic situation. *Journal of the American Psychoanalytic Association*, 39: 557–582.

McLaughlin, J. (1991) Clinical and theoretical aspects of enactment. *Journal of the American Psychoanalytic Association*, 39: 595–614.

Ogden, T. H. (1979) On projective identification. *International Journal of Psychoanalysis*, 60: 357–373.

Panel (1992) Enactments in psychoanalysis. *Journal of the American Psychoanalytic Association*, 40: 827–841.

Racker, H. (1968) *Transference and Countertransference*. London: Maresfield Library.

Roughton, R. (1993) Useful aspects of acting out: repetition, enactment and actualisation. *Journal of the American Psychoanalytic Association*, 41: 443–472.

Sandler, J. (1976) Countertransference and role-responsiveness. *International Review of Psychoanalysis*, 3: 43–47.

Weiss, H. (2002) Reporting a dream accompanying an enactment in the transference situation. *International Journal of Psychoanalysis*, 83: 633–644.

Winnicott, D. W. (1971) The use of an object. In *Playing and Reality*. Harmondsworth, UK: Penguin, 1985.

2 Mutual enactments within the therapeutic relationship

Valerie Cunningham

During my client work there have been occasions when a noteworthy outcome has been threatened or even negated by the process of enactment. The two case studies which I provide later in this chapter illustrate this unwelcome force and show how an enactment in one relationship may even overflow and infiltrate into another.

In the midst of an enactment process when it would seem that the combination of our difficulties was threatening to derail the process of therapy, I reflected on my distress and that of my client. I wanted to hold some compassion towards us all, in order to continue to believe in the efficacy of not just those instances but of psychotherapeutic work in general.

Freud originally (1914) wished to avoid transferences, of which a strong component is enactments. However, as I read through the analytic literature, I am heartened to discover that I can view the phenomenon of enactment as a mutual desire to remember traumas in order to resolve the ongoing effect of them. Also, in a hopeful comment, Boesky (cited in Hirsch, 1996) says: 'If the analyst does not get emotionally involved sooner or later, in a manner he had not intended, that analysis will not proceed to a successful conclusion' (Boesky, 1982, p. 573).

Most notably, Carl Rogers devoted his theoretical work to promoting a relational approach in therapeutic encounters (1951). However he, Laura and Fritz Perls, and Eric Berne did not provide a consistent theoretical structure to explain or cope with the vicissitudes of unconscious interactions (Ellenberger, 1994). Nor did they consider that a third dimension might emerge, as Winnicott identified (1965), a place which contains the intersubjective interplay of unconscious processes between client and psychotherapist. The psychodynamic and relational approaches in TA have joined together broadening the original body of theory (as illustrated by Moiso, 1985; Novellino, 1984; and Hargaden and Sills, 2002). The roots of these developments combined are based in the relational psychoanalytic tradition.

Listening to the 'In Our Time' programme on the radio (30 November 2006), I heard a group discussing the discovery and perception of the speed of light and its connection to time and physical matter. I was persuaded how complex this process is, and reflected that in a similar way, what can seem to be straightforward communications between people in relationships involve other dimensions which are not fully understood by anyone – yet. Aspects of psychological enactments seem to come in this category. For example, Gestalt field theory returns us to the psychological arena, suggesting that 'a person is never independent or isolated' but is 'always in contact and connected with everything else in the known world in a real sense' (Joyce and Sills, 2001, p. 24; Lewin, 1952).

If I may make an analogy with art, drawing objects involves considering the spaces both around and between them when creating the essence of a picture. This allows the objects to emerge fully formed in relationship with the overall space: all components are of equal importance and necessity.

Jacobs (1993, unpublished, quoted in Roughton) was the first to bring enactment into the analytic arena. He stated that an enactment is 'the transformation of a wish or idea into a performance'. Roughton (1993) added that 'as a general term, [it] means simply putting into behaviour that which one is experiencing internally'. The consensus in analytic circles is that enactments are inevitable and that their 'usefulness depends on close observation of the interaction between analyst and patient in the session' and that the harmful effects may be mitigated if we know 'in which areas enactments are likely to occur' (Steiner, 2006). Acknowledging the necessity of therapists engaging in personal psychotherapy seems obvious for this form of work.

David Mann defined an 'enactment' as 'a trauma enacted in the therapeutic relationship whereby both client and therapist find they are caught in an unconscious process as though a trauma is revisited or enacted in the therapy itself. The enactment is a re-edition of the past, not an exact replica' (personal communication, Mann, 2005). This interactive view is held also by Greenberg (1986), Stolorow and Atwood (1992), Chused (1997), Renik (1993), Jacobs (1986), McLaughlin (1987), and Friedman and Natterson (1999). I agree, and think the enactment process becomes alive during therapy because a core aspect of the trauma awakens something archaic which belongs to both client and psychotherapist and is unconsciously being negotiated by both into awareness, with the fundamental hope that a mutual resolution will be reached. Friedman and Natterson (1999) state that 'although analyst and patient are separate psychological entities, they are incomplete, and they, like all people, need to complete themselves in their relationships, including the analytic relationship' (p. 222). Therefore they emphasise that enactments are 'jointly-created' (p. 225). It is inevitable that this is so, because the therapist and client struggle to form a relationship, despite their problems probably occurring as a result of neglectful, misattuned and false relationships. The mutual, open exploration of the effect of an enactment process potentially leads to a shift towards a genuinely felt relationship in the present which both can carry forward into other relationships. Psychotherapists may believe that they know all about their life traumas from their own experience of psychotherapy, but the combination of both traumatic histories may actually constellate and collide together, exposing more layers of difficulty.

So far, I have noted different theoretical approaches and their relationship to unconscious processes. I shall now refer to the types of trauma which we generally see in ourselves and our clients.

The *American Heritage Dictionary* (2000) defines trauma in physical, emotional and psychological terms thus:

1   A serious injury or shock to the body, as from violence or an accident.
2   An emotional wound or shock that creates substantial, lasting damage to the psychological development of a person, often leading to neurosis.
3   An event or situation that causes great distress and disruption.

Further to perceiving that a trauma describes a one-off event, we should understand that, if left unrecognised, the effects of a trauma or more than one trauma can also accumulate over time (Khan, 1973). In addition, extreme versions of trauma, such as Post Traumatic Stress Syndrome, reside in domains of additional complexity, and the diagnosis of this condition is being reviewed as more survivors come forward for medical and psychological consideration (Kinchin, 2005; Scott and Stradling, 2004).

Any disturbance in the attachment process between family members can be experienced as traumatic by a child, especially when the main parental figures fail to notice the effect or grasp the significance that this disturbance has on the child concerned.

To illustrate my points, I have chosen to discuss two clients in relation to myself so that I can understand more fully why one relationship weathered the enactment storms and the other one did not. I have altered the clients' names to preserve their identities. The first example of an *enactment* precipitated an ending in psychotherapy and failed to achieve a sufficiently open self-disclosure. The second example shows a series of *short enactments* which resulted in deepening the quality of the relationship. I shall refer to effects of accumulative trauma both on myself and on each client.

Paul

I realised at the start that trouble lay ahead when I agreed to work with Paul. I thought I was experienced enough to manage the challenges he presented, as if that was sufficient for what lay in store. He wanted to see me on an intermittent basis. When I explained that was not my style of working, he stated he would look for a more 'flexible' therapist, then changed his mind and began sessions with me.

The previous history of his therapy was that in each case either he or his therapists had ended the work prematurely. He was only coming to me because he was 'desperate'. He thought he was locked in a relationship battle with a senior, female manager from which he did not know how to extricate himself and thought I could help him. This problem was more important to him than the fact that his mother left him for several months in the care of his father and paternal grandmother when he was an infant. He reported this – to me – significant experience (though fairly common in practice) in a seemingly casual, matter-of-fact way, reassuring himself that any distress he might have felt was alright, for the prize he had gained was to become his father's 'favourite'.

In addition, Paul needed to keep an idealised image of both his historical and current family to, I initially assumed, mask his despair and rage in reaction to the early separation trauma he did not want fully to acknowledge, and also to protect himself from the effect of therapists ending work with him and his own contribution to this process.

For my part, I was continually anxious, for I knew consciously that it was highly likely, because of his history, that Paul would find a way to end the work, citing 'how hard and unyielding I was' because I was charging him for missed sessions according to our contract, and would not tell him how well he was doing when he demanded this acknowledgement from me. Attempts at exploration of his underlying need to have a consistently nurturing, encouraging and emotionally present mother rather than the self-absorbed one he reportedly had had to contend with, fell on stony ground. A power struggle set the tone for all that was to follow in our time together.

Paul found many other ways of criticising me, regarding my appearance and my consulting room. He was regularly late and missed many sessions, and all attempts to explore his behaviour and the impact he was having upon me were fruitless to both of us. I began to dread the times he did arrive. I struggled to concentrate on the task of emptying my mind of any preconceived notions I might have about what was happening between us with the hope that I could stay in any given moment sufficiently to pick up a relevant strand in his comments which would illuminate the mutual process. No! His mother had been fun and had always told him that amongst all his brothers he was the good-looking one and so very bright. The door to the family skeleton cupboard was kept firmly closed each step of the way.

As I expected, Paul ended psychotherapy after he had gained enough insight into the transference process to achieve the resolution of the problems he had with his colleague, which led to a longed-for work promotion. However, he returned some months later. To my considerable surprise, he wanted to understand more about 'why and how he mixed up his reactions to people from his past in the present'. Had Paul understood that the roots of his struggle with his colleague lay in unresolved issues between himself and his mother and father and me? Perhaps Paul was at last wanting to attach to me, and perhaps his previous ambivalence (Bowlby, 1979;

Holmes, 1993) had dissolved enough for him to do so? Had he developed sufficient trust in me for us to enter the unknown together?

Though he had told me more of the details of his early separation from his mother, we had found little opportunity to explore the emotional consequences of it. Would he be willing to take some steps towards regaining early memories and making sense of them in the here-and-now within our relationship?

We both wove in and out of times of what, I thought, was good contact with each other during the next stage of our relationship. These 'now moments' as described by Stern (1998) became part of my empathic attunement with Paul as he expressed his feelings at the recent deaths of both his father and his mother (Rogers, 1951; Clark, 1991; Erskine et al., 1999). These times together allowed air to circulate through his psyche so that he began partially to express his grief too about being left as an infant and about not receiving the mothering he especially needed and wanted.

A chain of events followed which Paul found unwelcome, seemingly as a result of his opening up to his memories and to present reality. The shiny edifice he had built and polished to preserve the appearance of a perfect home and family life began outwardly to crumble. The role of being the 'ever giving, present, loving' father, who wanted nothing more than to provide for his family, was not working in reality.

Now Paul began to oscillate between the usual evasion of me and criticism of his wife and children. He also acknowledged the possibility that the whole purpose of his father taking on the shared parenting role with Paul's grandmother was to ensure his wife would return to him. Confronting within himself that he might not have been the most favoured son in the family deeply distressed him.

I found his revelation profoundly moving, and in tune with an image I had held from the start, of a bewildered, highly anxious and excited Paul as an infant child being with his 'daddy', who was partially in the shadows. I would shore up my confidence by returning to this image at the times of Paul's fiercest criticism of me, in order to assuage my desire to retaliate and transferentially shoot back at him.

However, despite my best intentions, I lost my footing and slithered down what seemed to be a hill of wet mud in the next stage of our relationship. He increasingly asked questions about the purpose and theory behind my interventions. I consistently fended off answering him directly: instead I shared that, though it was partly understandable in the light of his recent painful insight, I was curious about his seeming to want to create distance between us. Despite my reservations about our progress, Paul stated he was now working at a greater level of creativity than ever before, both in his profession and with his colleagues, in the manner I was doing with him. This seemed to be a further attempt to avoid grappling with being in a therapeutic relationship with me.

I surmised that Paul wanted some respite from immersing himself in the problems of his family life. He might also be avoiding putting any real effort into discovering his inner world, which would potentially be the key to finding his identity, and also to discovering his part in the family crises.

The emergence of my own history now touched upon his in an insidious way. My mother and father too had been, at strategic times, unavailable emotionally for me, as were their parents before for them. I was mainly recognised for what I could do for them from a very early age. I thought that if I did enough for my mother, she would not leave me and the family as she threatened to over time. To lose my mother would mean my survival in the world would be at risk. The echo in my mind of her threatened intention, together with the image of her pained expression when exhausted, had traumatised me, and the pain and trauma had accumulated as I lived unconsciously, before psychotherapy, in this state of impending danger.

Paul's and my rage at our parents using us for their own ends became enmeshed. I commented to him that it would seem that he believed if he 'rubbed shoulders' enough with those he thought were more developed people than himself, their evolution would eventually rub off onto him. I was experiencing him parasitically adhering himself to me, taking a notion of 'okayness' from me on a surface level. My reaction, as I moved swiftly between archaic Parent to Child ego state in the countertransference, confirmed the experience I had of my mother using me. Although I knew in reality I could not stop Paul leaving if he really wanted to, however skilled I was, just as he could not have stopped his mother leaving him, however delightful and bright he intrinsically was, I became fascinated, helplessly observing, retrospectively, that I had behaved in complete opposition to my conscious desires. By verbally attacking the adhesive behaviour, I took a step towards pushing him away emotionally, thereby repeating Paul's early trauma of being left, which mirrored my constant childhood anxiety. Surely, I soothed myself, mine was a justifiable and natural response to the accumulation of contemptuous avoidance Paul had directed towards me over years? Another layer of myself was now exposed. Had I envied him for having an ostensibly special time with his father and been angry with him for gloating about it too?

Paul heard my comment as criticism, and he was right. He retaliated: he said had always known that I did not admire him. I did what I could to repair my attack. I owned up again to my sadness and frustration at the ways he had avoided me. I did not include precisely how his early life touched mine. I did not want to give him any more of myself. We were repeating a pattern of withholding vital information, which both of us had learned to do early on in our lives. Instead, we agreed in future to disentangle as close to the moment as possible when Paul thought he heard me criticise him: we valiantly held to this aim. I felt raw with sadness and irritation that I had not contained myself sufficiently to hold him, and had then faced in psycho-therapy, yet again, the effect of my early experiences with my mother.

Paul continued to come to sessions until he had successfully achieved the promotion he most desired, though he was contemplating divorce. He had chosen me to confirm that parental figures only pretended to want him, and I had unwillingly fulfilled his expectations (Berne, 1968). To me, Paul confirmed that being seen in the world as a successful senior manager was more important to him than establishing a genuine relationship with himself and others.

Esther Bick's and Donald Meltzer's ideas, as cited by Meltzer (1975), are particularly helpful in understanding the nature of Paul's presentation to me and how it contributed to our enactment. They noticed that many people in their practice learned only by imitating other people. All their relationships were governed by external values and principles rather than from an internalised felt experience of being in a relationship with another person. Bick and Meltzer decided to name this narcissism, a form earlier than the previously identified Adhesive Identification.

Barry Proner (1988, p. 144) developed the notion further and stated that he noticed he struggled to form relationships with particular clients as 'what I may be offering is not devalued as much as it is by-passed. It may feel to me as if my patient is sticking on to me and/or entering me, in preference to taking me inside him'. Paul's sense of self had been impeded at a primitive stage of his development before he could reasonably understand what this meant to him. The only way he could defend himself from the effect of his losses was to get some semblance of relational sustenance by adhering himself to those people he held in high esteem socially or professionally. Ray Little (2006, p. 304) chooses a particularly apt quote when he cites Symington's (1993) view: 'in its hatred of the relational, one of the ways that narcissism operates is to destroy separateness' (p. 18).

Despite Paul's attempt to evade unconscious processes which could destabilise him, they emerged between us anyway. We both had wanted this, from a co-creative perspective (Hoffman, 1983; Summers and Tudor, 2000; Allen and Allen, 1995), in order to resolve what we could of our past traumas, and we had considerably heightened our awareness of these as a result of our meeting.

Further reflections

One way of considering how our relationship ended in the way it did, is to acknowledge that we held different views about what was the desired outcome for our work. For my part, I knew that a major factor in Paul's relationship difficulties, at work and in his family, lay in the early separation from his mother. This act, on the mother's part, also raised questions about the quality of parenting beforehand. Bick, cited by Meltzer (p. 295), observed catastrophic states of anxiety in some infants' observations, which resulted from mothers being unable to understand their infants and hold them emotionally. Paul had also stated how frightened he was engaging in psychotherapy, for would I be able to hold and contain him? Therefore, he mostly avoided dream work and certainly image making, for he saw that these forms of making contact with his unconscious could threaten his equilibrium. The necessary developmental stage of Paul seeing himself as separate from his mother, with a natural but not excessive state of anxiety about this, was seriously hindered by his mother absenting herself for months. His father's and grandmother's quality of presence further skewed matters. His ability to form an identity and feel secure within himself was impeded by not experiencing a consistent reflection of his mother's love for him, and by his mother's failure to contain her own and her son's feelings, particularly his rage, fear and envy, which could have led Paul to discern which emotion and which state of being belonged to whom. This example of transgenerational scripting is well documented by Berne (1975) and Bowlby (1979).

He did not like his grandmother, who he thought was mainly interested in her son's advancement in business. His father, in this regard, was constantly trying to please his mother by achieving ever-greater financial goals. Neither his father nor his grandmother appeared to think there was any lack of care for him. All family discussion about this event was avoided and further repressed by emphasising his specialness above his siblings. Emotional delving into experiences was not part of the family repertoire. I did not want to parallel this evasion, and thought that his urge towards and interest in resolving his transference towards me and others implicitly gave me the go-ahead to explore these dynamics in depth. I also thought I had explicitly checked with him at various stages whether this was indeed what he was wanting too. Paul recognised I had been a party to his work achievements, which prompted him to stay in therapy with me in order to achieve even greater successes, but not at the risk of a genuine relationship developing between us. Though bringing unaccustomed relief, when we shared moments of mutual understanding, our collaboration had also generated, in his mind, unnecessary pain, disappointment and disillusionment when his long-held beliefs were shattered. The terror of becoming psychologically fragmented and thus not able to function in the world is a strong deterrent to psychotherapeutic depth work. If he had already experienced breakdown in infancy when overwhelmed with powerful feelings which he could not yet express verbally, this would not have surprised me (Winnicott, 1965). I held considerable empathy with his stance. His continued involvement in psychotherapy ended with his longed-for work promotion. To some extent, he stayed as long as he did to please me, thereby repeating his father's behaviour with his wife and mother. Though he stayed for several years, any tenuous form of attachment Paul might have felt towards me was easily severed by my incautious remarks. He eluded moving with me into more unknown areas of his life by consciously ending a therapeutic relationship on his terms. It was an avenging move which reflected the rage and despair he felt towards me and the other women in his life.

I sincerely regret how I behaved towards Paul in venting my frustration at his need to protect himself from my probings into emotionally unfathomable areas. I continue to remember my client and his deep disappointment with me and my sorrow for adding to his distress. For this I am truly sorry.

Philip

There was nothing poetic or extraordinary about the context of the following series of enactments. I imagine the ordinary nature of them may be familiar, though most unwelcome, to all psychotherapists. During these difficult times with Paul, Philip, in his late thirties, arrived.

Philip was married, with children. He described having a lonely childhood in which he and his siblings were left to their own devices by a mother who was more interested in extending her social life than spending time with her children. When she did want to be with him, she made many emotional demands for comfort in order to alleviate the deep distress she felt at her husband's infidelity. She disclosed, to Philip, her intimate feelings towards her husband and the woman he was having an affair with, who had once been her best friend. Desperate for her attention, he listened attentively but described the cost to him as being 'sucked dry' as his mother drew upon his energies to assuage herself. He recounted also being left by his father – a cold, emotionally distant, high-flying business man who managed to maintain this ménage à trois for many years before he finally left his wife. Philip longed for his father's recognition of his creative talents; instead, he received polite indifference and bewilderment at his disinclination to follow in his father's footsteps. Neither parent was available emotionally. Both parents wanted the outside world to see them as a still-intact family. Philip's mother would not tell her mother that she lived with her husband in 'name only'. Philip's father did not want him to disclose that his second wife had been his long-term lover. Philip believed he held the family secrets for most of his life and was exhausted by accommodating them all. As a result, he had developed a finely tuned sense of responsibility, the stress of which led to his physical and emotional breakdown.

As a child, Philip looked for spiritual care and nurturing by observing the changing colours, shapes and scents in nature, for physical comfort from the household cats and for encouragement and interest from his school chums' mothers, and he felt deeply sad and ashamed that this was so. Even though he had not revealed the family secrets, he thought that people must have known about the abysmal situation which existed between his parents. I felt immense sadness when I heard Philip's story. I saw him as a small child continually waiting for his parents to notice him bearing the neglect of both a distracted mother and an indifferent father. I remained with him. He later remembered his mother remarking that Philip 'although good otherwise, was always a hungry baby who could never be satisfied'. This led

Philip to recall a recent dream of being almost suffocated by two large breasts and his subsequent terror and loathing at this experience. He preferred large breasts and was baffled by his extreme revulsion in the dream. On further exploration, he understood how much he had wanted his mum's loving feeding but had had to endure her smothering and neglectful mothering which threatened getting his hunger needs met and also his life. I wondered how he was seeing me. Was I sufficiently present or intrusive? A series of dreams followed, of himself as an infant in the womb. To begin with he hardly moved whilst sucking his thumb voraciously. He interspersed the dreams with drawings of himself as an infant growing, then moving around the womb, gradually playing and using the space. I understood that Philip wanted extra protection as he touched upon primitive states of himself with me.

Already, Philips's story was echoing Paul's and my history. We had all faced and been traumatised by the absence of an emotionally warm, reliable, consistently available mother and father and had all been used by them. The difference between us was whereas Paul was unaware of this, both Philip and I consciously knew it to be so.

A series of short enactments between us followed. Philip cancelled a session, and I charged him for this; he thought he could not ask for an alternative time. Despite my wondering what the effect was upon him, he held onto his feelings about both this and my forthcoming planned break. He rationalised my absence by telling me it was hard to miss a mother who hadn't properly mothered him, thereby expressing his anger towards his mother and myself for being unavailable, and 'using him' by charging for that privilege. His irritation grew indirectly in his transference towards me. However ambivalently attached Philip was to me as a result of being parented both inconsistently and intrusively by his mother (Holmes, 1993), he believed that his strong desire to maintain 'integrity and truthfulness in relationships' had developed as a reaction to the lack of these qualities in both parents. In making this statement, he intimated that he wanted this from me, which I thought boded well for the future. I also thought he was likely to be, unconsciously, deciding whether I could sustain his full frontal rage and disappointment without actually withdrawing, looking hurt and vulnerable in the process, or by counter-attacking him in return. These were behaviours both his wife and mother used in order to thwart him.

He cancelled again and we arranged an alternative time. Philip was simultaneously highly pleased and uncomfortable that he could instigate getting his needs met so easily. Was I accommodating him too easily to avoid his rage, or was I providing him with a reparative experience whereby I responded appropriately to him, or a mixture of both? At that moment, I could not answer these questions with certainty.

Due to his new work commitments, we negotiated another time to meet. Regrettably, the only time available was when I was also attending a course on a monthly basis, which resulted in us meeting less frequently. I highlighted that between us we were repeating the paucity of his parenting by agreeing to have less contact, but on balance we agreed that continuing the relationship was more desirable than ending it. These changes affected us both and contributed to us muddling session times and dates.

To my chagrin, I was the first, seemingly, to miscalculate the date of our next meeting. I found myself unwilling to agree that I had been entirely at fault as I was usually so careful about ensuring that changes to sessions were mutually logged, but then I repeated the process. On both occasions, Philip owned up to particularly looking forward to seeing me, hoping that he would find a warm welcome and acceptance of him: instead he found a closed door. My negligence mirrored his parents' behaviour. Each time, I took as much care as possible to be sufficiently sensitive to Philip's loss and fear that he had driven me away, and to be open to acknowledging his obvious fury at my crassness, and I apologised thoroughly. We seemed to settle for a short while, then it was Philip's turn to miss a session. He was mortified, as only people who say they care, but don't really, behave in such ways and he was too honest for that, and then proceeded to soften towards me: perhaps I did care about him after all?

We took more time to pick over and pick up any floating strands of the pattern we had recently woven together. I disclosed that I could understand, from first-hand experience, a mother's unconcern which matched aspects of his, and I apologised again for mixing up our histories. My disclosure affected him significantly, since he was used to his own mother consistently withdrawing from contact when she felt criticised. Philip revealed the strength of his mixed feelings about my planned breaks, as he missed me, whilst also feeling very angry that I 'left him' at regular times. He made a direct connection between me and the early experiences of being emotionally left by his mother. Gradually he believed that he could be more himself and I would not crumple under the onslaught of his feelings. This was particularly important to him, as he had held the idea of having unlimited power by making his mother happy by holding the family secrets and by averting his father's rage which might have resulted in him leaving the family much earlier than he actually did. He now thought his own rage and fear surpassed that of both parents, and who would be able to help him manage such forceful emotions?

Philips's investment into and involvement with discovering more about himself was evident. He showed me that he could receive my offerings and in so doing moved a step nearer to attaching himself securely to me (Bowlby, 1979). In that process he became aware that I was Valerie and had particular frailties similar to though separate from himself. Clearly the early ego state development of self had not remained split between the omnipotently able and the useless aspects of self versus him settling for being ordinary and special enough in his own uniqueness. Gradually, the losses he had endured were revealed, the deepest being having been emotionally left by both parents. Much later, Philip used the image of himself as an 'enraged baby' screaming out at those who had both left him with so much responsibility in his early years and had not wanted to know who he truly was.

Further reflections

Retrospectively, I am in little doubt that my difficulties with Paul, and continual unpicking of these difficulties in personal psychotherapy, did facilitate my relationship with Philip. Also a key reason why this therapeutic relationship continued despite the series of short enactments was the determined willingness Philip had to explore unpalatable areas of his life. He held a vision that his life could be different, that he could have another chance at it by first learning, in his dreams and drawings, how he could nurture himself in the womb under my interested gaze. From a positive transferential perspective, he liked the idea of coming to see a psychotherapist from an art background, who he believed would understand and appreciate his creativity. He also accepted that we both could be creative on our own terms and that engaging in psychotherapy could enhance his creativity yet further.

I was also particularly sensitive about my failure with Paul, and began with Philip by overcompensating for it by becoming ultra-present until I found my natural rhythm of working again. He tested my unconditional acceptance and resilience whenever he expressed a full range and strength of feelings. This was new behaviour for him and led to a new experience of being received empathically, unconditionally and congruently (Rogers, 1951). I think I was so irritated with Paul's lack of consideration that I unconsciously and inadvertently leaked my feelings over into my relationship with Philip by forgetting our sessions. A combination of Philip's apparent thoughtlessness and my past experience of neglect metamorphosed into my neglect of him in the present. A turning point came when, rather than keeping a pertinent aspect of my history secret, which would have conformed with his family system, I shared myself and apologised in a heartfelt way.

Philip's history of trauma was also accumulative. Although extreme traumas had touched him later in life, unlike Paul he had not suffered the combination of the actual and emotional loss of his mother at an early, strategic stage of development, which might have arrested his ability to receive, digest and enjoy being with me which he could then make use of in other relationships. Because of this he wanted, and was more able, to recover from the effects of the enactment process. In time, he was able to establish a genuine attachment to both me and others (Bowlby, 1979).

Conclusion

Friedman and Natterson (1999) summarise that, in their opinion, 'Intersubjectivity is the overarching theory which can explain the process of enactments'. A colleague wryly remarked, 'Ah yes! Intersubjectivity is about me knowing what you know, and you knowing what I know, and so on.' However, enactments arise from the unconscious, so it would be more accurate to say, 'I did not know at the time that I knew', but became conscious later of the original life experience which the enactment process revealed on its completion, or later was discovered through the analysis of mutual transferences and self-exploration in psychotherapy.

The dissatisfaction which follows yet another failure to satisfy unmet needs, by projecting these onto another person, may represent our desire to recreate and resolve original traumas. This device mirrors Berne's theory of games (1968) which he drew from Freud's notion of repetition compulsion (1926). The game moves the transferential drama of an individual's life script on to its inevitable conclusion as both protagonists switch their role positions of rescuer, persecutor and victim on the Drama Triangle (Karpman, 1968). Berne, I think, was in an optimistic frame of mind when he considered that once we knew our central game, which harbours our repressed feelings and needs from past traumas and so probably underlies any enactments we might engage in, it was possible to interrupt its outcome by analysing mutual transactions and then shifting ego states in order to find an alternative, less harmful, conclusion in the present.

It is no easy matter to change deeply-held beliefs made in reaction to our experience of parenting, social circumstances and genetic disposition. The best possible outcome is that both client and psychotherapist invest in change by being open to, in their respective psychotherapies, the known and the unknown pleasant and less pleasant sides of their respective natures. Bollas's notion of the 'unthought known' (1987, p. 278) refers not only to resurrecting aspects of repressed experiences within the trans-ferential relationship, but also to 'living through, for the first time, elements of psychic life that have not been previously thought'. These are memories which are held somatically in the body before the ability to conceptualise their meaning has developed. Later, 'fundamentally new experiences' emerge, given time and space to do so. In this spirit within the psycho-therapeutic relationship, shared associations, with carefully proffered self-disclosure on the part of the psychotherapist during the mutual exchange of experience, may lead to greater awareness so that shifts can occur.

Clearly, the earlier the relational failure is formed, the more challenging the work is, because it is more difficult to express ourselves using symbolic language at primitive, developmental stages. Both image making and dream analysis can provide an alternative conduit from the unconscious which helps to form symbolic thoughts and feelings consciously. When severe enactments occur they are likely to be experienced as overwhelming for both participants. The psychotherapist, however, is required to facilitate both herself and her clients into a conscious understanding of the past trauma whilst living through a present one which piercingly imitates the original (personal communication, Mann, 2005). This undertaking requires considerable self-awareness, the willingness of both participants and a sufficiently good attachment to navigate agonising psychological territory. Without a reasonable level of attachment, or a desire and hope for one, this task can be unworkable. Psychotherapists also need to have an understanding of the necessary holding and containing skills to facilitate the therapeutic alliance which fosters the process of attachment. Being authentic and fully engaged in personal psychotherapy lays the necessary foundation for this ability.

A considerable amount of research has taken place since the early days of infant and mother observations (Ainsworth et al., 1978; Bowlby, 1979; Winnicott, 1965; Stern, 1998). Stern noticed that early failures to make contact between mother and infant could be addressed in an ongoing manner throughout the early months, providing parenting figures had a willingness to engage differently, by being sufficiently aware, and accordingly responsive, to their infant's needs. However, when traumas remain unnoticed, especially at an early stage in an infant's life, brain development is affected; in severe cases irreparably so (Schore, 1994). This makes the attachment process doubly difficult if not impossible to repair, and enactments doubly counter-productive.

As previously stated, Steiner believes that as psychotherapists we can at least prepare for the likelihood of an enactment occurring: a client does not have the advantage of this prior information.

To see clients more than once a week, whilst taking into account the possible difficulties this might present, is more customary in analytic than humanistic practice, though it is likely to be the most effective way of working with primitive forms of ego state development. But no matter how willing I am to do this, or how thorough I am in assessing the readiness of clients to engage in psychotherapy, my level of ability and my commitment to the relationship, I cannot prevent times of enactment.

Paradoxically, Meltzer (1975) states the importance of casting aside all preconceptions and theories so that we can be open to fresh ways of thinking about what is happening between our clients and ourselves and so behave differently. Whilst acknowledging Meltzer's philosophical stance, I remain convinced, as research has confirmed (Kahn, 1997; Lambert, 1992), that the quality of the relationship which develops, and which is sustained despite unwanted enactment experiences, is the consummating factor for successful therapeutic outcomes, whichever theoretical or scientific model is referred to.

In this chapter I aimed to show how I became clearer about my part in the above processes and particularly about which aspect of my history can become unwittingly entwined in my clients', however many times I visit and wrestle with this particular trauma in my invaluable experiences of psychotherapy.

I wanted to remain compassionate towards myself, clients and colleagues and so remind myself of the story in Henry James's novel *The Golden Bowl*.

Though beautiful, this golden bowl wrought from one piece of crystal has a flaw which has a profound parallel effect in the protagonists' relationships. The bowl is bought by a person whose companion already sees the fault. This person likes it so much that the flaw, when perceived, is acceptable. This embracing of inevitable imperfection lies at the heart of psychotherapy (Kearney, 1996, p. 151–178).

References

Ainsworth, M., Blehar, M., Waters, E. and Wall, S. (1978) *Patterns of Attachment: Assessed in the Strange Situation and at Home.* Hillsdale, NJ: Lawrence Erlbaum.

Allen, J. R., and Allen, B. A. (1995) Narrative theory, redecision therapy, and postmodernism. *Transactional Analysis Journal*, 25: 327–334.

Berne, E. (1968) *Games People Play: The Psychology of Human Relationships.* Harmondsworth: Penguin. (Original work published 1964)

Berne, E. (1975) *Transactional Analysis in Psychotherapy: A Systematic Individual and Social Psychiatry.* London: Souvenir Press. (Original work published 1961)

Boesky, D. (1982) Acting Out: a reconsideration of the concept. *International Journal of Psychoanalysis*, 63: 39–55.

Bollas, C. (1987) *The Shadow of the Object: Psychoanalysis of the Unthought Known.* London: Free Association Books.

Bowlby, J. (1979) *The Making and Breaking of Affectional Bonds.* London: Tavistock.

Chused, J. F. (1997) Discussion of 'Observing-participation, mutual enactment, and the new classical models' by Irwin Hirsch. *Contemporary Psychoanalysis*, 33(2).

Clark, B. D. (1991) Empathic transactions in the deconfusion of the Child ego state. *Transactional Analysis Journal*, 21: 92–8.

Ellenberger, H. F. (1994) *The Discovery of the Unconscious: The History and Evolution of Dynamic Psychiatry.* London: Fontana Press. (Original work published 1970)

Erskine, R. G., Moursund, J. P. and Trautmann, R. L. (1999) *Beyond Empathy: A Theory of Contact-in-Relationship.* Philadelphia: Brunner/Mazel.

Freidman, R. and Natterson, J. (1999) Enactments: an intersubjective perspective. *Psychoanalytic Quarterly*, 68.

Freud, S. (1914) *Fausse Reconnaissance (Deja Raconte) in Psycho-Analytic Treatment,* Standard Edition, Vol. 12. London: Hogarth Press, 1958.

Freud, S. (1926) *Inhibitions, Symptoms and Anxiety,* Standard Edition, Vol. 20. London: Hogarth Press, 1959.

Greenberg, J. R. (1986) Theoretical models and the analyst's neutrality. *Contemporary Psychoanalysis*, 24: 689–704.

Hargaden, H. and Sills, C. (2002) *Transactional Analysis: A Relational Perspective.* Hove, UK: Brunner/Routledge.

Hirsch, I. (1996) Observing-participation, mutual enactment, and the new classical models. *Contemporary Psychoanalysis*, 32(3).

Hoffman, I. Z. (1983) The patient as interpreter of the analyst's experience. *Contemporary Psychoanalysis*, 19: 389–422.

Holmes, J. (1993) *John Bowlby and Attachment Theory.* London: Routledge.

Jacobs, T. (1986) On countertransference enactments. *Journal of American Psychoanalytic Association*, 34: 289–387.

James, H. (1904/1966) *The Golden Bowl*. Harmondsworth, UK: Penguin.

Joyce, P. and Sills, C. (2001) *Skills in Gestalt Counselling & Psychotherapy*. London: Sage.

Karpman, S. (1968) Fairy tales and script drama analysis. *Transactional Analysis Bulletin*, 7(26): 39–43.

Kearney, M. (1996) *Mortally Wounded*. Dublin, Ireland: Marino Books.

Kinchin, D. (2005) *Post Traumatic Stress Disorder: The Invisible Injury*. Didcot, UK: Success Unlimited.

Khan, M. M. R. (1973) The concept of cumulative trauma. *The Psychoanalytic Study of the Child*, 18: 286–306.

Kahn, M. M. R. (1997) *Between Therapist and Client: The New Relationship*. New York: Freeman.

Lambert, J. J. (1992) Psychotherapy outcome research: Implications for integrative and eclectic therapists. In J. Norcross and M. R. Goldfried (eds.), *Handbook of Psychotherapy Integration* (pp. 94–129). New York: Basic Books.

Lewin, K. (1952) *Field Theory in Social Science*. London: Tavistock.

Little, R. (2006) Treatment considerations when working with pathological narcissism. *Transactional Analysis Journal*, 36: 303–317.

McLaughlin, J. (1987) The play of transference: some reflections on enactment in the psychoanalytic situation. *Journal of the American Psychoanalytic Association*, 39: 557–582.

Meltzer, D. (1975) Adhesive identification. *Contemporary Psychoanalysis*, 11: 259–310.

Moiso, C. (1985) Ego states and transference. *Transactional Analysis Journal*, 15(3): 194.

Novellino, M. (1984) The analysis of countertransference. *Transactional Analysis Journal*, 14: 63–67.

Proner, B. (1988) Envy of oneself, adhesive identification and pseudo-adult states. *Journal of Analytical Psychology*, 33: 143–163.

Renik, O. (1993) Analytic interaction: conceptualizing technique in light of the analyst's irreducible subjectivity. *Psychoanalytic Quarterly*, 62: 553–571.

Rogers, C. (1951) *Client-centred therapy: its current practice, implications, and theory*. London: Constable.

Roughton, R. E. (1993) Useful aspects of acting out: repetition, enactment and actualisation. *Journal of American Psychoanalytic Association*, 41: 443–447.

Schore, A. N. (1994) *Affect Regulation and the Origin of the Self: The Neurobiology of Emotional Development*. Mahwah, NJ: Erlbaum.

Scott, M. and Stradling, S. (2004) *Counselling for Post Traumatic Stress Disorder*. London: Sage.

Steiner, J. (2006) Interpretive enactments and the analytic setting. *International Journal of Psychoanalysis*, 87: 315–20.

Stern, D. N. (1985) *The Interpersonal World of the Infant: A View from Psychoanalysis and Developmental Psychology*. New York: Basic Books.

Stolorow, R. and Attwood, G. (1996) *A Meeting of Minds: Mutuality in Psychoanalysis*. Hillsdale, NJ: Analytic Press.

Summers, G. and Tudor, K. (2000) Co-creative transactional analysis. *Transactional Analysis Journal*, 30: 23–40.

Symington, N. (1993) *Narcissism: A New Theory*. London: Karnac Books.

Winnicott, D. W. (1965) *The Maturational Processes and the Facilitating Environment*. New York: Universities Press.

Winnicott, D. W. (1974) Fear of breakdown. *International Review of Psychoanalysis*, 1: 103.

3   The abandonment

Enactments from the patient's sadism and the therapist's collusion

Marie Adams

Every therapist's nightmare is the professional complaint. At the very least a complaint will inspire shame in the therapist. At worst it could mean the end of their professional career. In this chapter I will look at how my own history formed a 'perfect' perverted match for my patient's archaic pattern of survival. This ultimately meant that the abandonment she so feared was repeated, rather than considered in the therapy, and together we enacted a sado-masochistic dance of attack and survival when she finally lodged a complaint against me. Enactment, as I will write here, is the unconscious playing out of archaic, unresolved conflict in the here and now *as if* it is in the past. In my view my patient's complaint against me was a symbolic act of revenge against those who perpetuated violence against her as a child. By this means she was still able to maintain the 'love' link where sadism replaces or equals affection in the unconscious mind of a helpless child.

Transference and counter-transference

How does it happen that the relationship between therapist and patient deteriorates to such an extent that a complaint is lodged? This is a messy business, because in most cases – and I am not speaking here of intentional exploitation, or a disregard of therapeutic boundaries – therapists work from the best of intentions. Our work is necessarily flawed (Winnicott, 1955–56, p. 298). We do let down our clients, and in most cases this is the grit of what we call the 'working through' of the transference. It is through the resolution of the transference/counter-transference struggle that our patients re-frame their view of the world and themselves; they lay the old ghosts to rest in the past and they emerge stronger, better equipped to manage the present. If this didn't happen often enough in our work, we could not stick at the job. I would argue that even the most altruistic of therapists needs some job satisfaction. As Winnicott (1947: 196) points out in his article on Hate in the Countertransference, therapists 'get immediate rewards through identi-fication with the patient, who is making progress, and I can see still greater rewards some way ahead, after the end of treatment'. If this is not forth-coming, hate often 'remains unexpressed and even unfelt'.

It is too easy to say that every complaint against a therapist is the direct result of a patient's history, unexpressed rage at an earlier trauma finding an outlet in the here and now. What about the therapist? What unresolved issues in their history are manifest in the dyad? What has drawn this therapist to this particular client group, which is more prone, perhaps, to overt acts of rage than some others? Why did this therapist take on this particular client when his instincts told him that trouble lay ahead, the shadow of defeat already obvious in that first meeting?

I saw Eileen on a weekly basis before a crisis precipitated her coming twice a week. I saw her for a total of three years, initially within a doctor's surgery before she asked to see me privately. This was agreed to by the surgery, even encouraged. When I first saw Eileen I was a qualified person-centred counsellor and in the middle of training as an Integrative psychotherapist. Throughout my work with Eileen I attended regular supervision and was in twice-weekly therapy. I had a strong, supportive network of colleagues and took advantage of reading material I thought might further my professional development and understanding. Despite this there was a fault line at the core of this relationship which, I believe now, was due to a profound interweaving of our unconscious processes, much of which could not have been avoided. My argument is not that unconscious processes can always be determined – by its very nature we cannot know our unconscious – but sometimes we may be able to recognise the signs that things beyond our grasp are at work. I believe that it is our recognition of this that may determine our worth as a therapist with those patients who speak so profoundly to the unresolved and unknown aspects of ourselves.

First impressions

Eileen presented with issues of low self-esteem ('I hate myself') and a comment that her husband of six years thought she was 'crazy'. This, she explained, was because she could not help herself when she was angry. 'I just lose it completely', she told me in a remarkably cheerful tone of voice. While I did pick up on the unconscious warning that she was likely to 'lose it completely' with me at some stage, I was not attuned to my own unconscious response – in the face of painful attack I historically respond by either withdrawing in shame or by working hard to win the protagonist over. In the first moments of this particular enactment, I made an effort to express warmth and acceptance, two qualities I understood to be fundamental to the therapeutic relationship (Rogers, 1957) but which in this instance might also be seen as an attempt to ensure my own safety. I don't believe that it was in the offering of these two 'core conditions' that the enactment resided, but in the paradoxically conscious effort I had to make to provide them. They did not come entirely easily.

The bare bones of her history were that she was the younger of two sisters. Eileen made a great point of telling me how much she cared for her parents, who lived in a privately rented house close to the estate where she had grown up. As evidence of her consideration of them she told me that she had been forced to badger the landlord into adapting the house to suit their needs, including building a ramp leading up to the front door to accommodate her ailing father's need for easy access.

I was less impressed by her generosity than I was struck by her assumption that the landlord should provide and pay for such exceptional services beyond the remit of the lease. I noted her sense of entitlement and what sounded to me like a paradoxical false note of concern. This evoked in me a powerful flash of disbelief and dislike towards her, my countertransferential response to the inauthenticity of the moment. Johnson (1987, p. 62) speaks of the narcissistic dilemma as a conflict between the 'false self' and the 'real self', where the first is mistaken for the other and any threat to the self-image, in Eileen's case her view of herself as a caring and dedicated daughter, is experienced as an attack on the real self. '[F]or the narcissist, if you threaten his self-image or self-concept, it is as if you are threatening his very being' (Johnson, 1987, p. 62).

Chassequet-Smirgel (1984, p. 25) adds to this, '[A]ll of us are open to the perverse solution which constitutes a balm for our wounded narcissism and a means of dissipating our feelings of smallness and inadequacy. This temptation can lead to our losing the love for truth and replacing it with a taste for sham.'

Eileen had received some therapy many years before, although she said it 'had not worked' and that the therapist had insisted that she attend regular group meetings. This had been in a hospital setting and she would not be pressed for further details. Why, for instance, had she been sent for a psychiatric referral? She simply shrugged her shoulders and said, 'I was going through a bad time, I guess.'

Her evasiveness intrigued me. I experienced a frisson of concern, but also a thrill. In a practice comprised largely of the neurotically distressed, I thought this patient would be interesting. I have always enjoyed a challenge – another element in my need to win over, or find some means of establishing mastery over unmanageable circumstances. Eileen's pathology and my own were already welding together through transference and countertransference to create a dyad where we could enact again our very different experiences of archaic abandonment, in my case the 'loss' of my mother to grief after the sudden death of my sister. I worked very hard as a child to win my mother 'back'.

Eileen worked for a building society. She was a quick thinker with a gift for numbers. She worked behind the scenes, and later I imagined that this was how her employers kept her out of the front line, away from the public with whom she had sometimes 'lost it'. Any hint that management might want to discipline her and Eileen visited her union representative or lawyer, sometimes both. Appointing her to a strictly clerical position was as safe a position as they could contrive to prevent her taking out any more grievances against those she worked for, or with. Their strategy was not successful, but it may have caused less disruption to the day-to-day running of the office. Eileen's career was littered with accusations and litigation, some of which she had won. Again this was a warning of what was likely to be enacted between us. While Eileen worked within the transference towards my attacking or abandoning her, I countertransferentially made it my goal to 'win' her over, to be the one person who did not let her down. I wonder now if I had been another therapist, with a different pathology, whether or not she would have continued with me. In order for the enactment to take place, both the patient and the therapist must have the potential within them for it to happen. I believe that in that first session Eileen was already unconsciously working to determine how I might fit into her particular drama. If I had failed the audition, she might have gone elsewhere.

Eileen's husband was wealthy and they lived in some luxury in an affluent neighbourhood within driving distance of her parents' home. She had no children, and in our first session she said this was a source of some sadness. This was stated without any affect, a matter of fact.

Throughout most of the session, however, she was cheerful, even chipper. She presented as very well groomed, even chic, and her clothes were tailored to fit her precisely. She wore very high shoes. Her features were a little pinched, and when I asked if she had ever suffered from an eating disorder she was enthusiastic, detailing a history of anorexia and bulimia going back years. In my experience, there is usually a tinge of shame when a client admits to a struggle with food or alcohol, but there was nothing but gleeful pride being expressed here. Shame, or at least sheepishness was evident concerning issues of self-harm. She had a history of cocaine abuse, and later I would see evidence of a deeper commitment to sado-masochism through illicit relationships and a history of profound violence in sexual contact. As Kreisman and Straus (1989), writing of the Borderline Personality Disorder point out, 'Borderlines form a kind of insulating bubble that not only protects them from emotional hurt but also serves as a barrier from the sensations of reality. The experience of pain, then, becomes an important link to existence.' They also point out that, 'self-destructing behaviour can also evolve from a manipulative need for sympathy or rescue' (p. 34).

My own history did not seem to link with hers on any level, other than a degree of professional success. I was born in relative comfort, the oldest of six children. For many years before training as a counsellor and psychotherapist I worked as a journalist, changing careers only in my early forties. The curiosity sparked in me by Eileen during that first session was not therapeutic concern, but journalistic curiosity, the excitement akin to entering a war zone, terrifying and titillating at the same time. Something deeper was also prodded, I believe now. In her perverse pride in her being 'crazy' and 'out of control', there was also a stroking of my narcissism, my own, unacknowledged and unwarranted confidence in the unhinged bits of my internal world. If she was 'crazy', so was I, but of a better sort. Unlike Eileen, I had hold of my temper and my life was steady. No one tried to shove me into the background because of what havoc I might wreak. My craziness was contained.

This was a process underground, not at all conscious. It was the horrible stroking of my tendency to prove I could always do things better than everyone else, the imperative to excel. If this served me well under most of life's circumstances, it clearly has its limits, and this was one of them.

Relief vs change

Patients do not tell us everything in detail in their first session, of course they don't, but they often show us what doors might be opened. They indicate what we might define as a curiosity about themselves, a willingness to begin the process of discovery, even as they shift into the familiar defences to keep us out. Rogers (1957) defines this in his six pre-conditions for therapy as the client's ability to 'receive empathy'. Masterson (1990, p. 129), with a more analytical perspective, understands the profound difficulty of establishing a 'therapeutic alliance' with patients who lack 'an explicitly conscious understanding that the patient and therapist are working together to help the patient achieve mature insight into the nature of his problems and the means to alleviate them'. He points out that this 'therapeutic alliance' is therefore the goal of the work in the first instance, which can take years (p. 130).

Eileen, however, spoke in absolutes, without any indication that she wanted to learn more about herself. She wanted relief from her symptomatic anger, which she admitted was out of control, but she was not concerned with developing insight. She showed a clear unwillingness to explore, a disinterest in determining a link between her history and her symptoms. Her distress at her uncontained rage was not that it happened, but that it threatened her relationship. She did not want to be abandoned.

Lorna Smith Benjamin (1996, p. 115) defines the Borderline process as 'my misery is your command'. In this lopsided dyad, the therapist works hard to understand, empathise and promote insight. The client, however, experiences interpretation as blame and the maintaining of the therapeutic boundary as rejection. Their response to what they perceive as abandonment is either to attack their therapist, or harm themselves. The therapist then becomes resentful or frightened, and often both. Eventually the relationship can be experienced as doomed, but there is no way out for the therapist. If she ends the relationship, she *is* abandoning her patient, but if she does not she is functioning with a metaphorical gun at her head – the terror that the patient will either hurt herself through self-harm, or hurt the therapist through litigation. These are not imagined possibilities, they are dead real.

Grandiosity vs. confidence

I began working with Eileen on a weekly basis. In ignorance I mistook my grandiosity for confidence and my perverse curiosity for concern.

Eileen was articulate and witty and was never late for her sessions. Within weeks of our working together her husband announced he was leaving Eileen for another woman. In a precursor to the anxiety I would later feel with Eileen he told her, 'I can't stand this any more. I'm even frightened you might kill me some day. I'm getting out.'

In the midst of this abandonment crisis Eileen decided to attend therapy twice a week.

Eileen could not connect any of her current distress to experiences in her past, despite a family history of violence and disruption. Eileen's mother walked out on her father a number of times, sometimes with the children, occasionally without them. 'This is about them, not me', Eileen insisted, disregarding how hard she worked to drive others, including her husband and eventually me, to enact these early, traumatic abandonments.

I held back on interpretation, noticing that empathy appeared to calm her. When she was soothed, I felt gratified. I told myself that I was doing my job and my client was feeling better. Although this process was fitting in very nicely with Rogerian notions of the therapeutic relationship (1957), instinct told me something was being avoided, and I also knew it wasn't just about her.

I was too inexperienced a therapist to recognise that an easy time in therapy often indicates collusion, a resistance on the therapist's part to name the struggle. Nor did I consider that what perversions are exercised outside of the therapy room will also be manifest within it. Chasseguet-Smirgel, writing of a client with perverse tendencies says, 'he does not seek in analysis to discover some truth as to his mental functioning; rather he seeks a support for finding a delinquent solution to his conflicts. We see that we are not in search of a therapeutic alliance but of a perverse one' (p. 113). She also notes that, 'there is a "perverse core" latent within each one of us that is capable of being activated under certain circumstances' (p. 1).

Eileen had only to hint at her rage for me to back down from awkward inquiry or the suggestion that her anger might be linked to early experience. In my effort to pacify her, I avoided the difficult issues altogether. While I convinced myself that her leaving the sessions 'soothed' was a marker of my 'success', it was in fact indicative of a power struggle, the first hint of a sado-masochistic dance being enacted between us.

There is also the notion of the therapist as miracle worker. A patient presents with distress and through counselling or therapy *with us* they will be made well, a kind of psychic laying on of hands. The therapist may also collude, consciously or unconsciously, with this myth. In this scenario it is our capacity to cure that is the focus, rather than the client's ability to change themselves through whatever insight or part of ourselves we make available for them to use. It is the old joke: God, in a wish to feel powerful, dresses up like a doctor (Peters, 1997, p. 269). If, in an effort to gratify our own need for *superiority* we become therapists, we deny our humanity and the authenticity through which we may truly be able to connect with our patients. We are also doomed to failure if, unconsciously, we actually become therapists in an effort to circumvent our own conflicts and to convince ourselves that we are better integrated, more together than our patients.

In my relationship with Eileen, she needed control and I craved success. We were a perfect match.

Litigation and complaints

A part of Eileen's struggle – and the source of some of her masochistic gratification – was derived from her conviction that she was persecuted. This included neighbours, dentists, electrical appliances, vehicles and those who looked after them and, of course, colleagues and employers. Anyone deemed in a position to *provide* for her inevitably let her down, at which point she would take out a professional complaint or sue. There was every reason to believe I was likely to fall victim to failure as well.

And yet my grandiosity, my determination to succeed pushed me forward. I was as blind as my client to the wider world, arguably just as crazy. I was an unconsciously willing participant in an enactment now so clear it is hard to imagine how it might have ended any way other than in a complaint, but I simply could not see that then. From my own historical position, I forever held out hope.

If, in fact, I deserved a complaint perhaps this is where it should have resided: in the arrogance to believe that in private practice, without the supportive cloak of a hospital setting which Eileen had already refused, I could work with someone with a history of violence, who displayed all the signs of Borderline Personality Disorder (DSM-IV) and used her rage and financial resources to sue anyone who disappointed her.

Searles (1986, pp. 510–511) suggests that the analyst 'will develop – hopefully, to a limited, self-analytically explorable degree' – a level of psychosis, a countertransferential response that is necessary to the work. He also emphasises that 'going crazy, whole hog' with the client can do great harm.

He, of course, is referring to when the work is in full swing, not at the very beginning when a decision must be made whether or not to work with a patient, and under what circumstances, in private practice or within a clinical or hospital setting. However, craziness in my view can kick in early, and the intensity of my determination to succeed with Eileen was certainly an indicator of some internal process. This was not out of character for me, but the visceral passion with which I was experiencing it was unusual. Main (1957, p. 135) speaks of this phenomenon when he says of a particular patient group, 'Not all severely ill patients are appealing, indeed, some are irritating, but all of these aroused, in the staff, wishes to help of an unusual order, so that the medical decision to treat the patient in spite of manifestly poor prognosis was rapidly made.' I was falling victim to the notion that I could be a saviour, despite the evidence that nothing and no one had ever succeeded before me.

And to what, after all, was I supposed to succeed? Was Eileen to rise up and walk, the crippling experiences of her childhood banished to such an extent that they would seem never to have happened? Or was I going to be the one that disappointed her without incurring her wrath? If that was so, no wonder that I worked empathy so hard, an unconscious effort to keep her rage at bay. In the countertransference I believe we were already enacting her history and, like her parents, I was more concerned with my own feelings of well-being than I was with Eileen's. However, that being so, what was I enacting within my own history?

Rage and insight

It was Eileen's rage that both interfered with her life and provided her with the most gratification. While anger was the currency that seemed to drive her early childhood, in my family all expression of rage was reduced out of existence through reason and understanding. Our experiences were polar opposites and yet, in those early days of our work together, Eileen and I played on what was a comfortable see-saw for both of us – through the use of *apparent* empathy (reason and understanding) I managed her rage out of existence and she was pacified. This was not true empathy, for I was not giving her what she needed, only what she wanted. I was feeding the bully in her, and as a result she felt powerful, rather than empowered. A more empathic response, for instance, might have been to reflect her struggle to look at her own process, to understand her anger and make sense of it, but of course that would have caused *me* discomfort. I would not have felt so superior, nor such a good therapist in those moments when she reared up in anger and accused me of being lousy at my job, of not understanding her. In *my* history, my parents were disappointed in themselves when their children were angry or expressed themselves without restraint. Any expression of complex emotion by me or one of my siblings was experienced as *their* failure, just as in a repetition of that history I tended to view any expression of rage from Eileen as a failure on my part rather than the unveiling of her process and a necessary part of the work, the working through of the transference.

In my view this process was less about my countertransference than it was about *my* transferential struggle with anyone who threatened anger towards me, this time projected onto Eileen. Another therapist, with a different history and more experience, might have understood the complexity of this process with Eileen. This is debatable, of course, as our unconscious processes can maintain such a stranglehold, but someone else might have been able to make sense of the experience earlier than I was, or at least to sit with it until some insight was given through the benefit of the emerging transference/countertransference dyad.

Over time my pattern with Eileen became uncomfortable for me, partly because my training in a more analytical frame was finally allowing me some insight into Eileen's deeper processes and also because, through my personal therapy, I was at long last coming into contact with my own repressed rage. Eileen and I, in those years, may have become like a couple who first come together in a perfect neurotic fit only to discover that at least one of them is changing and the arrangement is no longer so comfortable. If the relationship is to continue, some adjustment needs to be made in the other to accommodate that change.

Sado-masochism

I believe it is important to consider how changes in the therapist may affect the patient. In healthy relationships there is plasticity, a capacity to shift and change and make room for the other, not necessarily easily or without pain, but there is a willingness to make an effort. I believe we ask that of our patients all the time, usually out of awareness, but just as they make demands on us according to their moods and experiences, so do we make unconscious demands on them. We have bad days, we are tired or pre-occupied with our own relationships; our children are worrying and our partners become ill. We have mortgages to pay and unexpected expenditures; we have mid-life crises and we go through the menopause. We fall in love and we fall out of love. All of this we bring with us into the room with our clients, whether we are determined to keep our personal lives separate or not. With Eileen, amongst the multitude of small and greater life events that I carried within me, I also brought a change in my professional perspective. I grew up a bit and began to recognise a little more my complicity in our relationship. I began to understand that I was contributing to an unhealthy part of her in order to maintain an unhealthy aspect of myself. Even my attraction to a person-centred philosophy, I believe, was an effort to maintain a positive view. There was no room for the shadow side (Jung, 1916) as I saw it when practising the core conditions (Rogers, 1957), and now I was coming face to face, through my own therapy and continuing training and experience, with the less savoury aspects of myself and the possibility that perversion is a creative effort to manage trauma (Chasseguet-Smirgel, 1984).While there were flagrant elements of that 'creative' process in Eileen, there were also aspects at work within me. What I rationalised as therapeutic curiosity may, at times, have been more closely linked to voyeurism, and what I termed empathy no doubt sometimes carried an element of sadistic pleasure in Eileen's suffering as well as masochistic gratification – it often *hurt* to hear of her sexual experiences, often violent and humiliating and involving physical beatings, the bully Eileen reduced to less than nothing in an overtly sado-masochistic coupling for which she sometimes even paid. For Eileen this might be seen as a reversal of her archaic experience, imposing a perverse mastery over her own suffering by somehow inflicting it on me. I, in turn, enacted her childhood role, and my own, by taking on board that pain.

As I developed insight into my collusion with Eileen's process I began to gain some understanding of how this process might be playing out in the room. Once again, while it might be easy to see what was being replicated in her history, it may be even more important to understand what was going on in mine. Why was I so easily seduced into the perversion? Why could I not step back and extricate myself from this unhealthy relationship without the violent ending that ensued? I should have seen it coming – certainly my supervisor was concerned, and colleagues I had taken into my confidence expressed worry that I might be heading for disaster. In hindsight, is there another way that this relationship might have continued in a healthy way, or ended on a more productive note?

Even as I write this article I wonder what unconscious elements might still be at work. Why on earth would I hold up my therapeutic failure to such exposure? In the name of understanding a complex therapeutic relationship, am I really only holding myself up for a professional (masochistic?) flogging, just as Eileen might have done in her sexual exploits? Am I, even now, enacting my own archaic struggle to gain mastery over archaic loss by trying to win you over in the face of likely criticism?

As a child my distress was often minimised and, in an unconscious effort to release my anxiety, I developed a number of neurotic defences. These diminished over the years, not necessarily because the issues were resolved but rather because I found other means of discharging my anxieties. I chose a profession where I was often forced to engage with people under difficult circumstances and who were often antagonistic towards the press. I travelled a good deal, and of course my work as a journalist was a perfect forum for both discharging and disregarding my process at the same time. Because I survived, often withdrawing from any real danger just in time, I always felt superior – certainly it gave me a sense of control, something Eileen spoke about in her description of her sado-masochistic contacts. 'The agreement is that we stop whenever the other one says so. Nobody goes further than the other one wants.' Control, or pseudo-control?

Eileen and I moved into the next stage of our enactment, leading directly to her abandonment crisis. As I began to collude less with her, she began, not surprisingly, to like me much less. She detested interpretations, probably because they were experienced by her as criticism. She retaliated with accusations and sometimes threats, including one incident when she brandished a counselling textbook. My job, she said, was to empathise with her, not to query or challenge. She had spoken to friends and they all agreed that my approach was unethical. 'You are supposed to support me', she said. 'Instead you go on holiday and leave me, you don't actually care whether I live or die.' When I pointed out that recently she had been missing sessions, perhaps in an effort to gain some control over me, she was livid, and when I suggested that her feelings might be archaic and indicative of earlier abandonment terrors, she was even more incensed.

I felt stronger as a therapist during this period but I was also increasingly aware of a sado-masochistic process being enacted. Had Eileen been with another therapist, this stage of the work would have been inevitable. With someone else, however, it is possible that the ending of the work might have been a more positive experience for Eileen, with at least something worked through in the therapy. Instead, the work ended with nothing having been achieved for Eileen, not even any particular insight, and I became just one more person for whom she gunned in an effort to punish those who had hurt her in the past.

As the months and even years went by, managing Eileen's hate and anger felt relentless. She was the continual focus of my supervision, often to the exclusion of my other patients. My own therapist noted how often I brought Eileen into the room, pointing out that this time I did not know how to withdraw from the threat of danger. Nor could I raise my hand to stop the sadistic violence in mid-flow, as Eileen claimed she could when engaged in violent sex, just because I felt I'd had enough. Increasingly I wanted Eileen to become so angry she would actually leave therapy. At the same time, I knew that if she left in anger a complaint would inevitably follow, though I couldn't for the life of me figure out on what grounds. I was caught between a rock and a hard place and I began to feel helpless, in itself a masochistic experience.

How long would this 'working through' need to go on before something shifted? By this time I knew I was not providing Eileen with anything except a vehicle to vent her rage. She was not interested in insight or change, only in the gratification of archaic pain, inflicted sometimes on herself but often on me. In fact, there was such gratification for her in this sado-masochistic process that I don't believe now that she could see any benefit in giving up her behaviour. In her mind, if she did not have this, what would she have left? She might have wanted relief from her suffering, but she did not want to give up the prime motivation of her life so far – revenge for the pain she experienced as a child enacted over and over again and now with me in the therapy room.

There were several years at the beginning of the work during which Eileen did not take out any complaints or sue anyone, not even her former husband. During the last year, however, she told me she had engaged a lawyer to help her instigate a number of grievances at work. Bullying, sexual harassment, and a request by her bosses to change her working practices (she often rang in 'ill', returning only on the last day before they were legally entitled to let her go on health grounds) were just some of her complaints.

Over that year there were a number of disruptions to our work. Along with my regular holiday breaks, there was also an unexpected illness within my immediate family. This resulted in my having to take an unplanned break, but a further consequence was that I was naturally affected by this illness and I imagine Eileen was able to sense this underlying preoccupation in me, although to my mind I was certainly present with her in the room. I know I was less willing to act as her punching bag at that point, even less equipped than usual perhaps to weather the storms of her attacks. I pointed out that she was working hard to have me abandon her, a direct repeat of her history. Eileen knew nothing of my recent concerns, although I had explained that a family crisis meant I would need to take this break, for a little less than a month as it happened. I am still of the mind that I did the right thing in not telling her why I had had to 'abandon' her for that period. Theoretically, this was a perfect opportunity to consider her distress and work through her struggle.

Instead, two weeks after my return Eileen marched out of my room halfway through a session with the parting shot, 'I hope you're happy now. I won't be back.' I was relieved. Gone, I thought, finally. I also felt guilty, as if I had abandoned her, which of course I had done simply in *wanting* her gone. This sentiment would be fine (Winnicott, 1947), natural even, had I also had a willingness to work this through with Eileen.

I did not hear from her and so I supposed the relationship had truly ended. I wrote her a letter a few weeks later expressing regret at the abruptness of our ending and an appreciation of the years we had worked together. I did not invite her in for a last session to say goodbye or to work through the ending. In this failure to invite her back to therapy I finally fulfilled the last act in the abandonment cycle. And a few months later it was on these grounds that Eileen took out her complaint, with the help of a lawyer, and began to enact the longed-for revenge against her persecutor, this time symbolised by me as the abandoning therapist. In the first line of her complaint she noted that I had 'repeated the earlier trauma' of abandonment for which she had originally come to see me, locating that abandonment not in her childhood but at the point when her husband had walked out.

Eventually Eileen dropped the case, but in the meantime the sado-masochistic dance was played out even further, to no one's benefit so far as I can see, except our lawyers, though I have no doubt there was some gratification for Eileen in the fact that she was wreaking such revenge. I was certainly traumatised by the experience, unsure of myself and terrified of the possible loss of my career. I could not imagine how I would survive the shame of any possible rejection by a panel of my peers. Like my childhood self, I would have to work hard to prove my worth and there was no guarantee at the end that anyone would notice.

Since those events I have also had to look at myself as a therapist and consider how it is that I ended up with a complaint, a profound wound to the narcissistic elements within me that caused me to take Eileen on as a client in the first place.

Conclusion

It is easy to say that this ending was a direct result of Eileen's history, her need to punish and be punished, a direct repetition of her violent past. In her building up to the final enactment of her earlier abandonment, she was also able to hold up her hand and say 'stop', as she did in filing the complaint. I believe it would have ultimately been too traumatic for her to actually witness how she was inflicting suffering on me at the panel, just as it might have been dangerous or too painful for her to have raged against her offending parent as a child. But the traumatic process and ending of the therapy was also the product of my story, an enactment of my history of avoidance and the need to excel and win her over in order to keep my horror of worthlessness at bay. Through the sado-masochism replicated in the room with Eileen, I was also able to discharge some of my own archaic distress.

As therapists we have a responsibility not only to consider our patients' inner world, but also our own. We are not blessed with super-powers, only information, and sometimes we're wrong. In the name of concern and good practice we sometimes avoid what is difficult or painful in order to maintain a more comfortable view of ourselves. If our patients invite enactment in the room, so do we – this is a dyad, and the nature of relationships is that they are played out *together*. We feed off one another and, like in a bad marriage, we can sometimes play off the worst of ourselves, rather than the best.

What else might lay underground waiting for us to repeat in our work with patients? The dreadful truth is that, through the process of the unconscious, we might never know.

References

Benjamin, L. S. (1996) *Interpersonal Diagnosis and Treatment of Personality Disorders*, 2nd ed. (pp. 115–140). New York: Guilford Press.

Chasseguet-Smirgel, J. (1984) *Creativity and Perversion*. London: Free Association Books.

Diagnostic and Statistical Manual of Mental Disorders (2000) DSM-IV-TR. Washington, DC: American Psychiatric Association.

Johnson, S. M. (1987) *Humanizing the Narcissistic Style*. New York: W. W. Norton.

Jung, C. (1916) *The Psychology of the Unconscious*. New York: Dover Publications, 2003.

Kreisman, J. K. & Straus, H. (1989) *I Hate You, Don't Leave Me*. New York: Avon Books.

Main, T. F. (1957) The ailment. *British Journal of Medical Psychology*, 30(3): 129–145.

Masterson, J. F. (1990) *The Search for the Real Self*. New York: The Free Press.

Peters, D. (1997) Self-care: stress and the practitioner. In Alan Watkins (ed.) *Mind–Body Medicine, a Clinician's Guide to Psychnoneuroimmunology*. New York: Churchill Livingstone.

Rogers, C. (1957) The necessary and sufficient conditions of therapeutic personality change. *Journal of Consulting Psychology*, 21(2): 95–103.

Searles, H. F. (1986) The countertransference with the borderline patient. In Michael H. Stone (ed.) *Essential Papers on Borderline Disorders*. New York: New York University Press.

Winncott, D. W. (1947) Hate in the countertransference. In *Through Paediatrics to Psychoanalysis: Collected Papers*. London: Karnac, 2002.

Winncott, D. W. (1955–56) Clinical varieties of transference. In *Through Paediatrics to Psychoanalysis: Collected Papers*. London: Karnac, 2002.

4 The ghost at the feast

Enactments of cumulative trauma in the therapeutic relationship

Celia Harding

Introduction

Enactment is understood here as an internalised relationship in the patient's mind which evokes its complementary aspect in the therapist and is actualised in the therapeutic relationship. In this chapter I make a distinction between positive and negative enactments. The following are examples of what I mean by 'positive enactments' in which the traumatising relationship is reincarnated between therapist and patient.

> The therapist becomes judgemental towards her patient, demanding that he explain himself. It transpires that the patient is psychically in thrall to a bullying father figure.

> The therapist finds herself wrong-footed by a patient, enacting a narcissistic mother so caught up in her destabilized state that she leaves the patient floundering and confused.

At other times, the therapist detects a subtle but compelling pressure to avoid meaningful emotional engagement with the patient. This requirement is communicated by the presence of an 'absence' in the relationship with the therapist. 'In Hindu philosophy, to find out who you are, you ask what are you not. Then you are left with what you are' (*The Economist*, 2 Sept 2006, p. 80). These I shall call negative enactments.

Negative enactments are massive defences against the possibility of a positive enactment of traumatising relationships with a primary object. These patients have little confidence in ordinary human relationships which balance self-interest with concern (Brenman, 2006, p. 3); therefore they treat the therapist as a neutral, objective professional motivated purely by the patient's best interests. The therapist is dealt with as a narcissistic object, incapable of tolerating and accommodating the demands of a separate other: it is as if making demands of the therapist will inadvertently cross 'a line' and detonate an explosive reaction. As a precautionary measure the danger – of reincarnating the traumatising relationship in the therapy – is pre-empted by excluding the respective narcissistic sensitivities of patient and therapist from the 'professional' relationship which consequently configures around, as it were, a negative space, otherwise occupied by human emotions and intentions.

Both parties enter into an enactment unwittingly and it may remain unconscious for some time in the treatment. We tend to regard enactments as untherapeutic, 'mistakes' redeemed only when they are understood by the therapeutic couple and repaired. However, I suggest that there may be occasions when enactments fulfil benign, even necessary, functions in some therapies.

Cumulative trauma

The concept of trauma encompasses the psychological and/or physical injuries sustained both from the impact of unexpected and shocking experiences and of cumulative damage accruing over periods of time. In this chapter I focus on cumulative trauma in primary relationships and its impact on personality development. However, traumatising early attachments may well predispose a person to sudden and unexpected traumatising experiences: 'accident proneness' may indicate underlying, cumulatively traumatic damage to the fabric of the patient's personality.

Freud (1920) wrote of the infant's need for a protective shield against stimuli overload. This idea connects with the concept of 'repetition compulsion' (Freud, 1920) as a means of mastering traumatising experiences, both of everyday varieties, such as separations from mother, and of episodic kinds such as exposure to violent wartime experiences. Freud's ideas, coupled with Winnicott's concept (1962) of the 'good-enough mother' who provides her infant with ego-support until they can manage their own experiences, formed the groundwork for Khan's (1964, 1973) concept of 'cumulative trauma'.

> [C]umulative trauma is the result of breaches in the mother's role as a protective shield over the whole course of the child's development . . . in all these areas of experience where the child continues to need the mother as an auxiliary ego to support his immature and unstable ego functions.
>
> (Khan, 1973, p. 290)

Infants need consistent, reliable, protective, responsive and attentive mothers in order to integrate emergent feelings and impulses into their personalities. Integral to mother's 'protective shield' function is her capacity to take in, and contain, her infant's feeling states within her own mind, to recognise and process them and then accurately re-present them to the infant in a form that the infant mind can manage (Bell, 2002). Children with mothers who provide a protective shield and container for overwhelming external and/or internal stimulation may internalise a containing and protective object enabling them to tolerate their vulnerabilities and dependency needs. This gives them the psychic equipment to think about, and express, feelings symbolically rather than acting on them (Parsons, 2006).

However, when mother's containing, 'protective shield' function fails, the infant's ego is exposed to internal and external experiences which overload their ego capacities and distort their development. Without a maternal protective object, dependency and vulnerability are dangerous (Parsons and Dermen, 1999), and these infants fend for themselves by precociously developing independence whilst hiding their unmet dependency needs. This leads to excessive preoccupation with outer reality at the expense of self-awareness. The synthesising function of the ego promoting psychic integration is sacrificed and development is predicated on splits within the personality (Winnicott, 1963; Khan, 1964, 1973). In Kalsched's terms (1996) these infants attempt to protect the self from further traumatisation by avoiding dependency on others: they develop a 'self-care' system which dissociates internal pain, fear and helplessness whilst punishing the self for exposures to any experience resonant of the original traumatising scenario.

The internalisation of cumulatively traumatic experiences

Cumulatively traumatic experiences sustained in primary attachments are unlikely to be accessible to memory but rather are represented in the person's way of relating especially to their significant others. These familiar patterns may go unremarked and unrecognised, or as Bollas (1987) elegantly put it, constitute 'unthought knowns'. Earliest experiences are accessed through re-enaction not thought (Freud, 1914, p. 150).

> [T]raumas can be caused by subtle and complicated interactions in the mother/child relationship which are often largely unconscious to the patient, as are the subsequent patterns of their repetition . . . These are powerful influences which are hidden in the internal world. The extent of the influence of an obscure period of trauma on development is often underestimated and its enduring effect may not be realised.
>
> (Temple, 2002, p. 159)

Our minds develop from identifications with our significant objects. Children attached to uncontaining and unprotective objects identify with, and internalise, traumatising relationships. Freud (1917) first elaborated this model of identification in the context of losing a loved object. When the containing capacities of the ego are either lacking or too overloaded to mourn, the ego manages loss by identification installing in the mind both the abandoning object and the forsaken subject.

> Thus the shadow of the object fell upon the ego, and the latter could henceforth be judged by a special agency, as though it were an object, the forsaken object. In this way an object loss was transformed into an ego-loss and the conflict between the ego and the loved person into a cleavage between the critical activity of the ego and the ego as altered by identification.
>
> (Freud, 1917, p. 249)

Through identification with the lost object (Freud, 1917) and its function as a mechanism of psychic organisation (Ferenczi, 1933; Fairbairn, 1952; Khan 1964, 1973; Kalsched, 1996; Frankel, 2002) the perpetrator and victim of trauma are internalised in the mind.

When mother's containing and protective functions fail, she becomes – through 'ignorance, weakness or deliberate fault' – the agent of her child's traumatic suffering. Since children *actually* depend on mother for survival they must establish an optimal proximity with mother even if she is unreliable or inconsistent, frightening or neglectful, whilst avoiding the dangers of getting too close (Holmes, 2001). It is unlikely to be safe or prudent for such children to express rage and protest at their mothers when their needs go unmet and distress is unnoticed or dismissed. The aggression mobilised in reaction to neglect, deprivation, or being used as mother's 'narcissistic object' is dealt with by identifying with the aggressor in one part of the mind and with the helpless victim in another. This diverts the rage from mother and redirects it inward (Fairbairn, 1952; Kalsched, 1996), targeting the dependency needs and vulnerability which exposed the child to the pain of deprivation and mother's attacks for needing her.

Trauma, by definition overwhelming and destabilising, threatens the self and activates self-preservative reactions. Self-preservative aggression originates in the hatred directed towards the unpleasurable, the repudiation from early childhood of anything experienced as 'not-me' (Freud, 1915, p. 136f). Need, dependency and vulnerability are liable to become experienced as 'not-me', and attacked as such, when neediness becomes associated with the pain of deprivation and fear of attack rather than the protective presence of a containing object. Self-preservative aggression is re-deployed to maintain the psychic splits which keep need and vulnerability apart from consciousness. The dissociation characteristic of traumatised people (Kalsched, 1996; Mollon, 1996) is driven by self-preservative aggression, parcelling up experience into benign and dangerous segments and maintaining these splits.

> Dissociation is a trick the psyche plays on itself. It allows life to go on by dividing up the unbearable experience and distributing it to different compartments of the mind and body. This means that the normally unified elements of consciousness (i.e. cognitive awareness, affect, sensation, imagery) are not allowed to integrate. Experience becomes discontinuous.
>
> (Kalshed 1996, pp. 13, 36f)

This represents a shift from the unbearable position of passive helplessness to becoming an active agent controlling both the perpetration and the victimisation. A sense of control and mastery over the traumatising experiences, an internalisation of the rage which would otherwise threaten the relationship with the caregiver, and an internal regulation of dangerous states of vulnerability and neediness are thereby simultaneously accomplished. However, this solution also keeps the traumatisation current and active in the mind.

Case material 1

Ms B's confused internal state was apparent from our first meeting when she mistook her early morning appointment for an evening one. When I realised that this confusion may have arisen and telephoned her I was struck by the defensive, abrasive tone and content of her answer-phone message. These pre-meeting impressions succinctly characterised Ms B's being: a vulnerable, bewildered self protected by an abrasive approach to the world. On meeting she told me that life had thrown too much at her to deal with: she had been 'stuffing stuff in the cupboard' of her head for so long that everything was spilling out. The last straw was the end of a long-term relationship with her partner which left her reeling behind defiant, resigned surprise: 'what took him so long?' Her prevailing sense of confusion was palpable and, in the early stages of her therapy, she would sit in the park near my consulting room, staring into space for hours after her sessions.

Over the months and years that followed, it became apparent that Ms B's interesting, colourful, enterprising business and private life was interspersed with protracted periods of withdrawal when she escaped into a world of novels, mindless television and vast quantities of junk food. Meanwhile work commitments were dropped whilst she tortured herself with fantasies of being exposed as the fraud she believed herself to be; family and friendships were neglected along with routine practicalities such as returning phone-calls, opening her mail, paying bills and household chores.

During active periods, she packed her sessions with fascinating stories about her activities at work, home and play, engaging us with interesting and colourful details, distracting us from an underlying emotional void. She was so adventurous and enterprising that it only slowly dawned on me that she filled her life with eventful and exciting things but did not really live it. She had a gift for story telling and animating the characters populating her world, including a vast cast of friends from every period in her life, but there was more glamour than substance to many of her relationships and her 'closest' friends lived long distances away. Her fecund descriptions of her experiences referred to sensations rather than emotions. These impressions were confirmed when I wondered about her feelings in given situations: 'Feelings? What feelings? What've feelings got to do with anything?'

We came to understand that she managed an aching emotional void inside by withdrawal and binge eating or keeping herself very active with an apparently stimulating and exciting life.

Her preoccupation with DIY home improvements represented her 'do it yourself' independence, and many years passed before she realised that underneath she expected others to look after, and out for, her. Her many imaginative and worthwhile ideas to socially and/or personally enrich her life invariably fizzled out as did more mundane plans to give up smoking, lose weight or decorate a room. She found it difficult to sustain her efforts and bring intentions to fruition as if her aspirations withered before taking root. She was fascinated by 'before' and 'after' weight loss pictures: as she succinctly put it 'I want it to happen without going through it'. She was bitterly aware of how her – sometimes brilliant – ideas were adopted and developed by others, usually without crediting her.

In retrospect, Ms B presented as a person whose psychic development had been distorted by cumulative trauma. She treated emotions as might a dismissive mother. Awareness of her emotional states was limited to voids or overwhelming confusion (Holmes, 2001). There was little evidence that she had experienced a containing mother who had received her states of mind, processed and returned them to her in a manageable form, helping her to recognise, process and manage her feelings and develop a sense of herself with an emotional core. Equally she conspicuously lacked an internalised protective and nurturing internal object: she oscillated between abrasive independence and dismissal of her vulnerability and a naïve trust that strangers and acquaintances would prioritise her interests.

The extent and depth of the dissociation between her mind and body, conscious and unconscious, internal and external reality was profound. She was incipiently aware of this in the disjunction she recalled in her youth between her friends' view of her as the confident leader of their gang and her view from inside: lonely, marginalised, not belonging, inadequate, in a haze of ignorance about herself and the way the world worked. Above all, she felt incapable of verbalising her inchoate feeling states. She reported observing herself from a distance as if she was living outside herself or watching herself from the wings as she acted in a play. She was incapable of assessing her physical state when unwell or when injured after her frequent accidents: one graphic example was when she stood on a garden rake and reported looking at her foot with the steel prongs poking through, wondering if there was something she should do about this. She treated her periodic enuresis, dating from early childhood, as a fact of life to be managed, and it was not until shortly before she finished therapy that she reported dreaming of urinating and her surprise on waking to find the bed dry.

Gradually she constructed a personal narrative (Holmes, 2001) from these impressions and sensations. In the latter months of her mother's pregnancy, Ms B's father, who worked long hours for the emergency services, sustained critical injury. Mrs B, who had managed virtually as a single mother with the older children, was probably traumatised, facing the prospect of widowhood with several young children and one on the way. Mr B survived and his convalescence coincided with Ms B's birth and early months of life. She was the first baby in the family to experience father's presence and involvement. She is told that her father adored her. She has no memory of this; only a sense of hostility from her mother and elder siblings which she came to understand as their jealousy and envy that she had captured her father's heart and was the recipient of his devotion.

According to her narrative, Ms B's mother felt extremely ambivalent towards her infant daughter. Mother is described as loud and opinionated, apparently incapable of expressing emotions beyond periodic violent outbursts or wordless tears over the sink; maintaining a strict regime of household chores and imposing a rigorous discipline over the family with an equally strict regime of house rules and regulations. It seems likely that this mother was too preoccupied with her own unmanageable internal states to have been emotionally available to mediate her infant daughter's needs and emotional states and protect her. These clues to the primary attachment with mother were given narrative endorsement in the story of Ms B aged around three years, pedalling backwards into an open fire, whilst mother was concentrating on hanging the clothes on the fireguard at the other side of the room. Ms B recalled her mother's anger with her when her dressings were changed and she screamed, as if her mother felt too tortured by the damage her daughter had sustained when her maternal attention lapsed to respond empathically to her daughter's suffering. On another occasion, Ms B recalled mother's disbelief that she had hurt her arm and how she had crouched, whimpering behind the sofa until father arrived home and took her to hospital where a broken arm was diagnosed. That she had internalised a hostile rejecting object rather than a containing loving object was also reflected in Ms B's description of her cat as 'me with fur on': the cat approached cautiously when called, only to back away as if she were about to be attacked. This mirrored Ms B's self-observation of the way she kept her friends at a distance, as if she were on an island, throwing stones at them as they approached, willing them both to turn away and to forge on undeterred. Equally telling was Ms B's suspicion and hostility towards young children who, at the beginning of her therapy, she regarded as manipulative, malicious, cunning: she had little idea of a child's need for protection and vulnerability, for attentiveness and responsiveness.

Enactment

Psychically unprocessed trauma is 'lived' in some way, through character style, life themes, attitudes and other forms of enactment (Laub and Auerhahn, 1993). In a traumatised state, psychological distance from the experience collapses, therefore any capacities for mentally processing and symbolising experiences are paralysed (Laub and Auerhahn, 1993; Garland, 2002). People who cannot internally process experience are bound to use the external world to represent their internal state. In particular, the traumatised mind may deal with the experience by 'identifying with the aggressor', 'becoming' the traumatising object in some important respect (Garland, 2002, p. 199) as a means of decanting unbearable helplessness into another for temporary relief.

Enactments in therapy actualise, between therapist and patient, an aspect or dimension of an internal relationship. In common with 'projective identification' (Ogden, 1979) the therapist's own psychic susceptibilities draw her into participating in an en-action. The therapist succumbs to pressures from within and from her patient, to enact rather than think and feel, shifting communication from the symbolic into action. The dimensions and functions of 'projective identification' (Ogden, 1979) also apply to enactment: it has a defensive function, 'acting out' to protect from the psychic distress that remembering would generate (Freud, 1914). Secondly, it is a mode of communication, effective in so far as it elicits a congruent response in the therapist. Thirdly, it actualises a primitive object relationship frequently with a strong aggressive component. Finally, it has transformative potential, unconsciously carrying the hope that the therapist can mentally process the enactment and make it available to the patient's mind. Enactment differs from projective identification in that it involves an actualisation in action between therapist and patient.

Enactment crosses from the psychic to action, thereby incurring the scrutiny and censure of the analytic superego (Racker, 1968; Colman, 2005), liable to prompt shame and guilt in the therapist and alarm in the patient. This makes it difficult to credit the enactment with potential to serve the therapy and the patient's progress. As with projective identification (Ogden, 1979) the patient attempts to communicate an 'unthought known' by inducing a complementary 'unthought known' in the therapist. Sometimes the optimal mode of communication may be through action, but when psychic material bypasses thought the therapist is caught off-balance, drawn into the raw qualities of actual engagement (Chused, 1991, p. 629; McLoughlin, 1991, p. 600), in an area of her psychic functioning which is largely unconscious or incompletely worked through. It could be argued that enactments have the potential for psychic transformation precisely because they emerge from the therapist's actual vulnerability in the therapeutic relationship, much as Polden describes in the potential she sees in a therapist's erotic counter-transference (Polden, 2005). Sometimes the symbolic cannot communicate clearly enough, with sufficient intensity and immediacy, what the patient needs the therapist to understand.

> Although not therapeutic in itself, an enactment can provide invaluable information and an immediacy of experience that can enrich the work. Viewed as yet another source of information, greeted with curiosity and

not guilt, enactments can become part of the analytic process from which we all learn.

(Chused, 1991, p. 638)

Nevertheless the therapist is responsible for becoming aware of, and processing, the interaction that has been enacted, whether she explicitly interprets this to the patient or not.

Enactments of cumulative trauma

In principle, analytic relationships provide patients with opportunities to discover and work through traumatic aspects of relating in their earliest attachments. Optimally this facilitates the patient to develop relationships with others encompassing both intimacy and autonomy (Holmes, 2001). But this opportunity necessitates emotional engagement with the therapist, which may threaten to actualise in the present the traumatic aspects of the primary relationship. In particular the patient approaches the therapist as if she will relate to them as a narcissistic object: any demands they make on her could destabilise her narcissistic equilibrium and provoke a self-preservative attack. When cumulative trauma was an ingredient of primary relationships, subsequent intimate relationships involving emotional contact with/dependency on/needs of/and vulnerability with another person activate alarm bells (Garland, 2002, p. 109). For many the therapeutic relationship is potentially intrinsically re-traumatising (Frankel, 2002).

Negative enactments in the transference and counter-transference

My first inkling that cumulative trauma characterises a primary attachment may be a sense that something is missing in the way a patient relates to me, as if the patient has no transference relationship to me. The patient describes what I am to them in neutral terms: 'a professional' or 'an oracle'. These patients talk *to* me but not *with* me. I have come to think of such transference situations as 'negative enactments' in the transference of a cumulatively traumatic primary attachment. *To ascertain who I am for the patient, I have to start with what I am not rather than what I am.* In this context, the term 'negative' refers to representations where presence is defined by absence. This is conveyed in the following description:

> [H]e was working on this new idea. He was filling empty packaging with plaster, using the bubble packs that used to have toys in them . . . and the foam boxes you get packed around a new T.V. set. He calls them negative spaces . . . I walked around there, in his studio . . . looking at those white sculptures, and I thought, that's what I am. Always waiting for someone or something, or some kind of real feeling to fill me up.

(Roberts, 2004, p. 841)

Other examples include the negative photographic image – black and white, dark and pale are reversed until light is applied to process when the image and the 'negged out' features appear – and the concept of a 'negative database', developed as a way to protect sensitive data. 'Instead of containing the information of interest, such a database would contain everything except that information'. This idea is derived from the body's immune system which 'relies on a negative database to tell it what to destroy. It learns early on which biological molecules are "self", in the sense that they are routine parts of the body it is protecting. Whenever it meets one that is "not self" and thus likely to be part of a pathogen, it destroys it' (*The Economist*, 2 Sept 2006, p. 80). This instructive analogy conveys the protective function of the negative screening out and the aggression towards the 'not-me' which could destabilise, perhaps destroy, the mind if it was accessed.

When patients negatively 'screen out' the possibility of emotional involvement with the therapist they may be expressing their need to establish a secure attachment with the therapist before they can risk encountering potentially traumatising aspects of relating with her. Paradoxically, real security is only discovered when the therapist has 'failed' the patient but, unlike the past traumatising object, is able to empathically attend and respond to the patient's distress. This involves the process of re-establishing a lost good object (Klein, 1940; Brenman, 2006) in the mind: the possibility of a good object seems to survive somewhere even for those patients who are psychically dominated by 'bad objects'. Ordinarily, the good object is established after splitting the benign and safe aspects of the mother from her negative aspects and treating these as separate objects. This healthy splitting enables the infant to idealise the good object and learn to trust in that goodness before testing the resilience of the good object by subjecting her to 'bad' feelings. Some cumulatively traumatised patients need to preserve an illusion, perhaps over an extensive period, of an emotionally neutral, benign, well-intentioned therapist with no personal investment or involvement in the therapeutic relationship. The therapist, in response, may find herself enacting a relationship with the patient which, for her own psychological reasons, excludes emotional interaction. When the therapist becomes conscious of the absent, 'negged out' aspects of their relationship, her task is initially to endure, discover and process the missing dimension before 'the ghost at the feast' can be acknowledged and take shape in the therapeutic relationship.

Could an observer distinguish between a 'negative enactment' in which both therapist and patient are participating from one where the de-traumatised relationship is a reality only in the mind of the patient? The degree of a therapist's participation in such 'negative enactments' is probably relative, depending on the therapist's awareness that an aspect or dimension of the therapeutic relationship is missing and of the subtle pressures she feels to maintain this absence, reminiscent of a 'counter-resistance' (Racker, 1968).

A concept of 'negative enactment' begs further questions about what may and/or may not be achieved whilst the relationship between therapist and patient exclude fundamental aspects or dimensions of emotional engagement. Offering traumatised patients a safe and reliable containing space within which to explore their thoughts and feelings, may enable them to discover a trustworthy figure in the therapist, based on an idea of professional reliability and integrity. Moreover patients experience in the therapeutic relationship many of the therapist's personal qualities such as integrity, interest, empathy, thoughtfulness, reliability, constancy and tolerance, which are also core values of ordinary relationships. Such experience may, in time, enable patients to internalise a protective, attentive, responsive object and a capacity for containing and processing previously unthinkable and unbearable states of mind within an – albeit denuded – attachment with the therapist. A greater capacity for self-acceptance, understanding and tolerance can develop and distinctions stabilise between internal and external, fantasy and reality.

The synthesising functions of the ego are severely compromised (Khan, 1964, 1973) by those suffering from early cumulative traumas. Such patients are unlikely to have processed the impact and meaning of what happened to them and lack a narrative which makes sense of their lives and how they are (Holmes, 2001). Blum (1980, p. 6) describes reconstruction of a narrative in therapy as 'an integrative act' serving the cohesion of the personality. When a therapist is preserved in the patient's mind as emotionally neutral and 'objective', she is nevertheless available for the collaborative process of reconstructing a narrative which makes sense of the patient's traumatic experiences. Making connections between past and present develops the synthetic function of the ego and enhances a sense of self-continuity.

These are considerable achievements. But something essential will remain missing unless or until therapist and patient become able to risk engaging emotionally with each other.

Case material 2

Ms B regarded her therapy as insulated from the rest of her life, distinguishing between 'in here' and 'out there' and positioning her therapy as a castle surrounded by a moat. Sometimes anxiety about continuing with her therapy would be expressed as a need to 'try out' in the real world what she had discovered in her therapy, as if she had to leave to achieve this.

I began working with Ms B as a newly qualified psychotherapist beset by the familiar anxieties of the newly qualified, still in her own analysis, anxious about being good enough and not damaging to my patients. Adhering rigidly to analytic boundaries seemed the safest course.

At the beginning and for some time into Ms B's therapy, I was largely unaware of the 'negative enactment' in which I was engaged with her. I understood that she had suffered multiple traumatic experiences but not the implications for her development, for example in the degree of dissociation she presented, and in her distancing of myself and others. I was however aware that something was missing from her detailed and very engaging material and wondered about the absence of 'live' feelings between us.

Whenever I suggested that Ms B could be alluding to feelings about me we drew a blank. She would describe me as a professional: a teacher, or medic in a white coat. This preserved me in her mind as someone to whom she could talk about herself protected from the dangers she expected from earlier relationships: rejection, neglect, regimentation out of existence, exploitation. She upheld me as a professional with expert knowledge who knew what was best for her, whose judgements were objective and beyond question, with no personal investment or involvement in the relationship.

Ms B used her therapy to discover and explore her feelings; to identify patterns in her behaviour, especially her problem about not allowing herself good things; to gradually talk to me about, and discover, distresses connected with certain traumatic experiences; to reconstruct a personal narrative of her life and relationships with members of her family; to begin to recognise her phobic anxieties about intimacy and her hatred and fear of her destructiveness which frequently took her hostage. It now seems to me that the 'negative enactment' underpinning our relationship had a substantially benign effect for Ms B, allowing her to experience a safe, consistent reliable object who tried to understand without unduly imposing a preconceived interpretation as she developed her personal narrative whilst conveying my presence and responsiveness to her (Holmes, 2001). In other words, she seems to have found in me a protective, reliable container to gain a more cohesive sense of herself and a 'witness' to that becoming (Holmes, 2001, p. 94). In writing this chapter I have wondered whether our development together – she as a patient and I as a therapist – inadvertently generated something benignly therapeutic for her. This contrasted with her childhood experience of sexual abuse, when her sexuality was precipitately aroused and she was deprived of both her childhood 'innocence' of adult sexual arousal and in adolescence, of mutual sexual initiation with young men of her own age.

However, many therapeutic opportunities were undoubtedly lost by my inexperience and my own anxieties. For example, in time triggers from various sources set her wondering about her view of me as 'the professional' and what this might mean. A friend had invited her therapist to her wedding reception. Ms B reported watching the therapist in wonderment: how could a therapist be at the same social occasion as her patient? Since Ms B lived in the same locality as my consulting room, she sometimes wondered about what would happen if we met between sessions. I was unable to explore with her these ideas and fantasies or even realities of meetings outside the consulting room. At that time, I managed them, rather than working with and using them, by emphasising the importance of maintaining the boundaries of our relationship, unwittingly enacting her remembered experience of how mother imposed rules on situations liable to provoke confusion or anxiety, excitement, desire or anger.

There came a point in the therapy when Ms B became alarmed by the depth of the depression she was entering. She was at this stage attending three sessions a week and using the couch. It was the time when the Western hostages in Lebanon were released, and Ms B became engrossed in their stories and highly identified with a hostage state of mind. This work was interrupted by a long summer break, and she returned resolved to finish or cut down her sessions to once a week and to stop using the couch. During the break her benign view of me as 'the professional' with her interests at heart, knowing what was best for her, had shifted and she admitted that she had associated me with the sinister 'professional' figure of Nurse Ratchett, from the film *One Flew Over the Cuckoo's Nest*. Although we worked through these anxieties sufficiently for her to settle back into therapy she never did return to the couch, which I respected as her assertion of what she thought was best for her rather than continuing to suppose that I automatically knew best.

Positive enactment in the transference and countertransference

I have suggested that a 'negative enactment' of internalised traumatising relationships may be a necessary stage towards establishing a secure attachment to the therapist whilst the emotional and psychic scaffolding is established for a real relationship. At some point either the therapist makes a demand of her patient which is experienced as a betrayal of trust or the patient makes a demand of the therapist which she cannot meet, either because of her personal limitations or the limitations of her role (Kalsched, 1996). This triggers a positive enactment of the traumatising relationship between therapist and patient.

The therapist is less equipped to circumscribe and contain a 'positive enactment' of the traumatising relationship for patients when she is unaware of her part in actualising the traumatising scenario. This eventuality is more likely when the 'positive enactment' is rationalised as a legitimate part of therapy and the relationship has become, in effect, a folie à deux. Examples of this may include the therapist who unconsciously enacts a sadistic superego to a patient's traumatised self overlaid by masochistic defences (as described by Colman (2005) in his account of the 'rabbit and the stick'); a therapist's lack of responsiveness in the name of therapeutic neutrality; an actual betrayal of the therapeutic boundaries by engagement in an extra-therapeutic relationship.

Containment of a positive enactment may also be compromised when the feared experience is actualised with the patient before the therapist has sufficiently understood it, undermining her capacity to hold the space for thought and the symbolic dimensions of the situation. The therapist's failure will be compounded when she is not sufficiently internalised in the patient's mind as a good, containing and protective object, leaving the patient unequipped to hold the pain and rage attendant on feeling re-traumatised and liable to enact it by abruptly terminating therapy.

> Nearly a year into his once-weekly therapy, Mr Y gave notice that he would be taking a holiday during session times. I had made clear at the beginning of treatment that my practice was to charge for all cancelled sessions whatever the reason. Now, I found myself unable to raise the issue of payment for the sessions he would miss when on holiday, feeling that to remind him would be infantilising. In due course I presented him with the monthly account including the sessions he had missed. The following week he returned saying I had made a mistake. He was furious to discover that I had knowingly charged him for the cancelled sessions. He felt that he would betray himself if he continued in therapy when I had betrayed him, but leaving would deprive himself of something he had valued and needed. Our efforts to continue thinking about what this meant to him collapsed, the enactment of a victim betrayed became completely concrete and he stormed out.

A positive enactment of the traumatising relationship is more likely to be containable when the therapist becomes aware of, and processes the 'negative enactment' before it shifts into its positive incarnation. The therapist may become conscious of a 'no-go area' and of her counter-resistance to addressing it. Something in the patient's material or in the unconscious communication between them may alert the therapist to the missing aspect and signal a potential readiness in both parties to begin to mentalise what has been negatively enacted in the relationship.

Sometimes therapist and patient are unable to make this transition to a positive enactment.

> Over six years in therapy Ms Z maintained a cordial, polite, distantly friendly, 'professional' relationship with me. Her precarious sense of self was dominated by anger with negligent, terrifying, unprotective and actively violent, parental figures. Her fury with them seemed unending. With time in therapy, her periods of withdrawal from the world became shorter and she began to take more charge of her affairs and make progress in her life, completing her degree, marrying and becoming pregnant. Shortly before she left therapy to move abroad the day of her session coincided with the London bombings. When she did not arrive for her session I was concerned and phoned her. She answered the phone; she had not been involved in the terrorist attacks and seemed oblivious to a possibility that I might be concerned about her. This impressed upon me that, even at this stage, she believed herself 'out of my sight, out of my mind', despite the fact that she clearly valued and relied on her relationship with me.

I can see in retrospect one occasion when this 'negative enactment' might have shifted: I sensed that she felt deeply hurt, angry and betrayed by me when I charged her for the sessions she missed around her mother's death. This was conveyed in reports of a friend who took umbrage when she was unavailable for her during that time. I was however unable to find a way to articulate her anger and painful disappointment at my 'callousness' for charging her for the missed sessions, and behind that her longing to be treated by me as special, so the negative enactment was perpetuated.

When the therapist has identified the 'negged out' traumatising dimension of the therapeutic relationship she can begin to process her resistance to connecting with it. This self-analysis may unconsciously prompt the emergence of the missing aspects in the patient and/or the relationship. At other times the therapist more consciously finds an opening in the patient's material to communicate the avoided aspect to the patient. However it comes about, the entry of the potentially traumatising scenario in the therapeutic relationship is liable to be experienced by the patient as a re-living of the traumatising relationship. For the patient, the symbolic level of the 'as if', the space in which to think and explore, collapses in the immediacy of feeling re-traumatised in the present. The enactment becomes a symbolic equivalent of the original trauma (Segal, 1981). When the therapist has already understood and processed the re-traumatising aspects of the experience she is more equipped to hold the space for thought and the 'as if' symbolic capacity in her mind and to contain the patient's distress and terror until the space for thought can be restored between them. However, the power of the feelings evoked and the strength of the resonance with the primary traumatising experience may put the symbolic dimensions of the current experience – for both therapist and patient – under enormous pressure such that reality seems to tip into the fantasy that the trauma is actually repeating.

Case material 3

For a long time I felt that to write about the work with Ms B would repeat her experience of being used as a narcissistic object by both her parents (in different ways), other members of her family, some of her business colleagues and friends. However I began to reconsider the issue as our work progressed, her capacity for self-reflection and insight grew, and her capacity for symbolic thought developed (Wharton, 2003). I found myself feeling that the therapeutic relationship between us had become sufficiently robust to risk asking her permission to write about our work together in the confidence that if she did experience this as my exploiting her we had a very sound basis to work it through.

The point came when her thoughts of leaving therapy denoted more a readiness to leave than a compulsion to placate an internal ogre who terrorised her needy self for wishing to continue. Ms B's traumatic history and legacy of experiencing relationships as exploitative however indicated to me that a request for permission to write about our work should be made within the therapy to allow an opportunity for working through what it meant to her. I therefore made my request as she began to plan an ending to her therapy but before it felt imminent. She was surprised when I raised the matter and shocked by the strength of her anger that suddenly erupted as she found herself telling a friend of this unprecedented event in her therapy. I had thrown a spanner in the works and, in effect, generated more work for her to do; she was furious with me and able to tell me in no uncertain terms. She was also able to defer her response, oscillating between a 'yes' to stop thinking and feeling about it and a reactive 'no' to punish me. Over subsequent sessions, she worked with what I had, in effect, 'demanded' of her. This included a new view of me as a person with my own mind, my own interests and investment in our relationship – a painfully enviable figure who was contemplating writing for publication when she had been unable to fulfil her ambitions to write, and she imagined publishing an article about her therapy in a magazine in retaliation. She raged at me for having asked her: why had I not just gone ahead and done it? She need never have known, or had to think about it. I was proposing to use her, for my own ends, in my own way and it had nothing to do with her.

In time she shelved the matter, unable to come to a decision about it. Meanwhile I noted in her material possible unconscious references to aspects of the meaning of my request to her: a collection found in the attic which no longer interested her and which she offered to someone for whom it was meaningful; work on a joint project with a colleague and her discovery that something creative could come out of their collaboration. Mindful of Ms B's tendency to deal with her destructiveness aroused by core complex anxieties in sado-masochistic relating (Glasser, 1996), I found alternative material for the paper I intended to write so that I should avoid getting into a masochistic position. In retrospect, I see that this may well have defended me from the sadistic impact of the time it took Ms B to come to her decision: a transference version of her tendency to vengefully and sadistically withhold information which she knew was important to her mother, thereby foreclosing another potential therapeutic opportunity.

Six months before the date agreed for her final session, Ms B asked me, on arrival for her session, if she could take a cutting from a plant in my front garden. I found myself responding immediately, 'Yes, I don't see why not', and then felt appalled that I had answered without pause for thought. We went on to think about what had happened during this and subsequent sessions. I understood this enactment initially in terms of the impending ending as her wish for something tangible to represent her continued nurturing of the psychic growth she had started in therapy. Ms B however saw a direct link with 'my request' of her. Why didn't I just do it without involving her; she need never have known? And the same applied to her wish to take a cutting from my plants; she could have taken it without asking and I would never have known. Yet when it came to it she couldn't do it; it felt only right to ask me first.

This places our demands of each other as enactments of a traumatising aspect of Ms B's relationships with her objects. Her experience of others as taking from her what they wanted without considering her needs and feelings was a common theme in her life from infancy to the present. She was left feeling misused and abused, exploited and betrayed. When taken unawares by a demand on her to fulfil another person's needs, she felt helpless and paralysed without a say in what was happening or being done to her. Only latterly had she realised her unconscious refusal to look after herself and her expectation that others would protect her interests. The humanising of her relationship with me which emerged from my request for permission to write about work brought this dilemma to the fore in our relationship: in her struggle to communicate this to me and understand it, she identified with me, as the aggressor, taking me unawares with her request to take and develop something of mine, just as she had experienced me as putting her on the spot with my request.

In this light I was caught in an enactment where the space for symbolic thought collapsed and I acted by assenting to her request without pause for thought. I now understand my susceptibility to this enactment as based in my unconscious guilt about asking for her permission to write about our work which at some level both she and I equated with abuse. My conscious priority was to maximise her opportunities to use my request to further her progress in the therapy by doing all I could to allow her freedom of choice to decide for herself. My conscious hope was that this experience would have transformative potential rather than being a simple repetition of earlier abuses. Unconsciously I was clearly anxious and guilty that I was exploiting her, betraying her trust in me as a protective object. I think my capacity to give myself the space to think and make a conscious choice about declining or assenting to her request was compromised by the fact that I had already made a request of her to which I hoped she would eventually agree. In effect, my own confusions and anxieties about giving and taking, using and abusing, and my continued unconscious conflicts about having made a demand on her, compromised my capacity to 'hold' her request of me. In my instant 'yes' to her I may have unconsciously done the very thing I was consciously trying to avoid and made it more difficult for her to respond freely to my request: that is I may have enacted a version of an exploitative relationship where the space for free choice is restricted at best, or closed at worst.

However, although writing about the work with Ms B has undoubtedly abusive aspects and resonances there are important differences which Ms B may well have been unconsciously communicating in her 'request' of me. The 'demands' made of each other were different from the abusive demands of the past in that we asked one another's permission for what we wanted to take from each other and we were able to talk together about what these experiences meant for her. She had frequently told me that the worst thing about her abusive experiences was that they happened in silence and could not be spoken about.

Conclusion

In reviewing the pattern of therapeutic relationships with patients whose psychic development was significantly distorted by early cumulative trauma, it seems to me that the 'negative enactment' of a traumatised attachment served a limited but essential therapeutic purpose. It enabled the traumatised self in the patient to experience the reliability, consistency, protective and containing qualities found in the therapist. For some patients this is the most they can achieve, and they leave the therapy, perhaps at the point when a 'demand' is unconsciously surfacing, perhaps ostensibly in response to an external demand. For other patients, the therapeutic relationship predicated on a 'negative enactment' served to restore hope in a good-enough relationship in which their distress would be heard and held by someone willing to 'go the distance' with them as they struggled together to make sense of it. The traumatised self was protected in the therapeutic relationship by the negative enactment until such time as either therapist or the patient felt (consciously or unconsciously) that the relationship was resilient enough to risk testing the reality of the 'good object' by making a demand on the other. The 'demand' inevitably constitutes a tip of an iceberg representing multiple unconscious meanings and significances and is liable to shift the 'negative enactment' into a positive enactment of traumatising features of primary relationship(s). The extent to which therapist and patient together can open and hold a space to make sense of the re-enactment, in the context of a secure attachment, will determine the extent to which the patient may experience in the therapist a new and real personalised relationship with its potential for enabling intimacy with others in their lives.

References

Bell, D. (2002) External injury and the internal world. In C. Garland (ed.) *Understanding Trauma: A Psychoanalytical Approach*. London: Karnac Books.

Blum, H. (1980) The value of reconstruction in adult analysis. *International Journal of Psychoanalysis*, 61: 39–54.

Bollas, C. (1987) *The Shadow of the Object: Psychoanalysis of the Unthought Known*. London: Free Association Books.

Brenman, E. (2006) *Recovery of the Lost-Good Object*. London and New York: Routledge.

Chused, J. F. (1991) The evocative power of enactment. *Journal of the American Psychoanalytic Association*, 39: 615–639.

Colman, W. (2005) The analytic super ego (unpublished paper).

Fairbairn, W. R. D. (1952) *Psychoanalytic Studies of the Personality*. London and New York: Routledge.

Ferenczi, S. (1933) Confusion of tongues between adults and the child. In M. Balint (ed.) *Final Contributions to the Problems and Methods of Psychoanalysis*. London: Karnac Books, 1980.

Frankel, J. (2002) Exploring Ferenczi's concept of identification with the aggressor: its role in trauma, everyday life, and the therapeutic relationship. *Psychoanalytic Dialogues*, 12: 101–139.

Freud, S. (1914) *Remembering, Repeating and Working Through*, Standard Edition 12. London: Hogarth Press.

Freud, S. (1915) *Instincts and their Vicissitudes*, Standard Edition 14. London: Hogarth Press.

Freud, S. (1917) *Mourning and Melancholia*, Standard Edition 14. London: Hogarth Press.

Freud, S. (1920) *Beyond the Pleasure Principle*, Standard Edition 18. London: Hogarth Press.

Garland, C. (2002) *Understanding Trauma: A Psychoanalytical Approach*. London: Karnac Books.

Glasser, M. (1996) Aggression and sadism in the perversions. In I. Rosen (ed.) *Sexual Deviation*, 3rd ed. Oxford: Oxford University Press.

Holmes, J. (2001) *The Search for a Secure Base: Attachment Theory and Psychotherapy*. Hove, UK: Brunner-Routledge.

Kalsched, D. (1996) *The Inner World of Trauma: Archetypal Defenses of the Personal Spirit*. London: Routledge.

Khan, M. M. R. (1964) Ego distortion, cumulative trauma and the role of reconstruction in the analytic situation. *Internal Journal of Psychoanalysis*, 45: 272–279.

Khan, M. M. R. (1973) The concept of cumulative trauma. *Psychoanalytic Study of the Child*, 18: 286–306.

Klein, M. (1940) Mourning and its relation to manic depressive states. In *Love, Guilt and Reparation*. London: Virago Press, 1988.

Laub, D. and Auerhahn, N. (1993) Knowing and not knowing massive psychic trauma: forms of traumatic memory. *International Journal of Psychoanalysis*, 74(2): 288–302.

McLaughlin, J. T. (1991) Clinical and theoretical aspects of enactment. *Journal of the American Psychoanalytic Association*, 39: 595–614.

Mollon, P. (1996) *Multiple Selves, Multiple Voices: Working with Trauma, Violation and Dissociation*. Chichester, UK: John Wiley.

Ogden, T. H. (1979) On projective identification. *International Journal of Psychoanalysis*, 60: 357–373.

Parsons, M. and Dermen, S. (1999) The violent child and adolescent. In M. Lanyado and A. Horne (eds.) *The Handbook of Child and Adolescent Psychotherapy*. London: Routledge.

Parsons, M. (2006) From biting teeth to biting wit. In C. Harding (ed.), *Aggression and Destructiveness: Psychoanalytic Perspectives*. Hove, UK: Routledge.

Polden, J. (2005) Reparation terminable and interminable. *British Journal of Psychotherapy*, 21(4).

Racker, H. (1968) *Transference and Countertransference*. London: Karnac Books, 1982.

Roberts, G. D. (2004) *Shantaram*. London: Abacus.

Segal, H. (1981) Notes on symbol formation. In E. Bott-Spillius (ed.), *Melanie Klein Today: Mainly Theory*. London and New York: Routledge, 1988.

Temple, N. (2002) Developmental injury: its effects on the inner world. In C. Garland (ed.), *Understanding Trauma: A Psychoanalytical Approach*. London: Karnac Books.

Wharton, B. (2003) The reporting of clinical material: ethical issues. In H. McFarland Solomon and M. Twyman (eds), *The Ethical Attitude and Analytic Practice*. London and New York: Free Association Books.

Winnicott, D. W. (1962) Ego integration in child development. In *The Maturational Processes and the Facilitating Environment*. London: The Hogarth Press.

Winnicott, D. W. (1963) From dependence towards independence in the development of the individual. In *The Maturational Processes and the Facilitating Environment*. London: The Hogarth Press.

5   Loves and losses

Enactments in the disavowal of intimate desires

William F. Cornell

As I have experienced it, the analyst's feeling and timely acknowledgment of the impact of the patient on him, and of the analyst's impact on the patient, can evoke in both parties powerful resonances of those oscillations of mutual influence and confluence that were central to our early relating. Such evocations lend particular intensities of immediacy and realness to the experience of being touched and touching, seen and seeing, moved and moving, influenced and influencing in the analytic dyad.

(McLaughlin, 2005, p. 187)

I found myself a patient in a psychoanalyst's office as much by default as by choice. My previous psychotherapy had been terminated by unexpected, unwanted changes in external circumstances that required an abrupt termination of what had been a very productive, long-term psychotherapy. In the small city where I lived, it was difficult to find a therapist with whom I did not have some degree of professional or personal familiarity. I knew that the most likely choice would be someone within the psychoanalytic community, in which my involvement at that time was minimal. At my request, I was referred to Dr. D by my clinical consultant, a Jungian trained analytical psychologist. I knew only that Dr. D was one of the senior psychoanalysts in the city and that he had been classically trained.

My initial session was inaugurated by a dream the night before the session. The dream took place in Dr. D's yet unseen office and was of our initial session. The office of my dream was large, handsome, full of good and varied artwork, the ceiling strung with lines of illuminated plastic fishes, lights which in fact decorated the bedroom of my oldest son. The dream office was considerably more interesting than Dr. D's actual office, which was rather nondescript. The dream analyst looked startlingly like my maternal grandfather, Grandpa Frank, a man I deeply loved. In the dream, I was immediately drawn to Dr. D and felt that he engaged me very directly, asking me questions that threw me back on myself. There was one anomaly in that office, a large curtain that covered most of one wall. When I inquired about the curtain, Dr. D seemed evasive. It continued to distract and disturb me. I finally left my chair and pulled back the curtain. There was a smaller office hidden behind the curtain; seated at the desk was my previous therapist and around him were several of my friends, all of whom had been listening intently to my session. I was stunned and enraged. The dream then seemed to end – at least my recollection of the dream ended there.

I began my actual initial session with a recounting of the disruption of my previous therapy and my marital conflicts. When I told the actual Dr. D that I had had an anticipatory dream the previous night, he said that he doesn't usually take up a dream in an initial session before a decision is made to work together, but that he was inclined here to make an exception. I told him the dream, and he asked for my associations.

My first associations were to the termination of my previous therapy. The termination was the result of rather bizarre circumstances of my therapist being sued by a patient whom I had treated in an earlier round of her psychotherapy. I had had no idea that this patient, who had left me in a state of considerable mutual conflict, had then gone on into therapy with my own therapist. I did not know if she had somehow known that the therapist she then saw after our termination was my therapist. Unbeknownst to me, she had been seeing my therapist at the same time I was seeing him, and he had spent many hours listening to her talk about me. In her lawsuit, she had named me on her list of previous therapists and had planned to depose me. My therapist had tried to keep me out of the proceedings, but the lawyers persisted in their own way. It became clear that I would be required to write a report, be deposed and very likely called to testify in his malpractice case. Our therapy seemed suddenly filled with conflicts of interest and too compromised to continue effectively.

With deep mutual regret, we terminated. I was very worried about my therapist's well-being and quite frightened of the impending legal proceedings, though they ultimately turned out in his favor. My therapy with this man had been marked by prolonged negative transferences, projections on him of my anger and distrust toward my father, whom I had experienced as a remote and unreliable figure in my life. For years I had resisted depending on this therapist, keeping a wary, often sarcastic, distance. He met my reluctance and resistance with patient skill. As my transference gradually changed, we had begun to establish a much closer and trusting relationship. The termination for me was decidedly unexpected, out of my control, premature. I was unable to acknowledge the loss of him or our work. Instead, I shifted to a familiar stance of worrying about him, writing an incisive report to the court on his behalf, and went on my way.

Other associations to the dream were to my grandfather, my father, and others whom I had loved and who had died young – and to myself as a father. There was, in fact, more than a passing resemblance between Dr. D and my grandfather who had pure white hair when he died at age 52, as did Dr. D who was in his early 70s when we began treatment. My grandfather's death from lung cancer when I was seven left deep wounds in the structure of my extended family. My maternal grandparents had been my primary caretakers until I was four, and the loss of their care with the onset of his advanced cancer was profound for me. In the face of her young husband's death my grandmother fell into a depression that consumed her through much of the remainder of my childhood. My grandfather, though not long in my life, was the closest I'd had to a loving, engaged father figure. As I began my work with Dr. D, I was filled with an unvoiced, anticipatory hope for the interest and engagement of an elder colleague.

My other association to the dream, to that of my previous therapist and friends in the hidden room, was of my struggle to make a decision to seek a divorce. All of my friends, and my previous therapist, were weighing in heavily with their opinions that I should get a divorce. I was desperate to talk with someone who did not know me, my wife or anyone else in my life, who could give me the psychological space to sort this out for myself. It felt essential to me that I understand both my motivations in the structure of the marriage as it had evolved and my reluctance to leave it before coming to a final decision.

There was no curtain and hidden room in Dr. D's actual office, but there was something he was clearly reluctant to say, something I immediately feared would be held out of view. With considerable hesitancy, Dr. D told me that the dream was uncanny. Just the day before my first appointment, Dr. D had agreed to be one of the expert witnesses to testify in my former therapist's case. This would mean, at the very least, that my former therapist would be an actual presence in the background of my work with Dr. D. He would be literally reviewing my report and testimony. We could even end up in a courtroom together.

Dr. D presented three options: he could refer me on; we could agree to work together under these circumstances, in which case he would bring his thoughts and experience of the court-related matters into our sessions directly; or he could withdraw as an expert witness. I chose the second option, expressing a desire to work with him and find some way to 'manage the mess'. He questioned my choice, observing that while he didn't really know me yet, he had the impression that I often paid a high price for managing other people's messes. He wondered if such an arrangement between us would create a parallel in our relationship to the kind of mess I was trying to address in my marriage. Dr. D chose to withdraw as an expert witness in my former therapist's case so as to preserve our therapeutic relationship. His decision had an impact on me at multiple levels. It was completely unexpected to me that a psychoanalyst (or anyone else for that matter) would act so decisively on my behalf. I felt secure in my privacy being preserved; no one would be listening in or intruding upon my psychotherapy. I felt deeply grateful. His intervention underscored a central theme in my personal defenses, very much relevant to my conflicts within my marriage, and we set to work. This intervention also underscored the immediate, external circumstances of my anticipatory dream. The more subtle and unconscious implications of the dream were lost for the moment. They would return.

For the first three years, we met twice a week, face to face. I was focused primarily on my marital conflicts and the severe financial pressures of being the sole financial provider for my family with one son in university, another soon to go, the third in a private school, and the possibility of divorce pending. Long an opponent of the intrusion of third party payment structures into psychotherapy, I had always paid for my personal psychotherapy out of pocket. Refusing to use my insurance coverage, I could only afford Dr. D's fee for a single weekly session. Both of us thought that twice a week was necessary, and Dr. D offered to see me twice for the fee of a single session. I felt deeply grateful (and ashamed); we analyzed my gratitude and its possible consequences, but my shame passed unacknowledged by me, unnoticed and unanalyzed by Dr. D.

In the early years I constantly sought Dr. D's approval for my parenting, professional activities, and writing. I gave him copies of articles I was writing, eager for his thoughts and approval. He gave me his approval. We began to form what we sometimes nervously joked was a 'mutual admiration society', which we both enjoyed rather than examined. Unconsciously I had yet again established a pattern of setting myself up (and to the side) as an object of idealization. We had fallen into what McLaughlin (2005), drawing upon Sandler (1976), refers to as a 'transference actualization', in which 'the patient views his analyst's behavior as having fulfilled his expectations' (p. 188). Dr. D and I were ensconced in the 'unobjectionable' (Stein, 1981) aspects of a positive transferential arrangement, which Stein suggests may seem innocuous but must come to be analyzed. McLaughlin termed such 'unobjectionable', positive transferences as transference actualizations, seeing them as a form of unconscious enactment involving both parties of the analytic dyad, thereby eluding either identification or analysis. Dr. D and I were to pay dearly later on for the comfort of the moment.

Most powerful for me during this period of our work was Dr. D's comprehension of the centrality of losses in the foundation of my character. Both the paternal and maternal sides of my family suffered premature deaths of parents, creating intergenerational patterns of depressive and schizoid withdrawal. When I was 18 my mother, seriously ill with leukemia, died suddenly as a result of a medical error. Dr. D also lost his mother to cancer at 18, creating an area of deep, mutual identification between us, which informed and shaped our work in many important ways. Dr. D knew within himself the impact of early parental loss, and he understood something in me that had not been recognized in any of my previous therapy. He said to me, in the midst of my internal conflicts about leaving my marriage, 'Your entire character is founded in the determination to avoid unnecessary loss – be those losses of your sons, your wife, or your own. You cannot discriminate, and you cannot think in the face of projected losses. Loss has always been unbearable to you, devastating to those around you.' With that interpretation, I began to think. I was able to end my marriage and care for my sons. I felt profound gratitude to Dr. D.

Once I had separated from my wife, Dr. D and I decided to move from face to face sessions to the couch, in the hope of shifting my attention from coping with daily life to more intrapsychic reflection and a more purely analytic process. With the shift to the couch, I found myself going silent, mute really, for long periods during many sessions. At first, Dr. D seemed to reluctantly accept my periods of silence. I found myself in the familiar state of mind I fall into when I am alone, of silent thought with little sense of the presence or usefulness of others. It was a difficult struggle to remember to talk in session, to feel that there was any point in talking. Dr. D became a kind of ghost to me. I lost track of him. I would have a session with him in my mind as I drove to the appointment (an hour's drive) and then feel I had nothing more to say in the session, as though it had all already been said.

In our face to face sessions, under the pressure of my needing to make a decision about my marriage, take care of my sons, and keep my life going, I had been acutely aware of Dr. D's presence and concern. I was able to allow myself to rely upon him, unlike with my previous therapist. I accepted both his interpretations and his advice. On the couch, my attention turned more inward. I could not feel his importance or his function. I can see now, in retrospect, how hurt, helpless and angry Dr. D, having given me so much, must have felt in the face of my silence. Dr. D would sometimes encourage me to talk more, challenging my silence as a resistance, but any real understanding/analysis of the power and peculiarities of my muteness remained out of reach for a long time. In retrospect, I suspect that Dr. D did not have enough distance and understanding of his own reactions to my silence to effectively engage and analyze it. This, like our unexamined idealizations, were to have consequences for the two of us.

Unknowingly, I had set in motion again – this time with Dr. D – two rather paradoxical modes of relating: one a silent, cut-off distancing and the other an idealized and idealizing engagement. Each kept the most vulnerable and lonely aspects of me out of view and reach. As I often felt deeply alone in my sessions (in the presence of my analyst), I also felt deeply alone in my life (in the midst of many friends). I was, however, determined to at least find a sexual partner, if not a new life partner. I knew that with the ending of the marriage I would be exploring sexual relationships with both genders. As an adolescent it was clear to me that I was attracted to both women and men. I came out to my parents as possibly gay while in college. Both were supportive of either choice of sexual partner. I spent my college years experimenting with straight and gay relationships, though I found my relationships with women significantly more sexually satisfying. I lived with one woman for nearly a year and then lived my senior year with the woman who was to become my wife. At the point of separation from my wife I became involved with a man who lived in another state, hoping for some distance and privacy from my professional and home life. I fell into an intense and complicated relationship.

As issues of my sexual choices and activities came up in the sessions, I began to experience what I considered to be countertransference reactions on Dr. D's part. When I told Dr. D of my sexual interest in men as well as women, he was visibly both taken aback and interested. I had little inclination to discuss issues of bisexuality, homosexuality, sexual preference, etc., as I had no particular conflict about it. I was very concerned that whether I became involved with male or female partners, I not repeat the symbiotic patterns I had created and was unable to break in my marriage. But throughout this process Dr. D would repeatedly inquire about my homosexual feelings, the history of my sexual activities, and my understanding of my same-sex desires. These were, to me, his needs and questions, not mine; he had not inquired into my heterosexual relations in a similar way. I told him on several occasions that he seemed more interested in my homosexual life than I was. I told him that I had fantasies, frustrated and hostile, to add an additional, unpaid session each week to respond to his questions about homosexuality, so that it wouldn't detract from my time on the couch and my own concerns.

Finally, I asked Dr. D to talk about himself, what this was all about for him. Reluctantly, he told me of doing an analysis early in his career with a gay candidate in analytic training, with whom he made an agreement to hide the patient's homosexuality so that would not interfere with his accreditation as an analyst. He had had deep respect for this patient's professional skill and had long felt guilty and conflicted about colluding with the hiding of his patient's sexual orientation. He was now trying to come to a better understanding of same-sex relationships, acknowledging that he had had real questions about the capacity of two men to love one another. Dr. D told me he was on a national task force advocating for gays and lesbians within the American Psychoanalytic Association and was a member of a small group of local analysts and psychotherapists discussing gay, lesbian and gender issues. It seemed clear to me that in the background for Dr. D were broader, vaguer issues of intimacy and passionate attachments between men. I continued to feel my familiar detachment and distance from him. I was losing track of why I was seeing him. I no longer found him so helpful. Quite to the contrary, I felt a growing irritation with him, which I lived with in silence. We did not talk about what was happening between us.

One evening, as I was cooking a birthday dinner for my youngest son, I received a panicked phone call from a client of mine, who (unbeknownst to me) was a member of the gay and lesbian study group to which Dr. D belonged. In the meeting the night before Dr. D had discussed his work with a patient who she realized was me. She left the meeting as soon as she realized Dr. D was talking about me, but by then she had heard details of my sexual history and that I had recently become involved with a man. A bit later I received an awkward phone call from the clinical supervisor of the gay and lesbian counseling center, telling me that I had been outed by my psychoanalyst in the previous night's meeting. It was a surreal birthday party that night. I later learned that a supervisee of mine was also in that meeting and recognized that it was me Dr. D was talking about.

I was furious. I was confused. I called Dr. D's answering machine to tell him what had happened, telling him under no circumstances to contact me before our next session, that I needed time to think and I hoped he would have as miserable a weekend as I was anticipating for myself. I called my clinical consultant and went to see him at his home the next evening. He had known of my recent relationship with my male lover and was shocked at Dr. D's lack of judgment. He said I would probably have to terminate and suggested I consider bringing ethics charges against Dr. D. I saw no sense in either possibility. I was certain this was not an ethical lapse but something extraordinarily stupid, unconsciously stupid, an acting out. I did not particularly care that Dr. D had 'outed' me. Most people who knew me knew I identified myself as bisexual. The violation for me was that he spoke of the privacy of our work in a setting where I was almost certain to be recognized without elaborate efforts to disguise my identity. The curtain in my initial, anticipatory dream of Dr. D's office and my 'first session' with him had indeed been ripped away.

In our first session after the mess, Dr. D explained that the discussion in the gay and lesbian study group had devolved into one of these classically intellectualized psychoanalytic discussions of the defensive functions of homosexuality. He had become intensely frustrated with the tone of the meeting and told the group that if the discussions continued in this vein, he would be leaving the group. He was not going to tolerate the pathologizing of same-sex love relationships. 'Suddenly,' he told me, 'I found myself telling that group that I was learning a great deal about homosexuality and love between men from one of my patients. I went on to talk about our work without ever thinking of the consequences.'

Dr. D went on to suggest that we might have to terminate, that this was an error from which we could not recover. This was not acceptable to me. We needed to recover, to sustain our work. I needed to understand how this had happened. We each had things to learn about ourselves in the creation of this situation. I was suddenly revisiting familiar relationship issues with great intensity. I felt thrown back upon myself to take care of myself in a way so familiar from my earliest memories. How could I continue to rely on this man? If I worked to preserve this relationship, was I creating another horridly compromised relationship? I knew in my gut that I should not remove myself, withdraw – compromise and withdrawal were far too familiar defensive reactions. I needed to hold Dr. D on the hook to account for himself. Dr. D assured me that he was engaged in a self-analysis to understand what had happened. I was not the least bit reassured by this. I insisted he get consultation.

Facing the music

> Among the ways of being that I value in the analytic setting . . . is the effort
> on the part of the analyst and the patient to face the truth, to be honest with
> themselves in the face of disturbing emotional experience . . . In the absence
> of the effort on the part of patient and analyst to 'face the music', what
> occurs in the analysis has a shallow, desultory, as-if quality to it.
>
> (Ogden, 2005, p. 21)

The following weekend I was having dinner with an analytic colleague from
Great Britain. With visible distress I told him what happened with Dr. D.
He began to laugh. He continued to laugh, occasionally muttering, 'Oh,
what a glorious fuckup. What a glorious fuckup.' His reaction was rather
unexpected, to say the least, but rather refreshing in an odd way. When he
eventually settled down, he said quite simply, 'We only fuck up this badly
with patients we love. We are always learning from our mistakes. What we
and our patients owe to each other is honesty and a willingness to learn
from what goes wrong. If we do everything right, if we have to be right, no
one is going to learn very much. But we do seem to save our biggest
mistakes for the patients we love. It's the patients we love the most, want
the most for, where we act without thinking. What you and he have to deal
with is how much you love each other. You're very lucky to have each
other. You know, Dr. D must be utterly in love with you. This was a rather
clumsy way of telling you he loves you. You must talk to each other about
your love for each other.'

I took this dinner conversation back to session. We began to unravel
what this enactment meant for each of us and between us. With considerable hesitation, Dr. D spoke more openly of his affection for me, his
admiration of how I moved rather aggressively in my professional world,
and his envy of my relations with other men, my male friends as well as
sexual partners. He talked in more detail of his guilt for his collusion with
his gay analytic candidate, the paradox of regret for his secrecy then and his
inadvertent exposure of me now. He told me about an enlisted man he had
grown close to while serving in the military. Dr. D, as a physician and an
officer, was not supposed to interact personally with the enlisted men, but
he was drawn to this one man in particular. Neither of them felt at ease
with the hyper-masculine military environment. Both shared many
interests, and they became close. The friendship was shrouded in secrecy
– a double transgression of an officer and an enlisted man and of male
affection. I did not see the relationship Dr. D described as homosexual in
nature, but as certainly deeply intimate and perhaps homoerotic. They did
not maintain the friendship after their military service ended.

It became clear how much Dr. D hungered for male companionship and
intimacy. He said it was not to be found within his psychoanalytic community, which he characterized as intellectual, competitive, secretly

disdainful – men going though the motions of camaraderie but no true caring for one another. He told me he hoped our relationship would continue after termination. Perhaps most importantly, he talked of the complex meanings and feelings of my being his final analytic patient at the end of his career. His emotional charge around my gay relationships began to take on very different meanings for me.

I, in turn, had to acknowledge and examine my feelings of not deserving his attention (let alone affection) as the crises in my life were now past. I was taking care of my sons, working hard, earning college and school tuitions, and back fully into my distant, manic coping style. I was oblivious to Dr. D's care and concern for me. I did not give him the space or opportunity to give any voice to how he was feeling toward me. He did not make that space for himself. I realized that I had closed him out (as I had so many others) and could see how his complex feelings toward me and our relationship spilled out in a different context. As we now spoke more openly of our feelings for each other, I started to feel my reactions to his aging, my admiration for the way he was living his life, now past 80. My admiration had been held too often in silence, as his going on living vigorously was such a painful contrast to the resignation and ending of my young father's life. I wanted to know more about how he maintained his vitality and enthusiasm for life. I wanted to witness his growing older, how he coped with it. I wanted to be with him when he died. I was finally able to give voice to these desires. I felt my own envy of his happiness in his second marriage after the death of his first wife and the despair it engendered in me about ever finding love and companionship in a new relationship, be it with a man or a woman.

I was thrown back on the dream I had the night before my first session with Dr. D. I could not quite believe that we had somehow ended up living out that dream, my therapy suddenly exposed to colleagues and friends. I had to face that ways in which I had communicated an invincibility, even in the face of the depth of the work I had been doing my therapy. I had managed to convey a false sense of resilience and invulnerability that fostered both Dr. D's losing track of me as a patient and his feelings of being cut off by me, which I think contributed substantially to the spilling over of his feelings in an enactment.

Our enactment and potential rupture demanded that we consciously attend to the field of desire, love and intimacy opening between us. Dr. D and I began to grapple with the task defined for us by my dinner companion – the examination of our unacknowledged and feared affections and desires.

I would imagine that many readers, as you have watched this case unfold, could see the danger points, read the signals, recognize opportunities for intervention and analysis, or wonder, 'Why doesn't he (one of them at least) say *something*?!' The fact that neither Dr. D nor I could see or say anything underscores the nature and the power of enactments. It was the behavioral manifestation that brought us to the surface, to the possibility of conscious recognition and exploration.

Ten years later

> Arrested in their capacity to love, subjects who are under the empire of the dead mother can only aspire to autonomy. Sharing remains forbidden to them. Thus, solitude, which was a situation creating anxiety and to be avoided, changes sign. From the negative it becomes positive. Having previously been shunned, it is now sought after. The subject nestles into it.
>
> (Green, 1983, p. 156)

Ten years have passed since the enactment I have described above. Dr. D regained his analytic stance and we continued for another four years of productive work together. I was his last patient, our work the end of his career. As we approached termination, I wrote up this incident for us to use as a reflection on the many layers of meaning about loss and anticipated endings embedded in our relationship.

Eigen (1998) cautions us that the

> dread of environmental failure is the outer shell of a deeper dread of the failure of one's own [psychological] equipment. The environment tries to make up for what the individual can not do (and vice versa), but never with more than partial success. We rely on each other all life long for help with agonies [and I would add passions] we can not handle.'
>
> (p. 97)

I was in my late 40s when this enactment with Dr. D unfolded. I had been with and loved, within my limits, a woman for more than 25 years, but I had never truly relied upon her. I had wished for but never truly expected reliability. I had many friends, but there were limits to my engagement with them as well. Solitude remained my most faithful companion. I was by then having sex quite happily with a man, but I did not open myself fully or rely upon my sexual partners, none of whom had even lived in the same city as I. I had not yet learned to truly love a man or receive the love of a man. Dr. D was approaching 80 and the end of his career; a man's love and companionship for him, and his for another man had eluded him as well.

Andre Green's brilliant essay, 'The Dead Mother' (1983) afforded us particular insight into the process between us. Green describes mothers who are unable to metabolize and transform the losses in their own lives, living then in a profound deadness while still alive. For me, in my growing up, such an account characterized not only my mother but my extended family. Deadness and depressive withdrawal permeates my early object relations.

Vitality seems impossible to the 'dead' parent, even hostile. The infant/child cannot bring life to the parent's being; the child often identifies with the parent's lifelessness or imagines himself as the cause of it. What is most desired becomes the deepest threat. Gerson (2003) eloquently evokes the dilemma addressed in Green's essay:

> The baby's lips are made moist by the mother's milk even while the mother's tears dampen them both. It is a confused joining as the good and the bad are internalized simultaneously into a combined experience that occurs prior to splitting . . . a whole object that is a product of the deadliness that was ingested together with life . . . In this scenario, where the source of life is mixed with its failure to sustain liveliness . . . the closer one gets, the more alone one feels . . . the more of life, the more of death.
>
> (p. 14)

During this period of work with Dr. D, I began to recognize how profoundly I had turned away from others, forming a primary and solitary relationship with my own mind (Winnicott, 1965; Corrigan and Gordon, 1995). Dr. D and I had lived our lives in the shadow of 'dead' mothers (psychically dead and then tragically, actually dead), with fathers who were unable to bring vitality and passion into the lives of their sons or themselves. The wish for a man's affection and passionate involvement, for the love of and for a man, to bring each of us more fully to life was more than either of us could bear, even in the deeply committed relationship that we did have. We each unconsciously disavowed our loving desires for the other. Desire burst out unconsciously in the enactment at the gay and lesbian study group.

Dr. D needed to examine his breach of my privacy and the meanings of his outburst about male love, not to be punished or chastised for it. I needed to remain engaged with Dr. D rather than withdraw into myself, in spite of the breach, and examine my part in what was unfolding, though at that point I could not have understood this as an enactment. Gradually we were each able to comprehend our own contributions to this enactment, face our parallel fears of loss and rejection, and in so doing to begin to find the capacities for love that we each so dearly sought and could finally relish.

Perspectives on enactment

> We both came out of this piece of analytic work with our own deep sense of having been changed by the impact of an intimacy with an other that was novel and disturbing, then acceptable and enhancing to us both. . . . In this core experience is a moving power, by and for the two participants, that I do not fully fathom.
>
> (McLaughlin, 2005, p. 220)

The term 'enactment' is still emergent and developing in our professional lexicon, and as such it is encumbered with a multiplicity of meanings that can render obscure what any particular author is meaning to convey. Beginning in the mid-1980s a series of clinical papers began to explore the experience and meanings of countertransferential enactment and to differentiate enactment from acting out (Boesky, 1982; Poland, 1984, 1988, 2005; Jacobs, 1986, 1991; McLaughlin, 1987, 1991; Chused, 1991; Elkind, 1992; Johan, 1992; Roughton, 1993; Renik, 1993a, 1993b, 1999). Over the past 20 years, the term 'enactment' has evolved to gradually replace the concept of 'acting out'. Acting out was historically seen, within the psychoanalytic paradigm of free association and bringing everything into words, as a patient's regressive use of *behavioral action* in a defensive refusal (or inability) to use language and cognition for self-expression. Gradually it came to be understood that while acting out could well serve a defensive function, it wasn't quite that simple or unilateral. *Action* in therapy was coming to be understood as a form of implicit or procedural memory, a form of nonverbal communication for experiences that were not yet available in language. One could move from behavioral action toward expression through words, but it was coming to be understood that emergent, foundational experience was often neither available nor communicative in language (Bucci, 1997a, 1997b, 2007). At the same time, the understanding of countertransference was undergoing a similar transformation of meaning, from that of a regressive/defensive emotional reaction on the part of the therapist to an informative and communicative unfolding of emotional and unconscious communication.

Writing about enactment necessitated analysts being willing to write quite openly about themselves and their own intrapsychic conflicts, characterological blind spots, and unconscious vulnerabilities. These initial articles demonstrated courage on the part of their authors and began to introduce a personal frankness and self-examination to psychoanalytic writing seldom seen since Freud and Ferenczi. Elkind (1992) and Kantrowitz (1996) undertook self-report surveys of psychotherapists and psychoanalysts to study 'therapeutic impasses' and ruptured terminations (Elkind) and the 'impact of patients' on their analysts (Kantrowitz). While not writing specifically from the vantage point of enactment, these two studies offer a great deal of insight into the frequency of the phenomena, their developmental roots, and intrapsychic and interpersonal meanings.

Elkind distributed a questionnaire to 330 therapist members of the Psychotherapy Institute in Berkeley, California, inquiring about experiences of rupture in long-term therapy relations ending 'in an impasse with accompanying feelings of rage, disappointment, or sense of failure' (p. 4). Somewhat to her surprise, 87.5% of the respondents said yes with regard to patients and 53% said yes with regard to their own personal therapies. The respondents frequently reported their own vulnerabilities to being wounded by patients. The survey demonstrated that many of these irreversible ruptures were not a result of severe psychopathology on the part of the patient or incompetence and lack of skill on the part of the therapist, but rather:

> The new perspective that I am emphasizing in this book views the unresolvable dilemmas – mismatches, impasses, and wounding – that can lead to ruptures, not as avoidable failures, but rather as *common, inevitable occurrences that present us with a special opportunity for new awareness and change as well as for the dangerous possibility of a wounding and disillusioning setback.*
>
> (italics in original, pp. 6–7)

While not drawing upon the psychoanalytic conceptualizations of enactment, Elkind concludes that many impasses are the result of areas of primary (developmental) vulnerabilities on the part of both therapist and client. The recognition of these vulnerabilities and the understanding of their effects one on the other is 'critically important if the wounding is to be worked through rather than allowed to disrupt the relationship altogether' (p. 133). Her study is replete with detailed case studies and examples of her consultations with troubled therapeutic couples. For those concerned with the process of enactments, much can be learned from this volume.

Kantrowitz, a psychoanalyst, distributed anonymous questionnaires to 1,100 members of the American Psychoanalytic Association inquiring about the analysts' experiences of the impact of patients upon them professionally and personally; 339 responded. Kantrowitz followed up the written, self-report survey with in-depth telephone interviews with 26 of the respondents; these interviews and Kantrowitz's reflections upon them were written up and given to the interviewees, so that a second, often deeper discussion could ensue. Kantrowitz came to conclude that 'the dividing line between what we define as a countertransference reaction and what we define as an enactment may at times be slim' (p. 73). She characterizes 'reactions' as those 'in which the analysts described recognition of affective responses that were cognitively contained' (p. 73) while enactments were countertransference responses that took a behavioral form. Kantrowitz captures the nature of the enactment dilemma vividly:

> the patient at this point is experienced as 'the other', providing the stimulus for the recognition of some unwanted aspect of the analyst. Under these circumstances, the final jolt of recognition of being caught in an emotional reaction causes distress. The analyst sees that he or she is not in conscious control . . . and that reaction has had behavioral or distressing emotional consequences.
>
> (p. 216)

It is not my intent here to offer the final and definitive definition of enactment but to be as concise and precise as I can be about how I am using the concept of enactment. I am indebted to the work of James McLaughlin (1987, 1991, 1994, 2005). No one has written more extensively or openly about transference, countertransference, therapeutic impasse, and enactment than McLaughlin (Cornell, 2005; Chodorow, 2007). McLaughlin (2005) conveys an understanding of the unconscious meanings of behavioral enactments in near poetic terms:

> Each has learned from infancy, long before the words were there for the saying, how to appeal, coerce, clarify, and dissimulate through the signals of body language, gestures, facial expression, and vocal qualities . . . whether we are analyst or patient, our deepest hopes for what we may find the world to be, as well as our worst fears of what it will be, reflect our transference expectancies as shaped by our developmental past.
>
> (p. 187)

We still tend to hope for the awareness and insight afforded by counter-transference rather than the unconscious blindness of countertransferential enactments, but we seem to be coming to terms with the frequency and inevitability of enactments and to be seeing the challenge and opportunity embedded in enactment.

I do not think that the concept of enactment should replace that of acting out. Clearly there are times when actions on the part of the therapist or the patient are defensive and interfere with the course of treatment. I tend to think of acting out as a unilateral action on the part of either patient or therapist, and I reserve the term enactment for a bilateral process between therapist and patient. McLaughlin (2005) articulates the bilateral nature of enactments:

> When at work, we bumble, stumble, and get lost. . . . From this view of the analyst as an involved and not invulnerable participant, I suggest we use the term *analytic enactment* (italics in original) . . . to refer to events occurring within the dyad that both parties experience as being the consequence of the behavior of the other. . . . Implicit in this perspective of enactment in the clinical situation is the expectation that close scrutiny of the interpersonal behaviors shaped between the pair will provide clues and cues leading to the latent intrapsychic conflicts and residues of prior object relations that one has helped stir into resonance in the other, and between them actualized for both.
>
> (pp. 188–189)

Yet, in his acknowledgement of the inevitability and necessity of analytic enactments and the mutuality of unconscious influences within the analytic pair, McLaughlin came to stress the recognition and articulation of the unique and quite separate subjectivities of the two participants, which Chodorow (2007) characterizes as 'two-person separate'. There is a necessary move from enactment to reflection, analysis and meaning-making, shifting from the unconscious merger and *mutuality of influence* to the developing capacity for *mutual recognition* and differentiation.

The enactment between Dr. D and me could be seen as an especially egregious error, an acting-out on the part of Dr. D. That was certainly my first reaction to it, as I felt myself to be a victim rather than an unwitting participant. In our willingness to 'face the music' Dr. D and I learned about ourselves and each other. In the rule-bound, litigious atmosphere of our current era, Dr. D's behavior could all too easily have been cast as a violation of my confidentiality (which it was), an irreversible ethical breach or even act of malpractice (which it wasn't). In my work as a consultant and trainer, therapists often bring me cases of impasse, countertransfer-ential knots, failure, or enactment, usually accompanied by shame or anxieties of ethical charges or a lawsuit. What so often unfolds in the exploration of these therapeutic dilemmas is some form of enactment between therapist and patient. When the enactment is unrecognized, I suspect it is all too often further acted out in the arenas of ethical charges, law suits, or premature terminations.

While I see the process of enactment as bilateral and as the expression of parallel patterns of unconscious disavowal, the resolution of enactments is not mutual and bilateral. The therapeutic relationship is fundamentally asymmetrical with the onus of therapeutic responsibility on the mind and shoulders of the therapist. Kantrowitz (1996) captures the asymmetrical nature of the resolution of enactments:

> The analyst cannot resolve this just within the analytic hours. As elaborated previously, self-reflective efforts, along with talking to colleagues and sometimes friends or spouse about personal, emotional distress stemming from the situation with the patient, are employed by the analyst to regain perspective in the analytic work.
>   . . . the actual process of work is not so different once the analyst becomes aware of what has been rekindled. When the patient rep-resents some emotionally important figure for the analyst in his or her countertransference, the reworking of earlier experiences is most parallel to the patient's reworking. The patient, however, unlike the analyst, has no reason to be empathically attuned or responsive to the personal meanings stirred in the analyst in reaction to him or her.
>
> (pp. 217–218)

While periods of enactment provide the occasion for deeper recognitions and more open communication between therapist and client, the undoing of an enactment does not mean a 'mutual analysis' as exemplified in the radical experiments undertaken by Ferenczi (Dupont, 1988). It remains the responsibility of the therapist through self-analysis, consultation, ongoing supervision, or perhaps a return to personal therapy to undo one's own unconscious blind spots so as to re-open one's capacity for unconscious receptivity, direct communication and the capacity to observe, analyze, and find meaning.

The enlivening transference (and countertransference)

> What I am sketching out here is how the enlivening transference facilitates the emergence of love for an other in patients who have cynically foreclosed and turned away from another's love and in the process have impoverished their own ability to love either themselves or others.
>
> (Gerson, 2003)

Gerson (2003), speaking of the continual and inevitable meshings of eros and thanatos within interplays of the transference and countertransference, observes that 'the more overt expression of this [erotic] force may be most prominently at play in transferences of those patients who feel, or most frequently suffer from, a hollowness at the heart of their vitality.' This force was certainly at play in my transference to Dr. D. As can be seen in the enactment between Dr. D and me, this force can be at play, albeit disavowed, in the countertransference as well. Gerson expands the concept of the erotic transference to that of the 'enlivening' transference, suggesting 'this idea and terminology because I think it contains the advantage of highlighting the aim of the transference rather than its content or even its object. In the enlivening transference the motive is the evocation of desire itself rather than the object.' Desiring is not so simple; it is inevitably intertwined with the possibility, the likelihood of loss. This is especially true when one's first and foundational loved ones are shot through with unresolved and unspoken grief.

What Dr. D and I most wished for and feared was the evocation of passionate attachment and desire – love, more simply stated – and a coming more fully to life with each other. It was the experience of myself coming more fully alive, not some exterior intrusion or disruption, that was traumatic for me, and so too for Dr. D. We are often too much for ourselves. For years, until the dam burst, neither of us could tolerate the force of that desire within ourselves and thus could not overtly seek it in the other.

Since the termination of my work with Dr. D, my readings on the analytic exploration of enlivening and deadening processes in therapy (Bollas, 1989, 1992; Bolognini, 1994; Eigen, 1996, 1998; Gerson, 2003, 2007; Green, 1980, 1983, 1995; Mann, 1997; Ogden, 1999) have deepened my understanding of what transpired not only in my therapy with Dr. D, but of the universality of these passions and vulnerabilities. What I hope most to have conveyed in this essay is the compelling, yet paradoxical interplay of the intensity of the wishes for enlivening and the forces of disavowal and deadening.

In conclusion

Dr. D and I decided that should the right circumstance arise I would publish an essay on enactment based on the narrative I wrote as part of our termination process. The invitation to contribute a chapter to this book seemed the right circumstance. We wanted to draw from our experience to explore both the disruptive impact of disavowed desires in both therapist and patient as well as the intimate and healing potentials of the emergence of such passions. This essay offers a rather unique perspective on enactment, written from the point of view of the patient rather than the therapist, centered on the disavowal and unmanageability of 'positive' rather than 'negative' feelings, and descriptive of the traumatic intrusiveness of internal experience and passionate attachment rather than the environmental intrusions and violations that we most often describe and relate to as traumatic.

Maroda (1991) has argued passionately that:

> One of the most important tasks of analytic treatment is to accept limitations, loss, and human frailty, but this does not mean that the patient should accept responsibility for the therapist's limitations as well as his own. . . . Many people believe that for the analytic therapist to admit her own pathology is dangerous. I believe that it is the need to preserve the mask of sanity that is dangerous.
>
> (p. 107)

Those masks of sanity are, however, in our chosen profession idealized and deeply seductive. Over the course of many painful, bluntly honest sessions, my work with Dr. D again deepened, my self-understanding grew, my capacity to sustain a passionate attachment in the face of severe disappointment became solidified. This was an opportunity for me to see Dr. D struggle with a serious error and come together more strongly and richly on my behalf. In so doing, he provided me with a startling contrast to repeatedly watching my parents (especially my father) disintegrate, withdraw and/ or become avoidant in the face of conflict, disappointment and potential loss. With the challenge and understanding offered me by my dinner companion, I did not retreat into myself this time. I did not retreat but came at Dr. D again and again with the expectation that we understand what this meant for each of us. I had broken ranks with my past and with my standard defenses of providing reason and comfort to others by sustaining this confrontation with Dr. D.

In my own practice, many of my clients are themselves psychotherapists. It is a complex business providing psychotherapy to psychotherapists, to provide a space within which those committed to sanity can experience and explore their areas of insanity. For Dr. D and me, our masks of sanity had fallen away. We had the guts and commitment to each other to face ourselves, talk to each other, and move through a period of intense denial, conflict, and vulnerability to reach for a more honest self-understanding.

I write here the story of myself as a patient, but what I learned for myself as a therapist was profound. I learned anew and at a more fundamental level through my experience of this enactment of the power of unconscious, disavowed desires and of passionate, loving engagement. I acquired a deep and abiding respect for the fundamental humanity of all of us in this practice of psychoanalysis, psychotherapy, counseling and human relations work. I internalized a deep and abiding regard for the unstoppable, and often disruptive, force of our unconscious passions. I learned a more realistic meaning of love and commitment. I still love solitude and still have access to my manic and idealizing defenses, but now other options for coping and closeness are more readily available. I remain forever seduced by my mind and the eloquent minds of others, but there is more compelling space in my experience of life and our work for the uncertain, for the mistaken, for human troubles, for needing and learning together, for honesty and self-scrutiny, for loving and being loved.

References

Boesky, D. (1982) Acting out: a reconsideration of the concept. *International Journal of Psycho-Analysis*, 63: 39–55.

Bollas, C. (1989) *Forces of Destiny*. London: Free Association Books.

Bollas, C. (1992) *Being a Character*. New York: Hill & Wang.

Bolognini, S. (1994) Transference: erotised, erotic, loving, affectionate. *International Journal of Psycho-Analysis*, 75: 73–86.

Bucci, W. (1997a) *Psychoanalysis and Cognitive Science: A Multiple Code Theory*. New York: Guilford Press.

Bucci, W. (1997b) Symptoms and symbols: a multiple code theory of somatization. *Psychoanalytic Inquiry*, 20: 40–70.

Bucci, W. (2007) Dissociation from the perspective of multiple code theory: psychological roots and implications for psychoanalytic treatment. *Contemporary Psychoanalysis*, 43: 164–184.

Chodorow, N. (2007) The healer's bent: solitude and dialogue in the clinical encounter, by James T. McLaughlin. *Psychoanalytic Quarterly*, 76: 617–629.

Chused, J. F. (1991) The evocative power of enactments. *Journal of the American Psychoanalytic Association*, 39: 615–640.

Cornell, W. F. (2005) Deep in the shed – an analyst's mind at work. Introduction to J. T. McLaughlin. In W. F. Cornell (ed.) *The Healer's Bent: Solitude and Dialogue in the Clinical Encounter* (pp. 1–16). Hillsdale, NJ: The Analytic Press.

Corrigan, G. & Gordon, P. (Eds.) (1995) *The Mind Object*. Northvale, NJ: Jason Aronson.

Dupont, J. (ed.) (1988) *The Clinical Diary of Sandor Ferenczi*. Cambridge, MA: Harvard University Press.

Eigen, M. (1996) *Psychic Deadness*. Northvale, NJ: Jason Aronson.

Eigen, M. (1998) *The Psychoanalytic Mystic*. Binghampton, NY: ESF Publishers.

Elkind, S. N. (1992) *Resolving Impasses in Therapeutic Relationships*. New York: Guilford Press.

Gerson, S. (2003) The enlivening transference and the shadow of deadliness. Paper delivered to the Boston Psychoanalytic Society and Institute, 3 May.

Gerson, S. (2007) When the third is dead: memory, mourning, and witnessing in the aftermath of the holocaust. Paper delivered to the International Psychoanalytic Association, Berlin, 26 July.

Green, A. (1980) Passions and their vicissitudes. In A. Green, *On Private Madness*. Madison, CT: International Universities Press, 1986.

Green, A. (1983) The dead mother. In A. Green, *On Private Madness*. Madison, CT: International Universities Press, 1986.

Green, A. (1995) Has sexuality anything to do with psychoanalysis? *International Journal of Psycho-Analysis*, 76: 871–883.

Jacobs, T. J. (1986) On countertransference enactments. *Journal of the American Psychoanalytic Association*, 34: 289–307.

Jacobs, T. J. (1991) *The Use of Self: Countertransference and Communication in the Analytic Situation*. Madison, CT: International Universities Press.

Johan, M., reporter. (1992) Enactments in psychoanalysis. *Journal of the American Psychoanalytic Association*, 40: 40–41.

Kantrowitz, J. L. (1996) *The Patient's Impact on the Analyst*. Hillsdale, NJ: The Analytic Press.

Mann, D. (1997) *Psychotherapy: An Erotic Relationship*. London: Routledge.

Maroda, K. (1991) *The Power of Countertransference: Innovations in Analytic Technique*. Chichester, UK: John Wiley & Sons.

McLaughlin, J. T. (1987) The play of transference: some reflections on enactment in the psychoanalytic situation. *Journal of the American Psychoanalytic Association*, 35: 557–582.

McLaughlin, J. T. (1991) Clinical and theoretical aspects of enactment. *Journal of the American Psychoanalytic Association*, 39: 595–614.

McLaughlin, J. T. (1994) Analytic impasse: the interplay of dyadic transferences. Paper presented to The Karen Horney Psychoanalytic Institute and Center and The Association for the Advancement of Psychoanalysis, 5 March.

McLaughlin, J. T. (2005) *The Healer's Bent: Solitude and Dialogue in the Clinical Encounter*, W. F. Cornell (ed.). Hillsdale, NJ: The Analytic Press.

Ogden, T. H. (1999) Analyzing forms of aliveness and deadness of the transference-countertransference. In G. Kohon (ed.) *The Dead Mother: The Work of Andre Green* (pp. 128–148). London: Routledge.

Ogden, T. H. (2005) *The Art of Psychoanalysis*. London: Routledge.

Poland, W. (1984) On the analyst's neutrality. *Journal of the American Psychoanalytic Association*, 32: 283–299.

Poland, W. (1988) Insight and the analytic dyad. *Psychoanalytic Quarterly*, 57: 341–369.

Poland, W. (2005) The analyst's fears. Paper presented at Generativity: Honoring the Contributions of James T. McLaughlin conference, Pittsburgh, PA, 15 October.

Renik, O. (1993a) Countertransference enactment and the psychoanalytic process. In M. J. Horowitz, O. F. Kernberg, & E. M. Weinshel (eds.) *Psychic Structure and Psychic Change: Essays in Honor of Robert S. Wallerstein, M.D.* (pp. 135–158). Madison, CT: International Universities Press.

Renik, O. (1993b) Analytic interaction: conceptualizing technique in the light of the analyst's irreducible subjectivity. *Psychoanalytic Quarterly*, 62: 553–571.

Renik, O. (1999) Playing one's cards face up in analysis. *Psychoanalytic Quarterly*, 68: 521–539.

Roughton, R. E. (1993) Useful aspects of acting out: repetition, enactment, and actualization. *Journal of the American Psychoanalytic Association*, 41: 443–472.

Sandler, J. (1976) Actualization and object relationships. *Journal of the Philadelphia Association for Psychoanalysis*, 3: 59–70.

Stein, M. (1981) The unobjectionable part of the transference. *Journal of the American Psychoanalytic Association*, 29: 869–892.

Winnicott, D. W. (1965) Ego distortion in terms of true and false self. In *The Maturational Process and the Facilitating Environment* (pp. 140–152). New York: International Universities Press.

6   Action, enactment and moments of meeting in therapy with children

Caroline Case

The focus of this chapter will be on action and enactment in therapy sessions in the context of previous trauma. Firstly, trauma will be outlined, before considering the potentially confusing use of different terms to do with enactment. My interest is in moments when we might act out aspects of the countertransference rather than stay with a reflective attitude. This could be thought about in terms of projective identification or the acting out or actualisation of intra-psychic and inter-psychic dynamics, inner figures, parts of the patient's and therapist's inner worlds. The notion of action – making a move – could encompass 'moments of meeting': what they have in common with enactments is that the therapist comes out of their usual professional role for a moment. How may these apparently different therapeutic phenomena be aligned or connected?

In previous writing I have explored a child bringing an escort into the room with my permission, to look at a particular piece of work, only to discover that the escort was deaf. Our struggles to communicate, which included my initial embarrassment and wrong-footing, mirrored and enacted the struggles of this child to communicate with a father who was 'deaf' to his son's needs (Case, 2005). He had needed to go to these lengths to make me understand his situation. This suggests that sometimes the 'action' is client led. In this case the 'deafness' was being enacted by myself, and I needed to be shown it by the client; the enactment occurred as it was not known in a verbal form by the client, but present as an unthought known (Bollas, 1987). However, the action can also be therapist led as an unconscious response of the therapist, which may demonstrate something useful to the client, as will be described.

Two pairs of vignettes have been selected in order to explore firstly, *action* in contrast to *staying with* in art psychotherapy groups with adults; and secondly, an enactment of trauma which felt like a potentially useful intervention to the therapist at the time and was confused with a planned moment of meeting, unfortunately a contradiction in terms. This will be contrasted with a moment of meeting which was successful, and by definition, not planned, which led to enactment of trauma through play; these latter two examples are both with children.

I have found that enactment can take many forms working with children in an art therapy room. One child who had had deep distress projected into her as a toddler by a traumatised mother made messy black paintings of a huge size that she then tried to wrap around me, to literally engulf the therapist in unprocessed grief. These paintings sometimes contained ghosts, 'that are frightening'. These sessions left both of us and the room in an almost unworkable state, as indeed had the family ground to a halt in the face of overwhelming distress (Case, 2003, 2005). Whereas in this situation the painting itself was the medium of enactment, it can also be a catalyst as a finished image for an aesthetically based enactment/moment of meeting as I will demonstrate.

Trauma

> The unconscious mind is constantly scanning the external world in a very active way, seeking out events and situations which can be used to represent these internal situations. . . . These representations manage to both express and hide these inner situations – or become objects of projection.
>
> (Bell, 1998, p. 168)

Trauma is caused when too much stimulus, more than the mind can process, breaks through the 'protective shield' (Freud, 1920). The model for this is the carer/mother shielding the baby and young child from excessive stimuli, whether in the larger environment or in terms of modulation of emotions. A traumatic event is one which floods the person with feeling and experience that cannot be made sense of, breaching ordinary defences, leaving the person vulnerable. 'Primitive fears, impulses and anxieties are all given fresh life' (Garland, 1998, p. 11). Coates and Moore define trauma as 'an overwhelming threat to the survival or integrity of the self that is accompanied by annihilation anxiety' (1997, p. 287). A psychoanalytic approach shows how the present trauma is linked structurally in the mind with similar early anxieties when the baby felt annihilating impulses due to failure of containment by the primary carer (Garland, 1998). These will be early non-verbal and pre-verbal experiences. In infancy, the expression of early needs is through the body: crying, kicking, trembles, and physical agitation express anxiety. As we develop, language is acquired, bringing the capacity to symbolise rather than to physically enact. However, there is a breakdown in symbolisation with the loss of a containing object (Segal, 1981).

Freud (1893) thought that certain very painful experiences, the memory of them, exist in the mind as a kind of 'foreign body'. They work an effect on us but we are not aware of them consciously, as they may take a form as a symptom. They need to be brought to consciousness with the accompanying affect, usually intense feeling, for the symptom then to disappear. Garland (1998) usefully reviews the development of Freud's thoughts on trauma, in particular his understanding of anxiety. An extreme external event impacts on mental organisation, obliterating all defences against anxiety. Freud then thought that the anxiety which overwhelms the mind comes from internal sources, listing five primary anxieties: birth, castration anxiety, loss of the loved object, loss of the object's love, and annihilation anxiety. When there is actual danger, automatic anxiety is triggered, compared to a situation where danger threatens, which results in signal anxiety. Garland suggests that once one has faced annihilation the ego cannot believe anymore in signal anxiety and goes straight to automatic anxiety. This leads to a loss of symbolic thinking. Then sounds, smells, a word or phrase, sights or situations can plunge the person directly into a previous traumatic situation, a flashback accompanied by immense anxiety. Working with children who have often been repeatedly traumatised through neglect or abuse, I find it is extremely difficult to talk, as words, a tone of voice, a picture they have made, a piece of play can unexpectedly plunge them into states of terror.

Traumatised children are rendered helpless and suffer a subsequent loss of faith that there is order and continuity in life (Stronach-Buschel, 1990). Victims of trauma may have many combinations of symptoms including nightmares, involuntary recollections of the event, numbing of responsiveness, reduced involvement in the external world, hyper-alertness, sleep disturbance, guilt, low concentration, fear of death, phobias, chronic anxiety (Van der Kolk, 1987). Normal development will be hampered as available energy is spent in warding off further vulnerability. Various defences may be used such as denial, isolation, regression, projection and splitting, spontaneous thought inhibited, affect constricted. There is often a loss of a capacity to symbolise and fantasise. Play may be restricted and repetitive of a scenario without words or storyline (Terr, 1983). Garland discusses that the aim of treatment in therapy is for the trauma to become part of the survivor's overall thinking and functioning, instead of remaining split off, encapsulated and avoided, a foreign body in the mind.

Enactment

In art psychotherapy and psychotherapy with children, enactments take many forms, both inside the session and around the transitions in and out of the sessions. 'In its play, the child acts instead of speaking. It puts actions – which originally took the place of thoughts – in the place of words: that is to say, that "acting out" is of utmost importance for it' (Klein, 1980, p. 9).

Freud's understanding of the transference in psychoanalysis was that 'psychological experiences are revived, not as belonging to the past, but as applying to the physician at the present moment'. These experiences need understanding and integration so that they become part of conscious ego-controlled content of psychic life. Freud came to understand that transference was linked to early traumas in the client's history and explored how the trauma is re-lived, re-experienced, and re-enacted as real life in the transference to the therapist.

In Klein's work in child psychoanalysis her interest was more on the development in the setting of the relationship which displayed all the mechanisms which characterise the client's way of dealing with life in the world outside. In children, and young children particularly, re-enactments may be from the immediate present. Children enact their fantasy life as a way of relating to their own worst fears and anxieties. Relationships enacted in the sessions are the expression of the children's efforts to encompass the traumatic way they experience their daily lives.

In current thinking an enactment is understood more as a particular key moment in therapy where therapist and patient are caught up unconsciously in enacting a traumatic moment in the patient's past, rather than as all transference/countertransference phenomena being a series of enactments. There has been a shift from the everyday meaning to the significant occasion, possibly a matter of intensity. Boundaries may be broken and the therapist has the feeling that they have 'acted unprofessionally' or out of their normal way of behaving as a therapist, so the moment or incident may induce guilt and uncomfortable feelings; however there can be moments of joy or better understanding as well. These moments are understood as symbolic interactions, like players on a stage without an audience, rather than as an observer in the therapist and eventually in the patient being able to reflect on current processes in the therapy. This throws into counterpoint reflection and action. It is also possible that symbolising or concretising is highlighted in a similar way to options when thinking about action and enactment.

Self-observation in therapy sessions suggests that action and enactment by the therapist and patient sometimes present ideas or aspects of the trauma in a new and sometimes palatable way, although this is not always successful. It seems to be a way forward in communication when 'words are not enough'. Bateman (1998) suggests that it is an inevitable occurrence. Possibly we have different names for a successful and unsuccessful action-intervention. Do we call a successful one a 'moment of meeting' and an unsuccessful one a therapist drawn into 'enactment', a coming out of role? Holmqvist (1996) in his research identifying conspicuous countertransference reactions concludes that a countertransference response should be evaluated against the therapist/patient norm, not against a professional norm. Cambray (2001) usefully comments on the ambiguity of terms, concluding 'use the term acting out to emphasise the "extra-psychic, action-behavioural" pole, and "actualisation" as a process term connoting the "intrapsychic subjective experience" of the transference or countertransference. The term enactment will be reserved for the non-verbal field aspects of transference/countertransference phenomena (which can include the *way* in which words or silences are used)' (Cambray, 2001, p. 277). The following vignette allows us to begin to think about some of the terms used.

Vignette 1

Pauline, an adolescent girl diagnosed with Asperger's came to see me for three sessions to explore whether she might be able to make use of child psychotherapy. People with Asperger's find change particularly difficult. In the first session she began to describe her extremely complex family story of parents who had split, and had had successions of partners all of who had their own children with previous partners. Added to this were further half-siblings. I became literally befuddled with strings of names, sometimes duplicated in the children of the next partner, and suddenly said, 'I need to write this down'. My patient was delighted in my confusion, and together we drew complex successive family trees. Crucial to this was noticing and commenting on her changing positions in the families, where she could be eldest, youngest, middle, fourth child etc. It was quite unusual for me to write this down and not to hold it in mind, enacting her evident tortuous sense of not knowing where she was in these changing families, or *who* she was, i.e. if there was a child of the same age in one configuration did that mean she was a twin? At the end there was a moment when our eyes met, we smiled, she stopped her delight in *my* confusion and we understood together how impossible this situation was for *her*.

In this example the therapist acts out, rather than holding something in mind, an actualisation of a traumatic situation, playing out the counter-transference rather than understanding and offering thought about it, although this came later, and there is a moment when their eyes meet as two people, out of role. In this way it is possible for there to be an entwining of action, enactment and moment of meeting. Crucial to this is the projection of distress and confusion and the therapist's response in projective-identification, contained on paper between us rather than internally by the therapist's mind. This could be understood as the actual-isation of intrapsychic phenomena. This child had very limited capacity to symbolise and may have needed to see a living object who could actively make a map of the situation, understand her difficulty and struggles and could bear to have contact with both it and her, as well as making it palatable (the maps). It is an example of showing a live part of oneself as a model (Bovensiepen, 2002; Case, 2008).

In an enactment, the therapist becomes a participant as well as an observer, as noted by McLaughlin (1991) and Roughton (1993). Devereux (2006) defines enactment as follows: 'The term "enactment" thus represents the conceptual uniting of Freud's concepts of transference and acting out, extending it to include both members of the analytic dyad, with a special emphasis on the non-verbal actualization of intrapsychic configurations' (p. 498). Gerrard (2007), writing about actual physical movement of the analyst in sessions, suggests that in these and enactments that take different forms the therapist is alerted to what they might not otherwise have understood.

Adult group art therapy examples

In the following two vignettes it may be easier to see action/enactment and
reflection from adult group work before going on to examples from work
with children, simply because as stated earlier there is naturally continual
enactment in play when working with children. In these the internal
processes of the therapist and the need to monitor through self-observation
of somatic processes and conversations with oneself are stressed.

Acting out on the part of the therapist may be a pull of curiosity which
can lead to moves outside the frame of usual activity, going with an
unconscious pull of which one is half aware. Here are two examples where
in one case I think it was essential to move, to act as a model to make
psychic movement possible, and another where it was essential not to act
but to stay with the unbearable. Both examples are from group art therapy
with adults.

Vignette 2

In one group, Patrick, a young man had from the first day presented in
a disturbed and persecuted manner. He wore heavy dark sunglasses and a
Sony Walkman, effectively shutting himself off from the rest of the group in
a slightly menacing way in that he could look at them and they not at him,
and it was also not really possible to know if he was listening or not.
Attempts to interpret his fears and anxieties and to bring him into the
group had not been successful, and the group felt paralysed by his increasingly brittle presence. As another silence grew and grew I stood up, and
walked across the room, saying that I needed to look at the pictures, laid in
a circle on the floor, from a different perspective. I was then able to say to
him that I thought that it was as if he was 'looking through a glass darkly'
(reference to the Rolling Stones rock band/his sunglasses) and that possibly
his picture (about which he hadn't spoken) could appear in a different light
if he could bear to look at it without the glasses. Now as I got up I was only
aware of a need to move, to take action. This was an enactment of his own
sense of feeling trapped in the group (a dark glass perspective); however
once standing and moving I was able to find an intervention to which he
could respond. He hesitantly began to say a little about his picture, glasses
on, Walkman turned off. Following that he was able to come to the next
group without the glasses or Walkman.

In this example I enacted the possibility of moving out of a trapped
feeling that is paralysing. This was also a concrete example of how to move,
externalised. This possibly added reinforcement to a paralysed part of the
young man that did want to move on internally and externally participate
in a different way in the group. I had been less aware of his anger and more
in touch with his fear. He was angry and frightened by his pictures and the
group (he did not want to see them or hear them); but as I moved I became

in touch with all this and was able to find words that would reach him. In group terms he was giving expression to the group's fear of exposure, but I had not been able to reach him with a group interpretation; it had needed a touch of humour and to be appropriate to this person. What is important is the concrete example that a change of perspective is possible without falling apart; words had not reached him – it needed to be non-verbal communication – and it did work in that he did come into the group and eventually was able to relate that he had been told that he ought to attend the group. It would be good for him, hence the anger. The expression of this and change of perspective allowed him to experiment with being there because he wanted to be there, i.e. not looking through a dark glass. In this example, client and therapist held two parts of one picture. The client was more aware of anger, but not of his fear; and the therapist more aware of his fear, but not his anger. The enactment brought these two aspects together.

Vignette 3

In another group, there was a problem with communication: eight out of ten members had spoken about their images in a session and before a lunch break two members remained to speak; both had been very silent in the group. We returned after the break to the images still lying out on the floor and sat down; a silence grew. Gradually I found I was losing my sight, as a headache descended and my sight broke up into segments like a fly's eye. This was so unbearable that I thought that I would have to leave the group, that I was too ill to go on. I had only once before suffered from a migraine, was this another? However, I then thought that I could not leave the group; I could remember the images from the morning session so I managed to ask if there was anything else to add to the morning's work. A member who had spoken earlier made some comments. Then I asked if there was something that one of the two silent participants would like to say, and said that I could feel how very difficult it was for them. Rowan then began to speak of the horrific death of her father in an accident, in her childhood. As she began to speak my vision and headache cleared. What became apparent was the nature of the accident to her father, which was impossible for her to visualise. This was a powerful somatic countertransference that I managed to not enact by leaving. If I had left I would have taken away the opportunity for this member to talk about her horror and grief. However it was also a gamble and a risk to stay in the group with impaired sight. I felt quite mad as I sat there, until she spoke. Interestingly, her image was foggy with a few broken lines, giving no indication of what was to be talked about: it was not possible to visualise.

I hope that these examples convey the nature of the unknown with which we work. In the first example action and movement, not pre-thought out, freed me to make a useful intervention. In the second example I stayed with the physical and mental pain, accepting the pain that could not be borne as a projection which enabled the participant to talk for the first time of her father's death, but at the time I had no conscious awareness that that was what I was doing; I thought I was ill. In both cases I think curiosity plays a strong role, i.e. what is going on here? In the first case there is an enactment of the countertransference; in the second case, a staying with the projection. In both cases, having made the decision to move and the decision not to move, I had conversations with myself: in the latter case, 'I cannot sit here a blind therapist in an art therapy group'. 'Yes, you can, you have a good memory of the morning's images'.

Important in these therapy situations is the capacity to think, for which one needs enough mental space. In both cases the group members were paralysed and unable to symbolise. A fear of exposure had led Patrick to cover ears and eyes, a psychotic anxiety about what might get into him through these orifices, or what might leak out; but his image of a landscape had led me to think that it might not be so bad as he imagined and that he would be received sympathetically by the group if he could uncover himself, and he was. Of course the fear of exposure leads him to draw attention to himself in an acute manner. In the second case one can see the trauma as an alien object in the mind of Rowan; the mangled body of her father is unthinkable and is lodged in the therapist as that which cannot be seen. The psychotic anxieties which accompany this experience can be understood through my experience of 'feeling quite mad' sitting there not able to see the group's images.

While writing this chapter a question has arisen about the use of the therapist's personality. How much is one submerged in the interpsychic and intrapsychic dynamics of the situation; how much is it to do with our own subjectivity? Enactments are in the interactive field between therapist and patient, and they do seem to be about what cannot be spoken. Are they at all related to 'moments of meeting', defined as moments when therapists and patients 'are meeting as persons relatively unhidden by their usual roles, for that moment' (Stern et al., 1998, p. 913; Case, 2002, 2005; Lanyado, 2004)?

Child therapy examples

Vignette 4

In the first case I was working intensively with a selective mute child aged ten, in child psychotherapy. We had been working together for 14 months when we had a long summer break. Suzie had not spoken in therapy but did manage to use art materials to communicate. Images present many constituents and are able to hold many different feelings and thoughts; and although I could talk about possibilities of meaning, these were never confirmed or denied verbally by her. Her whole symptom was constructed around hiding feelings and fear of exposure. The worst thing for her, which was traumatic, was to be wrong, and by not talking, nothing was let out. Suzie was a child who had to know everything; to not know was to be put in touch with being a child in relation to the parental couple, and was unbearable. She exerted enormous control upon the adults around her by not speaking, although able to physically.

After the summer break she drew a picture of a girl swimming in the sea and an adult sitting on the beach. The girl's arm is raised in a wave. At first glance it could be a happy holiday picture of a child swimming and an adult on the beach – or is it a picture of a child drowning, all at sea, and an adult in the sun, enjoying herself, ignoring, or not seeing the child in crisis? Sitting in the silence with her I began to think about a poem which I thought was by Sylvia Plath, 'Not waving but drowning'. (In fact I had conflated two poets, as it is by Stevie Smith. Both poets wrote about intense emotion. I thought that the drowning person was a child talking to 'Daddy', while in fact, 'Daddy' is a different poem by Sylvia Plath.) I began to speak about the poem, by a woman, which shows us that two people may try to communicate but how difficult it is to know at a distance if someone is waving in fun or waving for help. I wondered if over the holiday Suzie had had a good time, but had also been thinking of my holiday and who I was with and what I had been doing. Was she showing me what a good time she had had or was she feeling left out of my holiday and drowning?

I was left, as I usually was with this patient, not knowing whether what I had talked about was helpful or not, or even if it had been taken in. After the session when I realised that I had confused two poems and two poets, I decided to read 'Not waving but drowning' to her the following day, in an effort to reach her. Suzie was half-arrested in her painting, listening, and then a deep silence with a stifling sense of depth took over. In this silence that followed I felt exposed, in the wrong. I had said the wrong thing, and felt embarrassed and ashamed, all of which I imagine she felt when she spoke and 'got it wrong', a humiliating error. Reading the poem was an attempt to reach the non-verbal, but revealed the limits of a 'teaching approach'. I think I had been motivated by an attempt to teach her, an actualisation of an internal figure 'who was always right' who prevented a child part of her from 'being a child'. I enacted 'the teacher' and then felt the excruciating sense of shame which prevented her from speaking, 'the child'. In this 'complete mess' I had been in touch with a depth of emotion present. Both poems are powerful, but had failed to find an adequate intervention.

It felt as if I had spilled out, 'I'd made a play, and failed'. Suzie's whole life was built around hiding feelings, afraid of exposure; was it helpful to show that one could make a mistake and survive, or a misattunement? At the moment of reading I was convinced that this was the right thing to do and that it would reach her – the grandiose therapist. Working with such controlled patients is extremely frustrating, so that if one component – the underlying despair of not reaching someone – led to a teacher's role, you would listen! An alternative way of construing this event is that it was a failed moment of meeting, i.e. if she had responded it would have been a moment where we came out of our usual ways of relating, when we met, and moved on. In making the enactment and my subsequent feeling of exposure I became more aware of her loss of security in taking a risk, but I do not believe it moved her on. It could be that I wished to surprise her, but she needed to surprise herself. For the moment of reading the poem I came completely out of my usual role. I think that I was in touch with the depth of her despair – in the deep silence that followed – but it was also an enactment and a moment of mis-attunement.

Vignette 5

The second child, a boy, also age 10 had been referred for therapy because he was having uncontrollable rages. He had a diagnosis of Asperger's and was on the autistic spectrum. In the first session he had built a room of Lego and put two figures sitting inside. His difficulties in thinking symbolically can be seen in that when I suggested that this was a little like us who were meeting together in this room he laughed and said 'don't be silly, they're too small'.

Toby presented as anxious, uncertain and walked rather robotically with a stiff physicality. The next session he drew a shape which became 'The Alien'. The legs are heavily reinforced with unsure and anxious lines. It was unclear how they would support weight. The eyes when first drawn were young in feel and looked scared. He was pleased with the drawing and said that it was an Alien from a science fiction story. In talking about 'the Alien', I wondered how he felt here on earth. Toby decided that the Alien might be speaking and added a speech bubble, writing 'Hello Stranger'. He said that because he was from another planet, everyone was a stranger to him. I talked about drawings generally and how they can relate to ourselves, here in therapy. I said that we are strangers and getting to know each other, although we feel different to each other. Then, I quite uncharacteristically put my hand out and said 'Hello Stranger', and he put his hand out and said, 'Hello Stranger' back, and we shook hands. A slow smile came to Toby's face. This moment of meeting was essential to the therapy. I said 'how alone the Alien must feel', and he nodded.

At the time I knew that at a few months old Toby had been hospitalised through failure of an organ and had nearly died. What I did not know was that he had been traumatised through essential hospital procedures to save him, and that his parents had been told that he was dying as they rushed to hospital where he was in intensive care. My understanding is that Toby's parents took in the loss of Toby as the baby who had died and continued to see him 'as without life'. He in his turn had been traumatised with unbearable intrusive procedures and had shut down on communication. It is difficult to know in such cases how the Asperger's should be understood. It is a tragedy of joint interacting trauma. Gaensbauer (2002; see also Drell, Siegel and Gaensbauer, 1993) describes infants experiencing painful medical procedures, as well as other specific abuse, physical and sexual, and explores how the traumatic experience is remembered. There is evidence for the persistence of somatic memories, and also that language can be superimposed on previously registered preverbal memories during enactment in therapy. In his work Gaensbauer (2002) defines the stages in representations of trauma in infancy: at 0–3 months, infants recognise stimulus cues; at 6–9 months infants have internal representation of a traumatic event that can be expressed in the form of sequentially meaningful play re-enactments at subsequent periods of time from months or years ahead. The re-enactments 'captured essential elements of the trauma' and were in multiple sensory modalities, i.e. visual, auditory, kinaesthetic, tactile and vestibular. They were not dependent on verbal learning, but children later superimposed verbal descriptors on their memories and play enactments (2002, p. 268). A traumatisation even when lost to conscious awareness will 'influence and potentially distort'.

Toby could not bear touch, and this was a continuing source of grief to his parents. Somehow my shaking hands with Toby at that moment allowed touch to develop, which continued through ball games and other ordinary interactions. Eventually the hospital trauma was enacted in play, and what became essential was that Toby would emerge from a hiding place in the therapy room saying, 'Describe what you see', and I would describe Toby, i.e. 'I see an *alive* curly haired boy who is coming out from under the blanket. He is looking out at the world and is smiling at me.' It was crucial to use the word, 'alive'.

It would be possible to look at both interventions, with the two children, Suzie and Toby, as changes in modality. In the first case I changed experience from painting to reading an experience in a poem, which was out of role, and it failed as an intervention, as it enacted a 'teacher' response to the muteness, confirming the trauma. In the second case I changed from drawing and talking to a handshake, touch, which was also out of role, and it worked as an intervention which became a moment of meeting. It created an avenue to a part of Toby that had become untouchable, bringing it into contact. It led directly to the possibility, months later, of greeting Toby as a live boy, when the trauma of the hospital procedures was re-visited in the therapy room, enacted in play. In the first example through the enactment we stayed stuck in the trauma, repeating aspects of it, and in the second through the enactment we broke new ground, doing the thing that was originally missing and traumatising – the lack of touch. This poses a question as to whether 'moments of meeting' are enactments that are *reversals* of trauma, as they are usually significant moments of change. Both these examples have a strong aesthetic component, in the former an evocative and intense language of picture and poetry, and in the latter an aesthetically-based response to the image and child.

Conclusion

The first two vignettes, of Pauline the adolescent with Asperger's and Patrick the young man with dark glasses, suggest that there was an actualisation, or action-behaviour when there was difficulty in the patient being able to symbolise. In both cases they were able to see the therapist modelling behaviour. Pauline saw me struggle to map information in order to understand her confusion and distress that had been projected into me. The case of Patrick showed a concrete example of movement being possible in the external world although it was an inner shift that was needed. The third example of Rowan, where the therapist did not move, is included to suggest that enactment is not necessarily to do with intensity, but also that in the complex work that we do, one has to think in the situation and have conversations with oneself, although this is not always possible as one can be gripped by powerful counter-transference, as in the example of Suzie.

Actions and enactments seem to be to do with what is, so far in the therapy, unspeakable, pre-verbal or not yet in the symbolic zone. It might be possible to think of all actions and enactments, moments of meeting, as changes of modality that are mediated through the mind and body of the therapist into communication to the patient. Putting language to counter-transference enactments verbalises the non-verbal or what has seemed unspeakable.

Garland discusses the Death Instinct when thinking about the effects of trauma on the personality, that there is the direction of constructiveness, connectedness and life and the direction of destructiveness, disintegration and ultimately, death. The wish to avoid pain can become very powerful. The working through of severely traumatising experiences can be very powerful in terms of countertransference on the therapist, including reversal of trauma, revenge, and evacuation. There are elements of these in Pauline's delight in my confusion and the projection of somatised experience into the therapist about Rowan's father; and in my experience of my mute patient Suzie's depth of despair or should this be understood as communication? Garland brings to our attention that in working with trauma there is a conversion of passive into active in play, as well as attempts at mastery. Repetition in play is an attempt to bring something not remembered or understood into conscious mental life. These features in play attempt to enlist the therapist's understanding, but there can be a pull to something more destructive – a reversal of the trauma, identification with the aggressor, or the repetition of a victim role (Garland, 1998: 27). Enactments occur all the time, in the sense that the transference/countertransference is a series of enactments. There are more specific times that we take action and come out of role for a moment. These moments may be an actualisation of the intrapsychic dynamics. They can re-confirm the trauma, show that movement is possible by change of modality, or can be moments of meeting that reverse a pull towards the death instinct, towards connectedness and life.

There are many psychic elements that might influence the success or not of such interventions. On the client's side there has to be an element of hope. To put this in terms of opposite extremes, one can meet a client who has been unconsciously searching for just such a person as the therapist, and in this situation one may be providing a previously missing experience; or, one can meet a client who one realises has come to therapy to have it confirmed that no change is possible. This latter client will be vulnerable to a failed moment of meeting which is a mis-attunement: the trauma confirmed. This is difficult to retrieve. Moments of meeting have both an aesthetic and a playful element, and therefore both client and therapist need a readiness to be playful. This needs a certain flexibility on the part of the therapist, as a severe super-ego supervisor on one's shoulder could inhibit 'coming out of role'. Timing on the part of the therapist seems to be crucial as these openings to moments of meeting cannot be pre-arranged. The work with the client to be at a readiness to play, and open to surprise, needs to be in place.

References

Bateman, A. (1998) Thick- and thin-skinned organisations and enactment in border-line and narcissistic disorders. *International Journal of Psychoanalysis*, 79: 13–25.

Bell, D. (1998) External injury and the internal world. In Caroline Garland (ed.) *Understanding Trauma: A Psychoanalytical Approach* (pp. 167–180). Tavistock Clinic Series. London: Duckworth.

Bollas, C. (1987) *The Shadow of the Object: Psychoanalysis of the Unthought Known*. London: Free Association Books.

Bovensiepen, G. (2002) Symbolic attitude and reverie: problems of symbolisation in children and adolescents. *Journal of Analytical Psychology*, 47: 241–257.

Cambray, J. (2001) Enactments and amplification. *Journal of Analytical Psychology*, 46: 275–303.

Case, C. (2002) Animation and the location of beauty. *Journal of Child Psychotherapy*, 28(3): 327–343.

Case, C. (2003) Authenticity and survival: working with children in chaos. *Inscape*, 8(1): 17–28.

Case, C. (2005) *Imagining Animals: Art, Psychotherapy and Primitive States of Mind*. London and New York: Routledge.

Case, C. (2008) Playing ball: oscillations within the potential space. In C. Case & T. Dalley (eds) *Art Therapy with Children – From Infancy to Adolescence*. London and New York: Routledge.

Coates, S. W. & Moore, M. S. (1997) The complexity of early trauma: representation and transformation. *Psychoanalytical Enquiry*, 17: 286–311.

Devereux, D. (2006) Enactment: some thoughts about the therapist's contribution. *British Journal of Psychotherapy*, 22(4): 497–507.

Drell, M. J., Siegel, C. H. & Gaensbauer, T. J. (1993) Post-traumatic stress disorders. In C. Zeanah (ed.) *Handbook of Infant Mental Health* (pp. 291–304). New York: Guilford Press.

Freud, S. (1893) *On the Psychical Mechanism of Hysterical Phenomena: A Lecture*, Standard Edition, vol. 3.

Freud, S. (1920) *Beyond the Pleasure Principle*, Standard Edition, vol. 18: 1–64.

Gaensbauer, T. J. (2002) Representations of trauma in infancy: clinical and theoretical implications for the understanding of early memory. *Infant Mental Health Journal*, 23(3): 259–277.

Garland, C. (1998) *Understanding Trauma: A Psychoanalytical Approach*. Tavistock Clinic Series. London: Duckworth.

Gerrard, J. (2007) Enactments in the countertransference: with special reference to rescue fantasies with hysterical patients. *British Journal of Psychotherapy*, 23(2): 217–230.

Holmqvist, R. (1996) Methods of identifying conspicuous countertransference reactions. *British Journal of Psychotherapy*, 12(4): 487–500.

Klein, M. (1980) *The Psychoanalysis of Children: The Writings of Melanie Klein*, vol. 2. London: The Hogarth Press and the Institute of Psychoanalysis.

Lanyado, M. (2004) *The Presence of the Therapist: Treating Childhood Trauma*. Hove, UK and New York: Brunner-Routledge.

McLaughlin, J. T. (1991) Clinical and theoretical aspects of enactment. *Journal of the American Psychoanalytic Association*, 39: 595–614.

Roughton, R. E. (1993) Useful aspects of acting out: repetition, enactment and actualisation. *Journal of the American Psychoanalytic Association*, 41: 443–472.

Segal, H. (1981) Notes on symbol formation, in *The Work of Hanna Segal: A Kleinian Approach to Clinical Practice*. New York and London: Jason Aronson, originally published in 1957, reprinted 1981.

Stern, D., Sander, L., Nahum, J., Harrison, A., Lyons-Ruth, K., Morgan, A., Bruschweiler-Stern, N., & Tronick, E. (1998) Non-interpretive mechanisms in psychoanalytic therapy: the 'something more' than interpretation. *International Journal of Psycho-Analysis*, 79: 903–921.

Stronach-Bashel, B. (1990) Trauma, children, and art. *The American Journal of Art Therapy*, 29: 48–52.

Terr, L. (1983) Play, therapy and psychic trauma: a preliminary report. In C. E. Schaefer and K. J. O'Conner (eds) *Handbook of Play Therapy* (pp. 308–319). New York: Wiley.

Van der Kolk, R. A. (1987) *Psychological Trauma*. Washington, DC: American Psychiatric Press.

7 Bad faith in practice

Enactments in existential psychotherapy

Raymond Kenward

Some psychotherapists, such as Irvin Yalom, have integrated existential ideas into what is essentially a psychoanalytic model (e.g. Yalom, 1980). Others, such as Medard Boss, have developed theories which deviate from psychoanalytic thinking (e.g. Boss, 1979), but remain largely content with the clinical method of psychoanalysis. Still others have developed fully-fledged existential theory and practice, for example, the British School of Existential Therapy. But just as there is a great range of psychoanalytic and psychodynamic theory, so there are many ideas influencing the practice of existential therapy, some of them complementary and some of them divergent. For this chapter, I shall lean towards a Sartrean existential approach, in an attempt to interest the reader in an alternative account of enactments. Sartre was a philosopher, and his keen interest in psychotherapy was purely theoretical, but his ideas have been put into practice by many existential therapists, most notable amongst them R. D. Laing, on whom Sartre was a notable influence (e.g. Laing, 1960).

In her monograph on Jean-Paul Sartre, Iris Murdoch writes that where a Freudian analyst might describe a patient's emotions as causing him to punish himself, a Sartrean analyst might describe the patient's behaviour as a chosen way of life, a semi-deliberate project (Murdoch, 1953, ch. 2). Be that as it may, one of the chief characteristics of existential psychotherapy, as Emmy van Deurzen and I have remarked elsewhere (van Deurzen and Kenward, 2005), is that it stresses personal choice. Consequently, it is also concerned with the evasion of choice, and the deliberate obscuring and disguising of reality. It is, of course, recognised that many choices are not made in full consciousness, but follow almost unnoticed from earlier choices. For Sartre, an existential psychoanalysis consists of an investigation into the patient's *original choice*, their chosen position in the world.

Like Freud, Sartre sees the psychoanalysis of the individual as an investigation of the meaning they give to the components of their lives. Sartre also stresses the holistic nature of the enterprise:

> It is not enough . . . to draw up a list of behavior patterns, of drives and inclinations, it is also necessary to decipher them . . . according to the

rules of a specific method. It is this method which we call existential psychoanalysis. The principle of this psychoanalysis is that man is a totality and not a collection.

(Sartre, 1943, p. 568)

If Freudian-derived analysis emphasises the patient's unsatisfactory resolving of childhood developmental phases, existential analysis emphasises the individual's present responses to his or her predicaments of existence. For Sartre, these choices constitute the individual's identity.

Sartre writes of the ways in which we evade the truth of the world. One of these is the active and deliberate use of emotions. According to Sartre, emotions are used as a strategy, to create change – or if not change, then an illusion of change:

> [An emotion] is a transformation of the world. When the ways before us become too difficult . . . All ways are barred and nevertheless we must act. So then we try to change the world; that is, to live it as though the relations between things and their potentialities were not governed by deterministic processes but by magic.

(Sartre, 1939, part III)

Such desperate and near-blind impulses create a false self and a false world, providing the potential for distorted re-enactments of earlier experiences. And any analysis of evasion is fraught with difficulty. What Sartre calls *bad faith* is just such an evasion of duty, being the individual's active denial or refusal to recognise his or her freedom. It is not a knowing deception, not role-playing as an actor plays his part, but it is a self-deception buried deep beneath the level of everyday awareness. Sartre goes on to describe the state of bad faith as living as though one was utterly helpless or entirely free, unwilling either to transcend the limiting factors of life, or to see them as any kind of obstacle to action: the person in bad faith ignores his own freedom of choice, or sees no hindrance to it, ignoring the practical constraints of the world. Sartre warns that we frequently avoid the discomfort of choice and freedom in favour of telling ourselves that our predicament was decided for us. So in this way we are in bad faith. And living in bad faith means one is likely to construe oneself as one imagines others construe oneself, and so lose one's flesh-and-blood reality and become no more than the idea of a person. Alternatively, in bad faith we might see ourselves as we used to be, and become bound in the past, losing present-day freedom of action through an anachronism that denies the truth of the present and ruins our potential for transcendence of the limits of our existence.

Of course, all this is too often thought to apply only to the psychotherapy patient. Armed with his theories and the success of his own training analysis, the therapist may assume him or herself to be well-adjusted, and his or her psychological vulnerabilities either resolved or at least well-understood. But the Sartrean existential therapist does not rest comfortably, for he sees bad faith as an inevitable part of the human condition, a state into which we are constantly prone to slip, against which all we can do is be alert. And yet he knows that alertness is no proof against self-deception, and what is often dealt with less well in the psychotherapeutic literature is the evasion – the covering-up, the bad faith – of the therapist.

Carol Holmes (Holmes, 1998) compares the Sartrean notion of bad faith with some of the ideas from Robert Langs's Communicative Psychoanalysis. Langs (in, for example, Langs, 1976) emphasises the difficulty therapists have in interpreting patients' negative communications concerning themselves, remarks at variance with the therapist's ideal self-image. In such circumstances, the therapist is likely to retreat into defensiveness.

The concept of bad faith may be of inestimable worth in the assessment of the psychological health of the patient. But it may be the focus of therapy itself. A short case study may illustrate some of this, and briefly explore the notion of bad faith as an explanation for enactments. But first, the practice of existential therapy needs to be briefly indicated:

> According to existential thinking, people are always in relation, so therapist and client face one another and engage in active conversation . . . It is a mutual dialogue, an encounter, albeit one where the focus of attention is constantly on the client's experience, and often on the client's emotions, for emotions are seen as a barometer of the person's values.
>
> (van Deurzen and Kenward, 2005, p. 71)

Existential psychotherapy has a deliberate, investigative approach. There are no set or required techniques, but therapy is not allowed to drift, and the therapist carefully monitors the patient's explorations of his life struggles, whether expressed in thought, feeling or action. Openness and authenticity are an ambition for the patients and a requirement for the therapist.

Bad faith in action

Like any case study, this one both flatters the therapist and does him an injustice. The subtlety of the process cannot be recreated, and the need to disguise identity weakens much of the sense of the original. Furthermore, the need to write concisely simplifies and makes neat a process that was far more complex and not always orderly. Lastly, the honesty of the account is limited by the therapist's own knowledge, and the degree of his bad faith.

Simone was 42 years old, and by profession a musician. In fact, she was a very successful violinist, as she explained when she first telephoned a psychotherapist, whose name was John. She had found John's name on the internet, and told him that he seemed to be the most qualified therapist in the area. They spoke for a minute or two, then he suggested that they meet for an assessment.

When they met, Simone, expensively-dressed and well-spoken, gave John a detailed and confident account of her career. She was the leader in an orchestra of international standing, and the founder-member of a string quartet with a recording contract with a very good record label. The quartet's recordings sold well, and she earned considerably more than her peers. She had written a variety of music, including an opera. And she had composed a number of solos for orchestral works. She also taught a few exceptional pupils, who worshipped her. She related to John how a number of composers were keen to compose for her. The name of one of these composers was known to John, and despite himself he was impressed.

John asked Simone what brought her to seek out a psychotherapist, and she paused and told him of the strain she felt at being so important to so many people. She felt very responsible for the happiness of others. Many of them relied upon her, depended on her. John silently wondered if this was boasting, or simply untrue. Such a consideration of the truth value of a patient's statements was not something John usually engaged in during a session, partly because it would distract his attention from hearing his patient, but also because his concern was with the subjective. John recovered himself sufficiently to regain his usual position of giving equal consideration to all the elements of his patient's account.

At the end of the first session, after Simone had left, John noticed an unusual mood in himself. He was excited and troubled. It seemed that his new client was a musician of more than technical genius, a gifted artist, and that she was greatly admired and in great demand. John had always enjoyed working with artistic and creative clients, but Simone was exceptional. But that earlier doubt had grown and John began afresh to doubt the accuracy of her claims. Were they grandiose? Was she too fond of looking into mirrors? John also found it hard to see what was troubling her. Was she depressed? It seemed certain she was holding back. John determined to be more sceptical than usual at the next session. Only in long retrospect did it occur to him that this itself was remarkable. As an existential-phenomenological therapist his natural stance was to take a position of scientific scepticism – that is, to rule out nothing, and question everything. Yet here he was, feeling an especial need to discover whether his new client was lying.

In the second session, Simone told John that people around her needed to see her as strong, as capable, as always able to be creative, always able to develop ideas, always able to take the lead. When she told him this she showed no sign of weariness or irritation, but seemed quite matter-of-fact. She knew a number of well-known and famous musicians, and recounted some amusing anecdotes about them. In subsequent sessions she would mention more names and recount more anecdotes.

Simone spent several early sessions treating John as a consultant, an adviser, asking help with handling her professional relationships. This flattered John's view of himself as an expert, but in time it rankled. He wondered whether he was at fault for the lack of what he felt was true psychotherapy. He was always careful not to advise her on particular courses of action, but nevertheless Simone would make her own deductions, and was sure she was following John's suggestions.

She told John of her desire to recapture her ability to dazzle audiences. John wondered if by 'audiences' she meant people in general, but he was sure she was not yet ready to hear such a question. She would leave each session with her lesson learned, and go away to practise it. She would return the following week and tell John just how helpful his lessons had been. Her students were now telling her they could not have learned half as much without her extraordinary teaching powers. This seemed to contradict her earlier statement that her students already worshipped her, but again John held back from challenging her.

It was clear Simone was a perfectionist, her ideals and standards exemplified in demonstrations of technical excellence and novel ideas. Much later, John was to see her boasts become fewer and less powerful. And later, she would reveal to him that she was dyslexic, and that reading had always been difficult. As a student she had got around the problem by instigating study groups with fellow students, when by listening to their discussions she picked up the theory she struggled to discover in books. A quick learner, she remembered everything, but she had an unusual view of herself in this regard. 'I'm a bloodsucker', she said, in their fifth meeting: 'I fasten onto people, and take from them; and when there's nothing left, I leave them empty'. This was a great claim, that she had the power to empty people. At face value, her assertion was that she was a parasite, preying on people and destroying them. Was this a boast or a warning, or was it both? But the consultations continued, with John helping her to explore her relationships and problems.

Had John become Simone's virtuoso teacher? Was this going to be a psychotherapy or an instruction course? He found it hard to know. He wondered if she would use up his entire stock of knowledge, then leave him. He prepared himself for this eventuality, and his preparedness kept him at a distance from Simone, and helped keep the therapy superficial.

The therapist increases his self-deceit

As a boy John had been seriously ill, and lost a great deal of schooling. Up till then, he had nursed the ambition of becoming a musician, but then it became impossible, for not only was his ordinary education hampered, but his music lessons had of necessity to cease. As an adult John sometimes told himself that he had not been very talented, but at the time his disappointment had been bitter. And abandoning his ambition provided John with the advantage that he would never face any practical examination of his ability, and he could retain the conviction that but for bad luck he might have enjoyed a fine career as a public performer. The burgeoning value John had placed on his future career as a musician developed into a pride in his cultured self. Not playing an instrument, he *consumed* music: he bought recordings and went to concerts; he continued to tell himself and others that he could have had an exciting career in the concert hall. Whether or not his friends and acquaintances accepted the truth of this, John was perfectly pleased with it. He had a satisfying role as a cultured and artistic person. His pleasure at this obscured his regard of himself as a psychotherapist, in which he was disappointed. There were interesting roots to all this in John's early life, but he seldom chose to consider it. And so John did not allow himself to see his ambivalence towards his own choice of profession.

John frequently used musical metaphors and analogies in his sessions with Simone. To some extent this was fair, since John usually tried to work with his client's own lexicon of ideas. However, it carried with it two disadvantages. Firstly, it did not allow her to step out of her professional role: she was always a musician, and less a person. Secondly, it allowed John to demonstrate a musical knowledge unusual in a psychotherapist. Such a demonstration, if not intended, might arguably be harmless, but John was slow to bring into full awareness that this was self-promotion, that he was boasting of his cultured status. Simone certainly responded to these turns of phrase and analogies, and twice asked John if he was also a musician. He was pleased by this question, and although usually attuned to any moves that shifted the spotlight away from his client and onto himself, this time he neglected the evidence before him. Instead of considering what was happening he merely analysed the meaning for Simone of her discovery that he was an artistic person. She told him how pleased she was to have found such an imaginative therapist.

John's client told him how she imagined psychotherapy would be 'all touchy-feelie', and that she was glad it was not like that. John was glad too, and left that session pleased he was not like other therapists.

Simone had many friends, and they looked to her to be the life and soul of the party. From this she extracted considerable confidence. But when John asked her to picture herself in the midst of her relationships, she wept long and loudly and told him how she knew people kept a distance from her. And she told him she realised she didn't really like herself. John then wondered if the trust and dependence others had in her was her solace, providing her with sufficient human contact to avoid facing her emptiness.

Simone talked of how she was materialistic, and how much she loved the violin she had bought with a second mortgage. Then she spoke of an affair she was having with the orchestra's conductor, David. There was a passion in her relationship with him that was missing in her marriage. She said: 'He says he worships me'. John was once again doubtful. There seemed in this an idealisation of some sort. And as for that from which she took solace, was it real or was it a fiction?

The therapist challenges himself

Using supervision and his own internal interrogation, John began more vigorously to debate what was going on in the therapy. He wondered if Simone overestimated his artistic nature. He felt a twinge of guilt, a pricking of conscience. He was again sure he was not an exceptional artist or psychotherapist.

'Do you know me? Because I don't think I know myself any more', she told John, and she explained how much she needed David, how much she missed him when she went home after concerts or rehearsals, and how lonely she felt with her husband. On a subsequent occasion she told John how clinging David was, and on yet another occasion she complained to John that David was uncommitted. She now, to her surprise, realised she valued commitment but avoided it. This revelation came to Simone as an epiphany. She sat gasping at the shock of it. She told John that she was no longer excited by striving – although in a later session she again said how much she wanted to rekindle the fire she once felt. But she came to the conclusion that she had what she had wanted, but didn't have what she now wanted. And what did she want? She didn't know. And furthermore, she realised she didn't really understand other people. 'They always surprise me', she said, and realised that she was always on her guard, and seldom expressed her sentiments to others.

John noticed that Simone boasted less and less. He suggested this to her, and she started, then blushed, though she said nothing.

For a while, John wondered if between them, he and Simone were perhaps fuelling a mutual need to be artists, a kind of *folie à deux*. She seemed to grant such a status to him, and he certainly granted it to her. Of course, Simone *was* an artist, a publicly recognised musician. He realised he was ascribing a false role to himself, and furthermore, a fixed condition, and attributing a false and fixed character to himself was an act of bad faith, a denial of freedom.

Facing reality is potentially traumatic, for it means accepting ultimate loneliness and responsibility. Simone had found the challenge too great, and had sought to overcome reality by generating a new life, finding her own salvation. It was in this way:

Simone's mother had died when Simone was two. Aged five, Simone had walked into her father's bedroom, to find her father on the bed with a strange woman. They were wearing no clothes, and they were laughing, and doing something odd. Her father at once told Simone to go outside, and she fled in tears, with a sick feeling in her stomach. His voice sounded cross. Later, the woman came and spoke to Simone. Then Simone's father joined them, and Simone noticed how much her father looked at the strange woman, and how he smiled when she spoke.

Simone's feelings of abandonment were terrible. Believing herself displaced by an adult woman, she determined to be an adult, and to impress her father, so that he would smile at her. This was Simone's original choice, to be someone else, or rather, the *idea* of someone else.

A few sessions after this, Simone began to dress less showily. She told John she boasted to people to make up the difference. They discussed and explored this interesting phrase of hers, *the difference*. There was clearly a difference between the little girl who had not felt *wanted* and the persona she had developed, but there was also a more profound difference, and that was between the real world of individual human freedom and the fixed world of an object. John and Simone at last saw how she had made herself an object, and dedicated themselves to examining the fact.

Simone wanted admiration, an adoration that would dazzle her eyes and deafen her with its noise, and so prove to her that she was flesh and blood. She was terrified of glimpsing the void of her assumed identity, and more terrified still of feeling the shock of the abandonment that little girl had felt. And her desire to recapture her ability to dazzle audiences had met John's own unfulfilled ambition to dazzle an audience. The therapist had fallen into his own boyhood fiction, a tempting ideal raised from its dormant state in John's meeting with Simone. This was a breakthrough for John, although as he developed this insight, he realised that in inchoate form he had known it from the start. John had at last taken off his blinkers. He had been playing a part, a part he had once given himself, that of the Artist.

This then is an alternative explanation of enactment in psychotherapy, of patient and therapist encouraging bad faith in the other. It does not displace other explanations, but is offered with the intention of stimulating further discussion. The trauma is that of facing the existential nothingness of human nature. Bad faith is fleeing from it.

Simone was trapped in her original choice to be an exciting object for others. She had continued to see herself as she imagined others saw her. The pleasure and relief of this escape had become a habit for her; she craved the persona of the artist. In the process she lost her real, fluid, ever-changing character. She made no effort to re-examine herself, for she could not find the courage to consider the situation afresh. In place of thought, she had chosen mechanical action, a *role*. This repetition was not caused, but chosen. It was a strategy, and could be described as a coping strategy. It might be thought that a childhood experience of rejection had caused Simone to develop certain maladaptive behaviour, and that this had played itself out in her therapy. John saw it as a flight from reality. She had misunderstood her father's dismissal of her, and been mistaken in her perception of her displacement. And she had been unable to deal directly with her life, but instead had taken action to abandon her own life for an idea of a life.

Simone had entered into an affair, hoping for freedom, but in this she had of course been treated as an exciting object and not a person. There seemed no escape from her self-imposed shackles, and little possibility of understanding her imprisonment. And in all this, she had given up much of

her freedom, until misery and conflict, and a dim sense of her own constricted humanity had induced her to enter therapy where she had indeed
found the courage to face reality. Her real success as an artist had been
eclipsed by the desire to yield her self and become a thing.

John, for his part, became caught up in a fiction of his own, the make-
believe of himself as an artist. He had entered into competition with
Simone, showing-off as best he could, deluding himself, and losing grasp of
his professionalism. The excitement of the situation overcame him for a
while, and he was lost to Simone as a fully-present psychotherapist, and for
a while denied Simone his assistance in helping her discover the truth.
Eventually, both patient and therapist wrenched themselves free of their
traumas and grasped hold of reality.

References

Boss, M. (1979) *Existential Foundations of Medicine and Psychology*, trans. S.
   Conway and A. Cleaves, 1994. Northvale, NJ: Jason Aronson.
Deurzen, E. van & Kenward, R. (2005) *Dictionary of Existential Psychotherapy and
   Counselling*. London: Sage.
Holmes, C. (1998) Bad faith in psychotherapy. *Existential Analysis*, 9(2): 24–34.
Laing, R. D. (1960) *The Divided Self: An Existential Study in Sanity and Madness*.
   Harmondsworth, UK: Penguin.
Langs, R. J. (1976) *The Bipersonal Field*. New York: Jason Aronson.
Murdoch, I. (1953) *Sartre*. London: Bowes & Bowes.
Sartre, J.-P. (1939) *Sketch for a Theory of the Emotions*, trans. P. Mairet, 1971.
   London: Routledge.
Sartre, J.-P. (1943) *Being and Nothingness: An Essay on Phenomenological Ontology*,
   trans. H. E. Barnes, 1958. London: Methuen.
Yalom, I. D. (1980) *Existential Psychotherapy*. New York: Basic Books.

8 Tangled webs

Enactments on an inpatient ward for eating disorders

Patricia Marsden and Alison Knight-Evans

Staff working within a multidisciplinary inpatient team are involved in a complex web of interpersonal interactions between patients and staff, between patients themselves and between different members of staff. Frequently, these relationships are interdependent. For example, the relationship between two members of staff may be affected by their separate relationships with a particular patient. Add to this a population of highly disturbed patients with severe eating disorders who engender powerful countertransference feelings in staff members, and the scene is set for the possible unconscious enactment of patients' transference fantasies within the staff team. It is these enactments which we will discuss in this chapter. We consider the way in which aspects of past relationships are replayed in the present and how unconscious fantasies can disrupt the therapeutic relationship.

A definition of enactments

There is agreement in the psychoanalytic literature that enactments occur when both patient and psychotherapist are caught up in an unconscious process resulting in a symbolic repetition of some aspect of the patient's past history. Some writers (e.g. Martin, 2002) suggest that this occurs only as a recreation of past trauma. Others broaden the definition. For instance, Bateman (1998) suggests that an enactment is any mutual action within the patient/analyst relationship that arises in the context of difficulties in the countertransference work.

There are also differences between writers in their understanding of whether the term enactment should be reserved for actions on the part of the psychotherapist or whether her thoughts and/or fantasies should be included in the definition. Steiner (2006, p. 315) writes: 'Enactments, by definition, cross the boundary from thought to action.' However, other writers seem to suggest that the term can encompass attitudes on the part of the psychotherapist in addition to actions. For example, Currin (2000) defines enactment as 'a term used to refer to a behaviour, attitude, or happening in which both patient and analyst find themselves functioning outside of the analytic frame, in which they enact a pathological adaptation to the psychic conflicts of both patient and analyst'.

Similarly, Gerrard (2007) discusses a fantasy about one of her patients as an enactment, despite the fact that this fantasy did not spill over into action. There seems to be some overlap here between this use of the terms enactment and countertransference. Gabbard (1995) describes countertransference as a 'joint creation' between patient and therapist in which the patient 'nudges' the therapist towards an unconscious transference fantasy and the therapist responds insofar as there is a fit between the role demanded by the patient and the psychotherapist's own unconscious conflicts.

In this chapter, we will regard the therapist's thoughts, fantasies and feelings towards the patient as falling within the definition of counter-transference reactions as defined by Gabbard, whilst a spilling over into action we will understand as an enactment. We will therefore use the term enactment to refer to *actions* (verbal or physical) occurring within a therapeutic relationship which involve an unconscious participation by both patient and clinician and which symbolically recreate an aspect of the patient's past history (not necessarily past trauma). The term enactment has usually been used to refer to happenings between patient and psychother-apist or analyst, and writers have tended to discuss enactments within the context of a one-to-one psychotherapy. In this chapter, we will broaden our definition to include the patient's interactions with all members of a multidisciplinary clinical team who are involved in a therapeutic relation-ship with her.

A brief view of eating disorders

The symptoms of eating disordered behaviour are varied, ranging from severe restriction, restriction with vomiting, or bingeing and vomiting, to binge eating. Whilst all patients with eating disorders use the control of food and weight as means of acting out internal conflicts, low weight is an essential differentiating feature between normal weight bulimia and anorexia, 'weight in the sense of closeness to death, whether consciously or unconsciously' (Farrell, 1995, p. 5).

Anorexia nervosa is behaviourally marked by the refusal to take in food. The internal world is characterised by a need to control difficult feelings, a refusal to take anything in, or a spoiling of what is offered. In the external world any relationships or dependency on others is denied, self sufficiency being the conscious goal, while the unconscious wish may be quite opposite: a wish for total care, and a merged relationship where no differences are acknowledged.

Some anorectic patients use vomiting as a means of keeping their weight at a low level, whilst bulimic patients tend to have a normal body weight but have lost control of their eating patterns. The binge/vomit ritual reflects an internal world of chaos and is sometimes associated with other impulse disorders (for example, use of street drugs, abuse of alcohol, self-harm). The symptom expresses an underlying psychological conflict. Guntrip (1968), drawing on Fairbairn, suggests that there is such a marked ambivalence about needs and desire that the person can never get what she really wants. He suggests that this dilemma can be understood in terms of the earliest relationship which the baby forms with its mother: 'The situation which calls out the reaction is that of being faced with a desired but deserting object'. The bulimic patient replays this early infantile experience, using food as a substitute for relationships she cannot control. Unlike the anorectic, who denies her needs completely, the bulimic acts out her desire for gratification secretly, devouring the food and then rejecting it through vomiting or purging.

Lawrence (2002) suggests that the problem has its origins in intrusion or invasion of different sorts. She suggests that women who suffer from anorexia have an intrusive object instated in their minds which may or may not be the result of actual intrusions in external reality. She examines the intrusiveness of these patients in the transference and suggests that they often harbour powerful fantasies of intruding between the parents – a wish to regain their special place with mother and to exclude father.

Williams (1997) identifies two themes. In the first, a reversal of the mother/baby dependency relationship, the infant 'is exposed to the experience of being used as a receptacle . . . for massive projections' (Williams, 1997, p. 103). The infant grows up feeling she has to contain her mother's anxieties, leading to resentment (possibly unconscious) and a dread of dependence. In the second, a reversal of the Oedipal shift, mother remains the desired object with no room for the paternal function of separation, leading to a wish to deny otherness through the fantasy of a merged relationship.

Enactments on the inpatient ward

An inpatient eating disorders ward is a fertile ground for enactments. A community of patients, many of whom are severely disturbed, live together and are treated by a multi-disciplinary team of nurses, psychiatrists, psychotherapists, psychologist, occupational therapists, family therapist, social worker, psychodrama psychotherapist and dietician. All these, both clinicians and patients, are potential recipients of transference projections. In the hospital setting the patient is required to give up all her behavioural symptoms in order to allow the underlying psychopathology to emerge, so that the issues can be addressed in groups and individual therapies. There is an intense therapeutic programme supporting the patient's recovery, and the central focus of the week is the ward round when the team discusses the patients, bringing the different focuses of work into a single forum in an attempt to understand the whole picture of the patient's relationships on the ward. Weight is measured twice a week and recorded on a chart, which represents the concrete picture of patients' progress in treatment. The aim of the programme is to help the patient to find new ways of dealing with previously unbearable internal issues. However, because the psychosomatic defences are often felt by the patient as egosyntonic, she is cut off from the very real danger of what she is doing to herself and to her objects. She is in a psychic retreat (Steiner, 1993), and possibly out of reach with 'No Entry' (Williams, 1997) on her door, so that, in extreme cases, she may need to be detained under a section of the Mental Health Act and fed by naso-gastric tube until she is well enough to grasp the danger she has put herself in.

The dynamics of coercion and control tend to be played out in the relationships on the Unit. Frequently, a patient will experience powerful transference feelings towards clinicians, responding to them as if they were figures from her earlier life, distorted by her own drives and conflicts. These transference projections are liable to engender equally powerful counter-transference reactions in staff members. Further, the patient may enact different transference fantasies with different staff members. This may take the form of multiple transferences, by which term we refer to the situation in which a patient relates to several staff members or other patients as if they were different figures from her earlier life (distorted by her own projections). Alternatively, the patient's transferences may be split so that staff and patients become vessels for the projection of the bad, unwanted parts of herself or, alternatively, the good parts of herself: 'The patient also avoids the pain of conflict by splitting her whole objects into part-objects, so that good feelings are kept separate from bad feelings by attaching them to separate part-objects' (Marsden, 2001, p. 227).

Staff, in their turn, find themselves reacting to the powerful transference projections of the patient. They may become aware of an internal pressure to respond in a certain way, or they may find themselves acting unchar-acteristically with a patient without being fully aware of the reason for this behaviour. Sandler used the term role responsiveness to describe the way in which the analyst responds to the active (though unconscious) attempts by the patient to manoeuvre her into a relationship which reflects earlier experiences.

> The role-relationship of the patient in analysis at any particular time consists of a role in which he casts himself and a *complementary* role in which he casts the analyst at that particular time. The patient's trans-ference would thus represent an attempt by him to impose an inter-action, an interrelationship (in the broadest sense of the word) between himself and the analyst.
>
> (Sandler, 1976, p. 108)

Such pressures towards role responsiveness are experienced not only by psychotherapists on the inpatient ward but also by all other members of the staff team. Moreover, Sandler's paper describes subtle interactions between patient and analyst which may not be recognised by the analyst until some time later. Whilst subtle manipulations of this kind can, of course, also happen in an inpatient setting, the severity of disturbance of the patients is reflected in the fact that staff members may feel violently propelled towards a particular response to the patient rather than gently nudged into it. For instance, the transference and countertransference may manifest deadly dynamics, often with a sado-masochistic flavour. Thus the staff member may feel attacked or infuriated by the patient, or helpless and deskilled or, alternatively, may feel powerfully pulled into a protective role in which she wishes to defend the patient from the perceived cruelty of other team members.

Another possibility is that staff may collude with the patient in adopting a very concrete view of her behaviour. One feature of the psychopathology of eating disorders is a tendency towards concrete thinking. Disturbances in the relationship between the ego and its objects are reflected in the developmental failure of the capacity to think symbolically. This results in a powerful tendency to repeat early object relationships in the present as if they were the original relationship (Segal, 1957), and staff may be drawn into colluding with the patient in this concrete thinking. For instance, they may find themselves concentrating exclusively on weight gain and practical issues rather than more flexibly considering the psychodynamics of the interpersonal situation.

If we understand enactments as happenings between the patient and any clinician within a therapeutic encounter, the result of the forceful projections from the patient may sometimes be simultaneous enactments by a number of staff members in which all may take different roles or, alternatively, 'gangs' of staff may act together. This may allow the patient to recreate a whole scenario from her past rather than a single relationship, and staff may find that they are acting out the patient's pathology between themselves.

Clinical examples

In the following clinical examples, a number of personal details have been altered to protect patient and staff confidentiality.

Case 1

The patient whom we will call Anne had had a number of admissions onto the unit and, on each occasion, had failed to reach her recovery target weight. Her psychotherapist reported that Anne was working very hard with her, dealing with some early traumatic experiences. However, Anne failed to gain weight. On a number of occasions there were team discussions in which most members of the staff team wished to discharge her, but the psychotherapist argued against this, saying that the unconscious sadistic feelings of the team were being acted out against the 'victim' patient. A decision was made, when the psychotherapist was not present, to send the patient on time out (time out consists of sending the patient off the ward for a week, with a sheet of questions to help her think about what emotional issues led up to her breaking the contract she has with the team). The psychotherapist was angry, arguing that the decision was not helpful. Some weeks later, when the patient's situation remained the same, she was discussed again and the psychotherapist argued forcefully against the other members of the team, who felt that the patient should be discharged. However, they were reluctant to over-rule the psychotherapist, and, as no real consensus could be reached, the patient remained on the unit, very resistant to putting on weight.

Anne had been seriously sexually abused as a child by the father. Anne's mother had apparently turned a blind eye to the sexual abuse, and Anne was unable to confide in anyone at the time. She developed anorexia as she approached puberty, and this continued, together with an obsessive compulsive disorder. She lived in a state of internal persecution, remaining awake most of each night, dealing with rituals and obsessive cleaning and using exercise both to burn up calories and to protect her mind against unwelcome thoughts and memories.

Anne would only talk about her abuse with her psychotherapist, refusing to trust anyone else with her story. The therapist felt very protective of her, feeling quite rightly that she was her only support in this matter and arguing for special arrangements for the patient, in which she would be allowed to gain weight at a slow pace. When the team was helped, in a case conference, to understand the dynamics staff were being drawn into, the psychotherapist was able to stand back and join the team in making decisions that were in the patient's best interest. The team together accepted that Anne was not able at that time to reach her target weight, and it was agreed with Anne that she should be helped to stabilise her weight at a relatively safe level with ongoing support from an out-patient nurse.

Discussion: The psychotherapist was drawn by Anne into a special relationship in which, for Anne, she became the wished-for good object who would protect her. The psychotherapist did indeed feel fiercely protective of her and felt that other staff members, who had not heard the details of her abusive history, could not understand Anne's needs and her inability to comply with the requirements of the treatment programme. Indeed, Anne's persistent refusal to engage with other members of the team created a situation in which other staff felt excluded from the one-to-one relationship between Anne and her psychotherapist, perhaps echoing the feelings of Anne's siblings about her special relationship with her abuser.

Case 2

Brenda was rewarding to work with, in that she was psychologically minded and seemed motivated to use the treatment programme. However, she repeatedly demanded special treatment from members of staff and felt extremely aggrieved when her requests were not granted. Brenda had had several admissions to the unit for chronic anorexia. Towards the end of what seemed to be a successful treatment, she had reached her target weight and was working well in the psychological therapies, although she was from time to time expressing bitterness about the nature of her relationships with members of staff. She felt she was 'just a patient' while she wished to become a friend.

Brenda was one of two children of a professional couple who were not happy together. She did well at school, while her sister had learning difficulties and needed more attention from their parents. Brenda was extremely envious of the attention her sister received, feeling it was unfair that she, Brenda, was left to get on with her studies without encouragement or praise, as she saw it. Her parents split up eventually, and she had a rather over-involved relationship with her mother and saw very little of her father, whom she blamed for the breakdown of the marriage. Because of her envy of her sister, Brenda also saw very little of her sister and family.

Brenda had asked for an extended period of outpatient treatment in order to consolidate the good work she had done in understanding the issues underlying her anorexia. She was returning to full-time employment and before her admission she had approached her job in an obsessive way, working very long hours. She had spent much of her free time exercising so that she had become isolated and lonely. During this admission she had made some good progress in developing interests and meeting people outside the hospital. She had even made a rather tentative relationship with a man with whom she wanted to go on a holiday. The staff team agreed to this, but the holiday went badly wrong, so that Brenda returned to the ward emotionally bruised and disappointed, feeling that this had been a serious setback and that she needed more time to repair the trauma. Again, the team agreed rather cautiously to her request, perhaps because she was generally doing well and also because we wanted to avoid her sour response if she were to be refused. However, the other patients were envious of her special treatment and turned against her. She discharged herself in a bitter state of mind, feeling let down by staff for not protecting her from her fellow patients, but unable and unwilling to see her part in this. She returned to employment but soon lost all the weight she had gained and later was admitted for more treatment in a different part of the service, again in a special arrangement.

Discussion: Whilst the team clearly made several decisions that turned out not to be in the best interest of this patient, it is hard to describe the internal pressure each one of the staff felt to grant her request. She elicited our sympathy but she also evoked an exasperation which resulted in a pull towards sadism in the staff. The team then, anxious to avoid a sadistic response, granted Brenda's requests but were unable to foresee how this would impact on her need for masochistic satisfaction. Thus, it seems

Brenda manoeuvred the staff team to put her in the position of the envied sister who had had special treatment and was also able to create a situation in which she felt punished for getting such treatment.

Case 3

Caroline suffered from anorexia nervosa with multi-impulsive features. She had been discharged from a number of other eating disorder units for behavioural problems. Caroline seemed to find a certain security on the unit, rather like boarding school, and she took a lead role with the other patients but also evoked their resentment, as they experienced her as bossy. In the first stage of her treatment on the eating disorders unit she was found to be using alcohol and drugs – behaviour that would usually result in discharge. However, Caroline was not discharged, and she gradually began to work at both the behavioural and emotional/psychological components of the programme, although her progress was erratic. During a summer holiday period when both her key nurse and her psychotherapist were away, Caroline was found to be water loading (i.e. drinking large quantities of water) and using weights to disguise her true weight. Caroline was discharged by the team whilst her key workers were still away.

Caroline was the oldest of four children. She described her parents as caring but rather stiff and formal. She was distressed by the birth of her siblings, feeling displaced, and tried desperately hard to please her parents by attempting to make her siblings behave as she thought they should. However, this caused arguments, thereby pleasing no one. She was sent to an all-girls' boarding school at the age of 11, which she loved, perhaps a defence against feelings of distress at being sent away from home. She made friends at school and was the leader of a group of four girls. Although she enjoyed her position as leader, she resented her friends' relying on her to make all the decisions. She protested and they turned on her, leaving her hurt and humiliated, feeling like an outcast. She became successful in the workplace and was able to hide her problems from her employers until she collapsed under the weight of her false self.

Discussion: At a conscious level, the staff team was committed to trying to penetrate Caroline's defences while recognising the fragility beneath her somewhat hard exterior – a typical thick skin covering a thin one. The staff members who worked closely with Caroline tended to feel sympathetic towards her, recognising that she had made progress, and wished to be lenient with her. However, those who saw her in group situations felt that she had a somewhat arrogant manner, and this resulted in countertransference feelings of anger and a wish to punish her. There was therefore a marked split within the team, reflecting the split both within Caroline and within the family. Caroline idealised her parents but also saw them as fragile and in need of her help. She therefore omnipotently denied both her own dependency needs and her aggressive and denigrating feelings. In treatment, Caroline was able to reveal her fragility to her psychotherapist and key nurse but regarded the other staff members as ineffectual. The anger and contempt she denied in relation to her parents was expressed towards these staff members who experienced countertransference feelings of hostility. Her relationship with the other patients repeated her childhood experiences at boarding school, in that she began by being in the position of leader but gradually became resented and excluded.

In retrospect it would seem that a series of enactments took place with this patient as each side of the staff split took precedence. Thus, the repeated decisions not to discharge Caroline despite her breaking the treatment boundaries could be seen as an enactment of the psychotherapist and key nurse's identification with the vulnerable aspects of the patient. On the other hand, Caroline evoked a punitive response from other staff members, and the final discharge took place in an atmosphere of hostility when those who knew her best were absent. She was sent away from the hospital as she was sent away to boarding school when her parents felt unable to cope with her. In this case the staff as a whole failed to come to a full enough understanding of the splits within the team and of the meaning of these splits in relation to Caroline's internal world. If this had been possible, it might have enabled staff to reach a true consensus about the best way forward for the patient.

Case 4

This was Deborah's second admission to the inpatient unit. At the beginning of this treatment she approached both her psychotherapist and her key nurse from the previous admission to ask if they would work with her again. She had a way of getting what she wanted, and both these requests were granted. She had a seductive manner, and her psychotherapist struggled to hold the boundaries as Deborah would push her relentlessly, usually asking for something rather subtle either at the beginning or the end of the session. Deborah was very attached to both her key nurse and to her psychotherapist. Both felt a powerful internal pressure to comply with Deborah's wish that they disclose personal information but both resisted this pressure, much to Deborah's frustration.

An inexperienced young nurse, new to eating disorders, joined the team. Deborah singled this nurse out and would talk to her frequently, again inviting the nurse to talk to Deborah about herself. The nurse found herself disclosing information that became quite compromising. In her psychotherapy sessions Deborah voiced her discomfort about her relationship with the nurse. Deborah was aware of feeling on difficult ground, believing that the nurse was becoming dependent on her and that she, Deborah, was caring for her rather than the other way round. Deborah talked to her psychotherapist about her dilemma. She did not want to cause the nurse trouble and decided to be direct with her about how she felt. The nurse also spoke to the psychotherapist, and was then able to respond appropriately to Deborah. Deborah eventually completed the treatment successfully.

Deborah was the eldest of three girls born to a couple who were already experiencing difficulties in their relationship. The father and mother lived quite separate lives and talked of splitting up, and Deborah lacked any real connection with either parent. Her mother had frequent angry outbursts, directed at Deborah, which she found terrifying, whilst her father communicated with her only in a distant and hostile way.

Discussion: Deborah was desperate for connection with others, particularly members of the staff, having felt throughout her life that her parents had been unavailable to her. However, she also wanted these connections to be on an equal basis, wishing to deny her vulnerability and her status as a patient in need of care. In her relationship with the young nurse she was able to reverse the roles of container and contained (Bion, 1959), achieving a sense of closeness whilst still denying her own needs. However, she was able to recognise that this was ultimately unsatisfactory and that she needed the boundary between patient and staff to remain firm so that she could feel contained and cared for. This enactment turned out to be constructive in that it resulted in a shift in Deborah's willingness to reveal her vulnerability and a growth in her capacity to take responsibility for her own needs.

Conclusion

The clinical examples given above indicate a few of the multiple ways in which enactments can occur in an inpatient setting. We would suggest that such enactments are inevitable. The task of the staff team is to attempt to come to a mutual understanding of the dynamics which lead to such events, and to use this understanding in their decisions about the patient's treatment and in their work with the patient. In the cases of patients Anne and Deborah this was achieved and the patients' treatment benefited. In such cases, it would seem that the enactment can become a constructive element of the ongoing treatment. However, sometimes, as for patients Brenda and Caroline, enactments result in discharge from treatment and there may be no opportunity for working through with the patient.

Working within a multidisciplinary team has the advantage that the ward round discussion, in which clinicians of different disciplines share their perceptions of the patient, can alert the psychotherapist or other staff member to the presence of a split or to unusual attitudes on the part of the staff team as a whole. This may herald the possibility of an enactment and enable the team to become aware of previously unconscious reactions to the patient. The psychotherapist has a particular role here in helping the team to consider the pattern of relationships developed by the patient on the ward and the meaning of this pattern in terms of the patient's internal world. Of course, this process is not always successful and sometimes enactments will occur which cannot be resolved or repaired.

References

Bateman, A. (1998) Thick- and thin-skinned organizations and enactment in borderline and narcissistic disorders. *International Journal of Psychoanalysis,* 79(1): 13–25.

Bion, W. (1959) Attacks on linking. *International Journal of Psychoanalysis,* 40: 308–315. Republished (1988) in E. Bott Spillius (ed.) *Melanie Klein Today,* Vol. 1, *Mainly Theory* (pp. 87–101). London: Routledge.

Currin, J. (2000) What are the essential characteristics of the analytic attitude? Insight, the use of enactments, and relationship. *Journal of Clinical Psychoanalysis,* 9(1): 75–91.

Farrell, E. (1995) *Lost for Words: The Psychoanalysis of Anorexia and Bulimia* (p. 5). London: Process Press.

Gabbard, G. (1995) Countertransference: The emerging common ground. *International Journal of Psychoanalysis,* 76: 475–485.

Gerrard, J. (2007) Enactments in the countertransference with special reference to rescue fantasies with hysterical patients. *British Journal of Psychotherapy,* 23(2): 217–230.

Guntrip, H. (1968) *The Schizoid Phenomena, Object Relations and the Self.* London: The Hogarth Press.

Lawrence, M. (2002) Body, mother, mind: Anorexia, femininity and the intrusive object. *International Journal of Psychoanalysis,* 83(4): 837–850.

Marsden, P. (2001) Food and violence: Childhood violence and emotional abuse as complicating factors in the inpatient treatment of eating disorders. *Psychoanalytic Psychotherapy,* 15(3): 225–242.

Martin, K. (2002) Mirror, mirror: An enactment that stalemated a psychotherapy. *The Annual of Psychoanalysis,* 30: 211–221.

Sandler, J. (1976) Countertransference and role-responsiveness. *International Review of Psycho-Analysis,* 3: 43–47.

Segal, H. (1957) Notes on symbol formation. *International Journal of Psychoanalysis* 38: 391–397. Republished (1988) in E. Bott Spillius (ed.) *Melanie Klein Today,* Vol. 1, *Mainly Theory* (pp. 160–177). London: Routledge.

Steiner, J. (1993) *Psychic Retreats: Pathological Organisations in Psychotic, Neurotic and Borderline Patients.* London: Routledge.

Steiner, J. (2006) Interpretative enactments and the analytic setting. *International Journal of Psychoanalysis,* 87: 315–320.

Williams, G. (1997) *Internal Landscapes and Foreign Bodies: Eating Disorders and Other Pathologies* (pp. 103–123). London: Karnac.

9 Past present

Person-centred therapy with trauma and enactment

Louise Embleton Tudor and Keith Tudor

Enactment may be viewed as 'acting in' (as in self-harm) or 'acting out' (as in anti-social behaviour). In the context of a therapeutic relationship, it may also be understood as 'acting across', or the enacting of the past in the present between client and therapist. This chapter examines the enactment of trauma from an organismic, person-centred perspective, exploring how clients enact past physical and psychological trauma within the therapeutic relationship. We introduce this perspective with regard to the nature of the organism and self over time, from which we identify a number of under-standings with regard to trauma. Then we discuss the principles of an organismic person-centred approach by way of introducing certain thera-peutic conditions originally identified by Rogers (1957, 1959). Finally, drawing on Levine with Frederick's (1997) work on healing trauma and our own practice, we discuss the application of the person-centred perspectives, and specifically the therapeutic conditions, to work with past trauma in the present.

Trauma – an organismic person-centred perspective

There are different ways to understand and to work with trauma and the enactment of trauma, as represented by the various vignettes in this chapter. We have drawn on organismic psychology, which in many ways is the lost tradition of twentieth-century psychology (see Tudor and Worrall, 2006). We think that this tradition – and, specifically, the view that human beings are organisms – provides us with a particular understanding of the nature of trauma and enactment and with ways of working therapeutically with clients. In this first part we discuss the nature of the organism as a background to a holistic view of the person in his or her environment.

Organism

The biological entity that is the organism is central to organismic and person-centred psychology. As Rogers (1953/1967a, p. 80) puts it: 'one of the fundamental directions taken by the process of therapy is the free experiencing of the actual sensory and visceral reactions of the organism without too much of an attempt to relate these experiences to the self.' Rogers is one of a number of psychologists who have expounded organismic theory. Thirty years ago, Hall and Lindzey (1978) recognised that he adopted an organismic orientation in his theory and practice, a view more recently explored by Fernald (2000) who claims Rogers as a body-oriented counsellor, and by Tudor and Worrall (2006) who elaborate the centrality of the organism to person-centred approaches to therapy.

According to Angyal (1941, p. 99), the organism (from organ = tool) refers to 'a system in which the parts are the instruments, the tools, of the whole'. Feldenkreis (1981, pp. 21–22), the founder of a form and method of bodywork, defines it as consisting of 'the skeleton, the muscles, the nervous system, and all that goes to nourish, warm, activate, and rest the whole of it'. In his foreword to the re-publication of Goldstein's work in 1995, Sacks traces a brief history of neurology, seeing Goldstein and others, including gestalt psychologists, as important in rebutting more modular views of neural organisation and the human organism. These people

> were intensely conscious of the plasticity of the nervous system, the organism's powers of coming to terms and adapting, and the general powers of symbolization, of conceptual thought, of perspective and consciousness, so developed in humans, which seemed to be irreducible to mere elementary or modular capacities.
>
> (Sacks, 1995, p. 8)

Damasio (1994/1996, p. 87) defines living organisms as 'changing continuously, assuming a succession of "states," each defined by varied patterns of ongoing activity in all its components.' In their book on healing trauma, Levine with Frederick (1997, p. 67) define the organism as 'a complex structure of interdependent and subordinate elements whose relation and properties are largely determined by their functions in the whole.'

This view, and other more recent developments in neuroscience, support the view that the experiencing human organism tends to actualise, that is, to maintain, enhance and reproduce itself. Tudor and Worrall (2006) elaborate this perspective: that, as human beings, we are holistic, experiential, interdependent organisms; that we are always in motion; that we construe reality according to our perception of it; that we differentiate, regulate, and behave according to need; and that we have an internal, organismic valuing process. Recognising these qualities of the organism/person supports person-centred approaches to understanding and working with people who experience trauma.

The organism cannot be understood outside of its environment. As Perls (1947/1969, p. 38) puts it: 'No organism is self-sufficient. It requires the world for the gratification of its needs . . . there is always an interdependency of the organism and its environment.' Our first environment is another – an other, usually, initially a mother – and, developmentally, we need this other to reflect and to regulate our experience. The value of experience is confirmed by the work of neurobiologists such as Schore (1994, p. 33) who says that: 'the core of the self lies in the patterns of affect regulation that integrate a sense of self . . . thereby allowing for a continuity of inner experience'. In this sense and on this basis, the human organism is, as Barrett-Lennard (1998, p. 75) describes, 'a purposeful, open system, in particularly active interchange with its environment'. Equally, any inter-ruption to what we would call organismic regulation, is an interruption to the relational system that is the organism/environment. From an organ-ismic perspective Angyal (1965/1973, p. 117) views trauma as:

> a biospheric event, an instance of interaction between the world and the organism, [which] can be defined only in terms of its outcome . . . An event must be regarded as traumatic if it has led to the formation of a neurotic nucleus.

Thus, trauma is a normal or, put more accurately, *usual* aspect of life. It is the degree of trauma, the context of the trauma, and how we experience and understand our experiencing of the trauma, that are all significant in whether it becomes a 'neurotic nucleus' and, as Angyal (1941) puts it, a source of 'bio-negativity'. How we experience and process our experience depends on how are regulated and then how we 'self'-regulate, and on the impact of bio-chemical processes. Several studies show that cortisol func-tions as an anti-stress hormone (see, for example, Resnick, Yehuda and Acierno, 1997); and the results of one particular study suggest that chronic and persistent stress or trauma inhibit cortisol release and the stress response and, therefore, induce desensitisation (Axelrod, 1984). Human beings cannot avoid being traumatised; it's how we deal with it that counts. As Angyal (1965/1973, p. 60) puts it: 'The reaction of the organism to the traumatic damage is an unusual condition, and as such it may act as a further trauma.' In this case, neurosis and negativity, expressed in different forms of alienation, then get acted out, acted in or enacted in therapy and, specifically, within the therapeutic relationship.

From the above we understand:

1   That all trauma is a trauma to the organism, whether or not it is also experienced and understood as a trauma to self (see next section).
2   That a trauma to one part of the person will have an impact on the whole organism.
3   That trauma can only be understood in the context of the environment or, more precisely, in the context of the interrelationship between the human organism and her or his environment – including the therapist and the therapeutic relationship.

From an organismic perspective and from organismic beginnings, as Rogers (1951, p. 497) puts it: 'A portion of the total perceptual field gradually becomes differentiated as the self.' This clearly places the concept of self within the context of the human organism. Although some have identified Rogers' theory as a self theory, Rogers' definition of self is ambiguous as are those of other theorists such as Kohut (1977). This organismic perspective of the origin of self leads to a view of self as self-awareness or consciousness of self. Some theorists and practitioners view person-centred psychology more as a self psychology and write and talk in terms of parts or configurations of self (even Self). From this we understand:

4   That a trauma may be experienced as a trauma or hurt to the self, in addition to and as distinct from a trauma to the organism.
5   That the concept of selves or parts may be helpful to both client and therapist to conceptualise the differentiated aspects of the traumatised organism.

An organismic, person-centred approach to the therapy of trauma and enactment

Person-centred psychology and psychotherapy rests on three principles (see Sanders, 2000; Tudor and Worrall, 2006):

1   That the human organism, as other organisms, tends to actualise.
2   That, therefore, in order to be facilitative of another, a therapist embodies a non-directive attitude to her client and, specifically, towards her client's experience.
3   That, together, therapist and client create, and continually co-create, certain conditions which are facilitative of the client's maintenance, growth and development.

When people are traumatised, they are also healthy or, in some way, expressing their health or authenticity; and, in exploring trauma, we think that it is important to acknowledge this. In response to trauma and adversity, people do the best they can in the circumstances as they experience and perceive them. Many reports of the most brutal and brutalising acts committed by men (and it is predominantly men) are also stories of the survival of the human spirit. Person-centred approaches acknowledge the impact of a traumatic environment on the human organism, whether in the form of accidents, surgery, neglect, abuse, violence, dislocation, natural disasters or war, whether individual or collective (see Audergon, 2004). We think it is important to acknowledge with clients the context of the trauma so as to be able to help them process their experience.

The significance of an organismic, person-centred approach is that it acknowledges and values the client's *experience* of trauma. In its third edition of the *Diagnostic and Statistical Manual of Mental Disorders* (*DSM-III*) the American Association of Psychiatry defines trauma as 'a psychologically distressing event that is outside the range of human experience' (APA, 1987, p. 247). This is vague and misleading. All trauma is *within* the range of human experience, even, sadly, in its extreme forms. As Levine with Frederick (1997, p. 24) put it: 'People don't need a definition of trauma; we need an experiential sense of how it feels.' Perhaps significantly, in its current (fourth) edition of the *DSM* the APA (1994/2000) has dropped this aspect of its definition. Rogers' emphasis on the priority and authority of experience (see Rogers, 1961/1967c) is supported by more recent developments in neuroscience. The value of experience is confirmed by the work of neurobiologists such as Schore (1994, p. 33) who states that: 'the core of the self lies in the patterns of affect regulation that integrate a sense of self . . . thereby allowing for a continuity of inner experience'. As Janet (1919/1976) puts it: 'a person is unable to make the neural recital that we call narrative memory, and yet he remains confronted with the difficult situation.' Recent research using brain imagery shows that unprocessed experiences of trauma are stored in the limbic system. As this is the non-verbal, emotional centre of the brain, it makes sense that any therapy which seeks to work with people who have experienced or who are enacting trauma must account for and address non-verbal and pre-verbal experience. This emphasis on the client's experience and experiencing and/or difficulty experiencing, rests on the therapist's respect for the client and her or his symptoms and on the view that the client is her or his own expert and that diagnosis is an ongoing client-centred process. As Rogers (1951, p. 223) puts it, 'therapy *is* diagnosis, and this diagnosis is a process which goes on in the experience of the client, rather than in the intellect of the clinician.'

Whilst we are committed to a non-directive approach, especially with regard to the client's experience and experiencing, we also recognise the importance of structure – and that both are compatible within the person-centred approach (see Coghlan and McIlduff, 1990). We recognise the findings of research studies which suggest that there are various components to the recovery from trauma. For instance, Cook et al. (2005) identify six core components of complex trauma treatment: safety, self-regulation, self-reflective information processing, traumatic experiences integration, relational engagement, and positive affect enhancement. We see these elements of 'treatment' as part of a process of recovery and movement from fixity and rigidity, as a result of trauma, to fluid processing and integrating of experience (see Rogers, 1958/1967b).

The therapeutic conditions

Person-centred therapy is the original relationship therapy (see Rogers, 1942) and, in two seminal papers, Rogers (1957/1990, 1959) sets out his hypothesis about the conditions of a therapeutic relationship which effects change in the client. In the first of these statements to be published Rogers (1957/1990) makes it clear that these conditions apply to any situation in which constructive personality change occurs – and, indeed, with any client and in any relationship. On this basis, the statement may be viewed as an integrative statement (see, for instance, Stubbs and Bozarth, 1996). Rogers' (1957/1990, p. 221) therapeutic conditions for constructive personality change are that:

1 Two persons are in psychological contact.
2 The first, whom we shall term the client, is in a state of incongruence, being vulnerable or anxious.
3 The second person, whom we shall term the therapist, is congruent or integrated in the relationship.
4 The therapist experiences unconditional positive regard for the client.
5 The therapist experiences an empathic understanding of the client's internal frame of reference and endeavors to communicate this experience to the client.
6 The communication to the client of the therapist's empathic understanding and unconditional positive regard is to a minimal degree achieved.

Here we consider therapeutic work with trauma and enactment in the context of these conditions.

Psychological contact

With regard to psychological contact, Rogers says that:

> All that is intended by this first condition is to specify that the two people are to some degree in contact, that each makes some perceived difference in the experiential field of the other . . . it is sufficient if each makes some 'subceived' difference, even though the individual may not be consciously aware of this impact.
>
> (Rogers, 1957/1990, p. 221)

This helps us to stay with and alongside the client who may be so traumatised that he cannot make contact, at least in an obvious, perceived way.

One client, a young man, arrived promptly for therapy, week after week. In the sessions, he sat, head down, not uttering a word for most of the meetings. The therapist accepted this and responded occasionally.

In such circumstances, some theory as well as examples of good practice can help the therapist to stay in contact. In his study of psychotherapy with schizophrenics Rogers (1967d) reports on his work with a silent young man. Prouty (1976) describes making contact with clients, who are out of contact by virtue of childhood trauma, by means of a series of contact reflections:

situational, facial, body or somatic, word-for-word, and reiterative. Coffeng (2002, p. 153) views contact as 'a central issue for dissociating and traumatized clients'. The importance of working with even minimal contact should not be underestimated; and, in this sense, we think that, as it proposes working with people who are out of contact or only minimally in contact, person-centred therapy is more radical than other therapies which rely on clients being present and in a certain state.

One client, on ending several years of therapy, said: 'You know, I don't remember much about the first couple of years. I was so out of it, but the thing that kept me going through those times was that you always, every single time, looked pleased to see me when you met me. I don't know what I would have done if you ever hadn't.'

These vignettes illustrate the necessity of paying attention to the client's state, especially the traumatised client's state of increased arousal and sensitivity during greeting and leave-taking (Schore, 2006).

A client who was frequently attacked verbally by his mentally ill mother, especially during bouts of alcohol induced collapse, said to a therapist who was working after a night of interrupted sleep because of her young child: 'Am I annoying you today? Something's different. You look a bit different. I don't know what it is. Is something wrong?' No other client that day had apparently picked up on the therapist's tiredness. The therapist decided to tell the client that she had had less sleep than she had planned and, knowing that the client would be likely to think that she (the therapist) had worries that kept her awake (as the client had), the therapist added that she had been woken up by her child. The client looked relieved, and both therapist and client acknowledged the client's concern about annoying the therapist and the therapist's robustness. Until he asked this question, there had been no hint in the client's demeanour that he was concerned or disturbed by what he thought he saw in the therapist. This interaction was particularly significant as it demonstrated that the client had begun to trust the therapist enough to share something of his inner experience, without fear of reprisal. One of the challenges of this therapeutic condition for the therapist is to maintain contact with the client in the various forms of incongruence (identified below), and to work through the inevitable ruptures in contact in the relationship.

Client incongruence

Incongruence describes the discrepancy between the individual's actual experience and her or his self-picture insofar as it represents that experience (Rogers, 1957/1990). In his major theoretical formulation of client-centred therapy Rogers (1959) describes the breakdown of organismic and self-development in terms of the development of incongruence; discrepancies in behaviour; the experience of threat and the process of defence; breakdown and disorganisation – a description of the breakdown and discrepancies involved in the bio-negativity that is trauma, and its enactment. The concept of incongruence is fundamental to person-centred approaches to psychopathology and illness (see Speierer, 1990, 1996), and its elaboration in terms of defences (Rogers, 1959), conditionality (Bozarth, 1998) and alienation (Tudor and Worrall, 2006).

In the field of trauma, the work of Levine with Frederick (1997) is close to the organismic approach of person-centred psychology and therapy. They suggest that there are four components to trauma which, to some degree, are always present in any traumatised person and which are normal or ordinary and sequential responses to threat: hyperarousal, constriction, dissociation, and helplessness, which we understand as forms of incongruence. Whilst we see these as responses, we don't see them as necessarily sequential. Most people operate most of the time within a certain range of response or arousal to stimuli. When, for whatever reason, we don't manage to remain within our 'comfort zone', we may have either an increased level of arousal (*hyper*arousal) or a decreased level of arousal (*hypo*arousal). Accordingly, we consider these forms of incongruence, but frame and order them a little differently from Levine with Frederick, thus: *hyperarousal*, including constriction; and *hypoarousal*, including dissociation and helplessness.

Hyperarousal

This describes a domination of the sympathetic nervous system, an escalation of feelings, and an inability to contain, manage or self-soothe. It manifests as a physiological state of arousal such as increased and fast heartbeat and respiration, and a general hypersensitivity of the senses which are part of the sympathetic nervous system's response to threat. As the senses have been overwhelmed in the past, the present is likely to be misperceived. This can lead to acute anxiety states, hypervigilance and/or paranoid states. Often a particular incident acts as a stimulus in response to which a person may feel guilty, and fearful. She may focus on particular thing such as repetitive images, and be unable to focus on anything else. This state is often accompanied by an inability to sleep, lack of appetite, and constant tearfulness. Usually, no amount of reassurance or logic (reminders, or 'facts') works.

One manifestation of hyperarousal is the escalation of feelings: thus, a little hurt often becomes overwhelming. We see this in a child who is inconsolable after what appears to be an ordinary physical injury. In a filmed filial therapy session (involving a child, her Mum and a therapist), a child plays excitedly a game with her Mum. Suddenly the child falls to the floor clutching her face: 'My nose, my nose, you hit my nose!' The mother had not hit the child's nose. As mother and therapist expected, a later replay of the video shows that the child's face was not touched by the mother or by the ball. The child finds an opportunity to demonstrate the hurt she feels was done to her by a previous (foster) mother. Now, she re-enacts an aspect of the trauma in the hope that this mother, her Mum, can soothe the pain and that she can respond appropriately. The mother starts by kissing the nose and murmuring consolation. This is not enough. There are other hurts, on her arms and her legs. The mother props her child up on cushions, and is allowed to swathe the child's limbs and head in makeshift bandages. Previously she has enacted injuries like this but has refused all soothing and physical contact in an attempt to recreate the original, lonely, painful experiences in which she had to look after herself – and an absent and abusive mother.

In an adult who is already traumatised, a small mishap dysregulates her or him, i.e. disturbs to a degree which compromises everyday functioning. One person following a mishap or disappointment may have elevated levels of cortisol for a few minutes; another, who has experienced a past unresolved trauma, may take hours, or even weeks, to re-establish her or his equilibrium. A person who has experienced regular and repeated trauma over a time may lose sensitivity to stress, as the stress-response system is overwhelmed, and her or his capacity to deal with subsequent stress is permanently altered by the previous exposure to events which have over-whelmed their system.

Constriction

When people are traumatised the hyperarousal response is often accom-panied by both physical and perceptual constriction. Tension alters the breathing, muscle tone and posture, leading to the constriction of blood vessels throughout the body. It affects perceptions, eyes, ears, the digestive system, the heart (so that it beats faster), and thinking. The organism, through its nervous system, in effect, focuses on the threat in order to deal with it, and shuts out other perceptual awareness. This is the 'neurotic nucleus' to which Angyal (1941) refers; or 'intensionality', the term Rogers (1959) uses to describe the individual's behaviour when she or he is in a defensive state. This perceptual constriction refers to the change in the *field* of consciousness which, as a result of hyperarousal, narrows, so that not all perceived information is available for recall (see Janet, 1907). A person in a constricted state or process, for example, may not hear as he usually does; he may find it impossible to wait to hear what the other is saying; and may try to manage this by attempting to control and/or predict. There is often a high level of distortion and denial (Rogers, 1951), which means that the therapist has to check understanding, often in some detail.

One therapist said to her client: 'I won't be here in August.' This was understood by the client as the therapist saying: 'I will be here in August.' The therapist was able to acknowledge the client's experience of the com-munication, his concerns about the forthcoming break, and the disappoint-ment of his expectations. Therapist and client then went on to consider how the client would spend the month, the difficulties he might encounter, and the resources he could draw on in order to manage the break. On further reflection, the therapist recognised that she had not sufficiently prepared the client for the break. She was taking a break later than usual and, in looking forward to it herself, had overlooked the possible impact on this particular client, a process which contributed to the client's enactment.

One of the positive aspects of constriction is this increased focus, the fact that the therapist can work sensitively and effectively with the detail of what is or has been understood and misunderstood, and use the opportunity to strengthen both the relationship and the client's resources. Equally, the detail and the rigidity with which the client may hold her or his distorted perception can be frustrating, with the result that the therapist too can become restricted. One client interpreted every change of position her therapist made as an indication of her waning interest in her. This perception grew rather than diminished, and the client began to believe that her therapist was deliberately causing her distress by crossing her legs, moving her arm, etc. Despite the therapist's empathically attuned responses and authentic expressions of concern for the client, and exploration of the client's issues of motivation and control, the client's belief did not change and she left therapy.

Hypoarousal

If hyperarousal is a state of increased sensitivity to external stimuli and to inner-generated experiences, hypoarousal describes what Schore (2007) refers to as an 'energy failure'. In the face of repeated experiences of extreme terror, if the emergency strategy of hyperarousal has been ineffective, the organism now conserves and immobilises. In this last resort, the person 'plays dead' in an attempt to avoid attention, disengaging from internal and external stimuli. This respite allows for a reorganisation and refuelling of the energy which has been depleted and for some repair of injury to the self-concept. At such times a person may gaze into space or indicate that they feel foggy, fuzzy, spaced out or even blank. This response represents an alteration in the *level* of consciousness (see Janet, 1907). This presents a huge challenge for the therapist, whose visceral empathic response is likely to be boredom, drowsiness, hopelessness and helplessness. Should she be unable to make sense and use of this, and betray these unassimilated experiences to the client, she is likely to compound the shame the client already feels. As Schore (2007) states: 'Clinical work with parasympathetic dissociation is always associated with parasympathetic shame dynamics.' Further, he describes shame as: 'a shock-induced deflation triggered by a relational mis-attunement' in response to which the client averts her gaze and attempts to hide from the therapist, 'to escape from this being seen or from the one who sees'. Bromberg (2006) suggests that the reason for the same repeated enactments in therapy is that the therapist is not attending to the arousal of shame, in herself or in the client.

Dissociation

This describes a spectrum of experience from being a bit absent or 'spaced out' to various dissociative disorders, including dissociative identity disorder (see APA, 1994/2000) which describes the condition or process when different aspects of a person live within the psyche as fully developed separate identities. Within the person-centred and experiential tradition, Warner (1998, 2000) and Coffeng (2005) have developed the practice and theory of therapeutic work with this level of dissociation.

There are ordinary dissociative experiences, which may temporarily be exacerbated by a stressful event. Examples include: daydreaming, forgetting a name or where one has placed things, or why one went upstairs. People dissociate when reality is overwhelmingly painful. The spectrum of dissociative experience includes the client who sometimes looks a bit spaced out, the client who forgets what they were talking about mid-sentence, the client who comes to sessions late because she has misplaced her car keys (again), and the client who frequently arrives at the wrong time or on the wrong day. Dissociation usually is not a complete absence, but one in which the individual observes reality, including her or himself, as if out of her or his own body, an experience often described by people who have been abused or tortured. In gestalt psychology this defence is referred to as egotism, a defence which strengthens the ego as distinct from the self or organism. Some people talk about themselves in the third person, a form of distancing and perceptual distortion which Rogers (1958/1967b) places at stage one of his seven-stage process conception of psychotherapy. Talking about oneself as 'one', more common amongst upper class people and royalty (as the royal 'we') are socially constructed and sanctioned, if dated, forms of distancing and dissociation.

In the case of multiple dissociative identities, each identity serves an important function for the client, such as that of a friend to the terrified abandoned infant, or a cruel adult who could not be coherently integrated. Usually the switch between identities can be observed by a sudden change in facial expression, tone of voice, or a vocabulary which seems to bear no relationship to the external reality. Often, when there is a rupture in self-experiencing, this is accompanied by a different sense of time and space.

One therapist, working with a 12-year-old client, reported quite early on in the therapy that she was beginning to discern when '20-year-old Kylie' (the way the client referred to this part of herself) had replaced her 12-year-old self, as the client (as 20-year-old Kylie) had a slightly forced laugh and unusually bright eyes. Sometimes this same client would try to pick a fight with the therapist and would generate distractions from the conversation in hand, in which case the therapist would know that 'Jenny' (another dissociated part of Kylie) had arrived. From a person-centred perspective the therapist needs to engage, accept, get to know and understand each identity or character and the relationships between them (see Warner, 1998, 2000). We also consider dis*association* as a form of dissociation: literally, the withdrawal from association, company or society.

Helplessness

This describes the situation and process when all other defences have been tried and failed, when thinking, feeling and behaviour are all blocked and the person becomes immobilised and helpless. Levine with Frederick (1997, p. 142) describe it poignantly:

> The helplessness that is experienced at such times is not the ordinary sense of helplessness that can affect anyone from time to time. The sense of being completely immobilized and helpless is not a perception, belief, or a trick of the imagination. It is real. The body cannot move. This is abject helplessness – a sense of paralysis so profound that the person cannot scream, move, or feel.

When, for whatever reason, a person is prevented from fight or flight, the only way she or he has of dealing with overwhelming events is to (try to) avoid them. Since, often, this cannot be achieved physically, the person deploys the primitive defence of freezing, either involuntarily or as a deliberate strategy. We see this when animals freeze or merge into their environment in order to avoid a predator (a defence which some view as a form of flight). When this defence has to be used regularly, it takes a lot of energy, with the result that the person who is feeling helpless has a lack of vitality or deadness, and often appears passive.

One client had sustained systematic emotional and physical abuse as a child, which had compromised her success and happiness throughout her life. In therapy, she reported being the victim of a sexual assault the other day, in a conversational tone and without the strong affect one might expect, particularly of someone whose early experience of abuse is being re-stimulated. Initially the therapist wondered what was going on, as if it hadn't really happened. The therapist very nearly didn't respond, catching herself dissociating from the impact of the recent assault. She quickly brought herself back and communicated her shock, which, in turn, helped the client to contact her feelings about both the recent assault and the previous early abuse.

Our emphasis on the significance of the environment on the organism means that we consider these responses to threat also on a wider, cultural level. We think that, by and large, Western society encourages both hyper-arousal and hypoarousal: constriction, dissociation, and helplessness. In order to counter these trends, we agree with Ogden and Minton (2000) who suggest that it is necessary to work at the boundaries of tolerance to states of emotional arousal, and that simply to stay or to support the client to remain within her or his 'comfort zone' precludes the possibility of access to stressful affects and, subsequently, to more effective regulation.

The therapist's congruence

That the therapist is congruent and integrated in the relationship means that she is genuine and authentic. In general, person-centred training places great emphasis on the personal development of the therapist and, in particular, her awareness. This enables her to know herself (self-awareness) and to work through any feelings, for instance, of disgust or disapproval of addictive, compulsive or impulsive behaviour – her own and others' – so that she does not get in the way of her clients and can attend to their communications. This, in turn, enables her to be able to access what clients are saying, both verbally and non-verbally (empathic awareness). At best we do this by means of developing our sensory, physiological, affective, behavioural and cognitive awareness, and fine observation skills, of both external and internal phenomena. In his work, Rogers emphasises the importance of the therapist's congruence or integration *in the therapeutic relationship*, a perspective which also encompasses the reality of the therapist not always being congruent or integrated and, in this sense and for our present interest, enacting (in, out or across) in the way she relates to the client. People who have been traumatised have, necessarily, highly developed powers of observation, so therapists need to be aware of themselves and what they communicate. Schore (1994) notes the particular sensitivity of people whose perceptions are dominated by the amygdala, that part of the limbic system which ascribes values to experience immediately and independently of cognitive processing. Similarly, there is also scientific evidence that clients pick up our true feelings and quickest reactions. In all listening and talking therapies the therapist relies on the use of self and their ability to communicate their own experience and experiencing, as a way of communicating acceptance and empathy, and offering feedback and challenge to clients. The therapist's authenticity is, for us, a quiet condition which forms the basis of her ability to be acceptant and empathic. It's also the condition which is the conceptual basis for the therapist's own development, whether in the form of personal development or personal therapy, before, during and after training.

The therapist's acceptance

That the therapist is acceptant means that she is willing to engage with all aspects of her client, including, for our present interest, expression of high levels and an intensity of emotion and behaviour, including withdrawal, dissociation, and levels of regression and dependence. This condition involves the therapist having a profound sense of the client as an autonomous, separate person, and facilitating a therapeutic relationship in which she frees the client as much as possible from external evaluation, disapproval or approval.

One client reported his mother as monstrous and annihilating in her rage, holding him accountable for her own disappointment and hurt, and expecting him to modify his engagement with the world to suit her. This young man recognised his need for ongoing therapy, but was unable to accept the frame of weekly appointments at the same time of the week on an ongoing basis, viewing this as an attack on his autonomy, and an attempt to manipulate him to suit the therapist's interests. The therapist negotiated some appointment changes when she could, but could not offer the amount of flexibility desired by the client. For a while this tension was enacted between the therapist and the client: the client experienced being restricted and controlled, and the therapist experienced him as uncompromising and attempting to control her; and they seemed irreconcilable. However, the therapist, unlike the client's mother, was empathic with the man's struggle to be in a relationship in which his needs were met, whilst his sense of autonomy was not compromised and, to some extent, he perceived this. She was empathic enough with his experiencing, past and present, for him to continue in this relationship, despite its threat. Together they continued to explore his issues in the light of both current and past relationships.

The therapist's empathic understanding

That the therapist is empathic means that she seeks to understand what Rogers refers to as the client's 'frame of reference' or way of perceiving and construing the world. The therapist responds not only to the content of what the client is saying, but also, and more importantly, to the felt sense of the client's communication, and is, thereby, empathic to the organismic state or process of the client, as well as to his self state and disintegrated process. In the example above there were times when the therapist sat with the client when he was silent and 'tuned in' to herself. In doing so, she began to get a sense of what it was like to be the client, 'as if' she were him, holding himself together. She began to resonate with the client and got a sense of his experience of anxiety and conflict, and then began to frame and time how she would communicate her sensing and understanding. Grinberg (1995) describes this beautifully:

> I attempt to pay attention to body-postures, gestures and movements. I try not to remember material from previous sessions or rely on well-known theories . . . rather, I try to wait with 'floating attention' attempting to listen to the silence until I can confidently connect.

This quality and level of empathic resonance is often referred to as attunement. Empathy without attunement – that is, responses which demonstrate a sensitivity to content without any sensitivity to unspoken process – is not useful to clients suffering from trauma. We may call this particular kind of empathic attunement of the body somatic or visceral empathy. The point is that the client has a sense of the therapist holding him, mind and body, in her mind, presently and over time. This is an important aspect of what Fonagy et al. (2002) refer to as mentalisation or reflective functioning. The effect of being accepted and understood is profound. In this sense the therapist both validates the client's alienating experience/s, and offers a present-centred, reparative experience. When the client experiences this, then he can begin to rediscover and reclaim empathy for himself which, again, is a crucial developmental process: the client's felt sense unifies and gives meaning to the 'scattered data' of his experiences. Rogers made a huge contribution to the development of an understanding of empathy, a concept and practice also referred to by Freud, Moreno, Jaspers, Winnicott and, notably, Kohut.

One client reported happy relationships and overall satisfaction with his life until an accident resulting in the death of a child, for which the client felt and held himself responsible. Colleagues and friends had told him that he was not responsible, a view supported by the findings of an independent enquiry. Nevertheless, almost a year after, the client was still experiencing unwanted images and thoughts about the accident; he could not sleep at night; he had a diminished appetite; and was generally agitated, which took the form of pacing his bedroom at night. In therapy, he discovered that the accident had evoked unmanageable guilt and fear, in part, because his role in his original family had been that of caretaker. Whenever he had tried to choose to follow his own inclinations above the needs of his mother and younger brothers, he had experienced strong disapproval. This was underpinned by earlier experiences which, both client and therapist surmised from their knowledge of his circumstances, were not moderated by an attuned (m)other.

This client had no experience of what Schore (1994) refers to as 'contingent mothering', that is, experience which promotes the development of the ability to self-soothe. In such circumstances, the therapist needs to be minutely sensitive to minor clues – such as fleeting changes of facial expression or colour, smell, shifts in body position and eye movement, and changes in prosody (the rhythm, pace, tone and pitch of language) – and to regulate psycho-biologically. In being acceptant and empathic, and in order to offer an attuned response, the therapist uses information derived from her organismic responses to these clues, from her somatic empathic resonance with the client's bodily experience, together with her cognitive understanding of both the client's communication and relevant theory. When there is little information available expressed verbally, it is usually enough for the therapist to make contact in some way and to remark on what she observes. The therapist's response has to resonate with/in the client as true for him, and as authentic (on the part of the therapist) in terms of the quality of her facial expression, her tone of voice, and her use of language, including metaphor, and not merely as a clinical observation. The client needs to sense the therapist's sensing of him, her acceptance of the totality that is him in that moment.

The client's perception

Rogers' sixth condition asserts the centrality of the client in therapy. In another paper (Rogers, 1958/1967b, p. 130) he refers to this as the central or '*assumed*' condition. It is the condition by which the process of therapy and the therapeutic relationship stands or falls. In other words, the therapist may be accepting and empathic of the client but, if the client doesn't experience these attitudes or conditions, then, in a phenomenological sense, they don't exist for the client.

One client, Ruth, had a childhood dominated by domestic violence and the effects of alcoholism; no-one talked about it, or was allowed to mention or show any emotion: denial was the order of the day. Ruth described this as being submerged in an 'emotional effluence' which was toxic. The way to survive was to do as she was told and, in effect and in practice, not to exist in her own right. Ruth felt paralysed, often physically nauseous, and became passive, believing that it was impossible to seek or receive help. She began to read some self-help books, and then came across some books by Carl Rogers. Eventually, she did approach a therapist. Whilst she had some good experiences with some different therapists, she describes how she 'managed' therapy:

> My hypersensitivity meant that I was hyperaroused and vigilant to any perceived threat. I would retreat quickly, freezing solid at times, dissociated due to the intense level of threat, fear and pain I was experiencing. I watched each counsellor like a hawk, convinced by my experiences that none of them could be trusted with the real me: that who I was, how I felt, what I thought would again be crushed.

Later, Ruth reflected on what enabled her to take the risk to disclose and work through her experiences with a person-centred therapist:

> On reflection, it was really important to me that I wasn't judged; that there was no agenda set by the counsellor; that I was able to follow my own emotional landscape and to navigate a way through which was right for me, in my own time; that, when I had difficulties, I was not criticized or pushed onto emotional landmines which I was not ready to feel. I was nurtured, supported, accepted, and given empathy. This process enabled me to discover who I was again, what I thought, how I felt; and to recognize that the fear I had experienced and had been paralysed by was a normal reaction to an abnormal set of circumstances.

What this condition demands is the fine empathic attunement of the therapist not only to the client's own process but also to the client's relational process with the therapist. This is the basis of a more organismic, relational approach to client- or person-centred therapy and, in our experience, is essential to work with people who have been traumatised in relationship.

Conclusion: process and fluidity

Person-centred psychology proposes an outcome which is a process. Rogers (1958/1967b) describes this as: 'new experiencing with immediacy [in which] feeling and cognition interpenetrate, self is subjectively present in the experience, volition is simply the subjective following of a harmonious balance of organismic direction'. With regard to the recovery from trauma this involves:

- The recovery of organismic and self regulation – which involves the gradual and increasing ability of the client to transfer from one state to another with decreasing amounts of external help.
- The decrease in denial of experience and distortion of perception.
- The development of healthy strategies for managing experience and feelings, and for problem-solving.
- The increased integration of experiencing with thinking.
- The increased ability to trust oneself and the other/the environment.

Acknowledgements

We are grateful to the editors Val Cunningham and David Mann, and to Rachel Freeth and Renate Geuzinge for their comments on an earlier draft of this chapter, and to 'Ruth' for her contribution.

References

American Psychiatric Association (1987) *Diagnostic and Statistical Manual of Mental Disorders*, 3rd ed. Washington, DC: APA.

American Psychiatric Association (2000) *Diagnostic and Statistical Manual of Mental Disorders*, 4th ed., text rev. Washington, DC: APA. (Original work published 1994)

Angyal, A. (1941) *Foundations for a Science of Personality*. New York: Commonwealth Fund.

Angyal, A. (1973) *Neurosis & Treatment: A Holistic Theory*. New York: John Wiley. (Original work published 1965)

Audergon, A. (2004) Collective trauma: the nightmare of history. *Psychotherapy and Politics International*, 2(1): 16–31.

Axelrod, R. (1984) *The Evolution of Cooperation*. New York: Basic Books.

Barrett-Lennard, G.T. (1998) *Carl Rogers' Helping System*. London: Sage.

Bozarth, J. D. (1998) Unconditional positive regard. In J. D. Bozarth, *Person-Centered Therapy: A Revolutionary Paradigm* (pp. 83–88). Ross-on-Wye, UK: PCCS Books.

Bromberg, P. M. (2006) *Awakening the Dreamer: Clinical Journeys.* London: Routledge.

Coffeng, T. (2002) Contact in the therapy of trauma and dissociation. In G. Wyatt & P. Sanders (eds), *Contact and Perception* (pp. 153–167). Ross-on-Wye, UK: PCCS Books.

Coffeng, T. (2005) The therapy of dissociation: its phases and problems. *Person-Centered & Experiential Psychotherapies*, 4(2): 90–105.

Coghlan, D. & McIlduff, E. (1990) Structuring and non directiveness in group facilitation. *Person-Centered Review*, 5: 13–29.

Cook, A., Spinazzola, J., Ford, J., Lanktree, C. et al. (2005) Complex trauma in children and adolescents. *Psychiatric Annals*, 35: 390–398.

Damasio, A. R. (1996) *Descartes' Error: Emotion, Reason and the Human Brain.* New York: Grosset/Putnam. (Original work published 1994)

Feldenkreis, M. (1981) *The Elusive Obvious.* Cupertino, CA: Meta Publications.

Fernald, P. S. (2000) Carl Rogers: body-centered counsellor. *Journal of Counselling & Development*, 78: 172–179.

Fonagy, P., Gergely, G., Jurist, E. L. & Target, M. (2002) *Affect Regulation, Mentalization, and the Development of the Self.* New York: Other Press.

Goldstein, K. (1995) *The Organism.* New York: Zone Books. (Original work published 1934)

Grinberg, L. (1995) Nonverbal communication in the clinic with borderline patients. *Contemporary Psychoanalysis*, 31: 92.

Hall, C. & Lindzey, G. (1978) *Theories of Personality*, 3rd edn. New York: Wiley.

Janet, P. (1907) *The Major Symptoms of Hysteria.* New York: Macmillan.

Janet, P. (1976) *Psychological Healing: A Historical and Clinical Study*, trans. E. and C. Paul, 2 vols. (Original work published in 1919)

Kohut, H. (1977) *The Restoration of the Self.* New York: International Universities Press.

Levine, P. A. with Frederick, A. (1997) *Waking the Tiger: Healing Trauma.* Berkeley, CA: North Atlantic Books.

Ogden, P. & Minton, K. (2000) Sensorimotor psychotherapy: one method for processing traumatic memory. *Traumatology*, 6(3).

Perls, F. (1969) *Ego, Hunger and Aggression.* New York: Vintage. (Original work published 1947)

Prouty, G. F. (1976) Pre-therapy, a method of treating pre-expressive, psychotic and retarded patients. *Psychotherapy: Theory, Research and Practice*, 13(3): 290–295.

Resnick, H., Yehuda, R. & Acierno, R. (1997) Acute post-rape plasma cortisol, alcohol use, and PTSD symptom profile among recent rape victims. *Annals of the New York Academy of Sciences*, 821: 433–436.

Rogers, C. R. (1942) *Counseling and Psychotherapy: Newer Concepts in Practice.* Boston: Houghton Mifflin.

Rogers, C. R. (1951) *Client-Centered Therapy.* London: Constable.

Rogers, C. R. (1959) A theory of therapy, personality and interpersonal relationships, as developed in the client-centred framework. In S. Koch (ed.), *Psychology: A Study of a Science.* Vol. 3: *Formulation of the Person and the Social Context* (pp. 184–256). New York: McGraw-Hill.

Rogers, C. R. (1967a) Some of the directions evident in therapy. In *On Becoming a Person* (pp. 73–106). London: Constable. (Original work published 1953)

Rogers, C. R. (1967b) A process conception of psychotherapy. In *On Becoming a Person* (pp. 125–159). London: Constable. (Original work published in 1958)

Rogers, C. R. (1967c) This is me. In *On Becoming a Person* (pp. 3–27). London: Constable. (Original work published 1961)

Rogers, C. R. (1967d) A silent young man. In C. R. Rogers, E. T. Gendlin, D. J. Kiesler & C. B. Truax (eds), *The Therapeutic Relationship and its Impact: A Study of Psychotherapy with Schizophrenics* (pp. 401–416). Madison, WI: University of Wisconsin Press.

Rogers, C. R. (1990) The necessary and sufficient conditions of therapeutic personality change. In H. Kirschenbaum & V. L. Henderson (eds) *The Carl Rogers Reader* (pp. 219–235). London: Constable. (Original work published 1957)

Sacks, O. (1995) Foreword. In K. Goldstein, *The Organism* (pp. 7–14). New York: Zone Books.

Sanders, P. (2000) Mapping person-centred approaches to counselling and psychotherapy. *Person-Centred Practice*, 8(2): 62–74.

Schore, A. N. (1994) *Affect Regulation and the Origin of the Self: The Neurobiology of Emotional Development*. Hillsdale, NJ: Lawrence Erlbaum Associates.

Schore, A. N. (2006) *The Art of the Science of Psychotherapy*. Workshop, London, 25–26 May.

Schore, A. N. (2007) *Attachment Trauma and the Developing Right Brain: Origins of Pathological Dissociation*. Lecture. Confer Trauma Conference, London, 16 September.

Speierer, G.-W. (1990) Toward a specific illness concept of client-centered therapy. In G. Lietaer, J. Rombauts & R. Van Balen (eds) *Client-Centered and Experiential Psychotherapy in the Nineties* (pp. 337–359). Leuven: Leuven University Press.

Speierer, G.-W. (1996) Client-centered psychotherapy according to the differential incongruence model (DIM). In R. Hutterer, G. Pawlowsky, P. F. Schmid & R. Stipsits (eds) *Client-Centered and Experiential Psychotherapy: A Paradigm in Motion* (pp. 299–311). Frankfurt am Main, Germany: Peter Lang.

Stubbs, J. P. & Bozarth, J. D. (1996) The integrative statement of Carl R. Rogers. In R. Hutterer, G. Pawlowsky, P. F. Schmid & R. Stipsits (eds) *Client-Centered and Experiential Psychotherapy: A Paradigm in Motion* (pp. 25–33). Frankfurt am Main, Germany: Peter Lang.

Tudor, K. & Worrall, M. (2006) *Person-Centred Therapy: A Clinical Philosophy*. London: Routledge.

Warner, M. S. (1998) A client-centered approach to therapeutic work with dissociated and fragile process. In L. Greenberg, J. Watson & G. Lietaer (eds), *Handbook of Experiential Psychotherapy* (pp. 368–387). New York: The Guilford Press.

Warner, M. S. (2000) Person-centred therapy at the difficult edge: a developmentally based model of fragile and dissociated process. In D. Mearns & B. Thorne, *Person-Centred Therapy Today: New Frontiers in Theory and Practice* (pp. 144–171). London: Sage.

10 The therapist as a 'bad object'

The use of countertransference enactment to facilitate psychoanalytic therapy

Penny Webster

So in the end we succeed by failing – failing the patient's way. This is a long distance from the simple theory of cure by corrective experience.

(Winnicott, 1965, p. 258)

The hypothesis presented here, perhaps somewhat paradoxically, is that it is traumatic for some patients when the damaging past *is not* in the present. In other words therapy enactments may actually facilitate therapy and prevent trauma with some patients. Patients who are attached to 'bad objects' are better able to make use of the therapy situation if the therapist behaves similarly to these objects. By behaving in a manner similar to the patient's 'bad objects' the therapist becomes familiar and therefore a 'good object' for the patient. These patients need their therapists to be similar to their original objects in order to feel safe in the therapeutic environment. Patients who are 'attached to bad objects' are often unable to tolerate interpretation, and therefore traditional approaches to intervention are not effective. I will suggest that through what I term a 'strategic/relational' approach to treatment to facilitate communication with patients who are attached to 'bad objects', a therapist may use the deliberate/strategic enactment of countertransference responses in the beginning stages of therapy.

The strategic use of the technique of 'joining', as expounded by Minuchin (1974) in the field of family therapy, may facilitate communication and the gradual development in the patient of the ability to tolerate interpretation within the psychotherapeutic relationship. This suggestion challenges the basic 'frame' of traditional psychoanalysis and also extends the notions of intervention associated with the relational psychoanalytic approach (Aron, 1996).

Alexander and French (1946) challenged the psychoanalytic ideals of abstinence and neutrality by proposing that psychotherapists should consciously adopt an attitude and behave in a manner *contrary* to their patient's negative transference expectations, since re-enactment of early object relations would be traumatic. Although this chapter also challenges psychoanalytic abstinence and neutrality it differs from Alexander and French in proposing that the therapist should deliberately adopt a mode of response that 'fits' with the patient's negative transference expectations. The therapist should utilize his countertransference feelings and enactments to plan strategies of intervention that are in keeping with the intra-psychic structure of the patient. This may involve active intervention, an altering of style or mode of communication, as well as verbal intervention, rather than the traditionally accepted technique of interpretation.

The theoretical context

The context for this chapter is based firstly on Fairbairn's (1952) conceptualization of psychopathology as an 'attachment to bad objects'. Ogden's (1994) view of interpretation will be mentioned briefly because it is my view that Ogden's changing conceptualizations of technique form a link between more traditional notions of technique and relational psychoanalysis. Relational psychoanalysis (Aron, 1996) serves as the conceptual framework for a new theory of intervention as proposed here, because relational psychoanalysis provides for the flexibility in technique required by the strategic use of enactment.

The context of this chapter is also based on my training as a clinical psychologist. A major influence was the understanding of psychopathology and psychotherapy from an interpersonal framework, based on the work of Sullivan (1953). From this perspective, the therapist is seen as a 'participant-observer'. The interpersonal approach that I adopted was also influenced by the Mental Research Institute, founded by Jackson in 1958 (Watzlawick et al., 1967). This institute developed the 'strategic model' of psychotherapy. Strategic psychotherapists believe that it is impossible not to influence or manipulate while interacting. The problem is, therefore, not how influence and manipulation can be avoided, but how they can best be comprehended and used in the interests of the patient. The therapist's main task is one of taking deliberate action to alter poorly functioning patterns of interaction as powerfully, effectively and efficiently as possible.

Another notion central to the strategic approach is that of 'fit' or 'structural coupling' (Dell, 1982, 1985). Maturana (Dell, 1982), a biologist, describes any system (the individual, the family, society, as well as non-human systems) as being more or less structurally plastic, a structurally plastic system being one that undergoes structural changes as a result of interacting with itself, its environment and other structurally plastic systems.

In the therapeutic environment this can be conceptualized as a patient system, which is (theoretically) less structurally plastic, and a therapist system, which, because of the therapist's relative ability to self-reflect and to reflect on the patient-therapist system, is more structurally plastic. Dell (1982) argues that psychotherapy helps individuals to develop to a new state if the interventions fit with the current system structure (structural coupling – Maturana). The therapist therefore needs to adapt his or her behaviour to 'fit' with that of the patient. However, Dell (1985) points out that in order to be successful in triggering system-transforming behaviour the therapist must also use behaviours (i.e. interventions) that differ from those being used within the system. Dell describes the individual's behavioural coherence as the lock and the interventions used as the key.

> It is always the lock that determines which keys will work. There is no truth (i.e. one key). There is no causality (i.e. the key that makes the lock open). There is only fit (i.e. those keys that are complementary to the lock).
>
> (Dell, 1985, p. 35)

The emphasis is thus on the therapist's structure being the same as the patient's structure (fit), as well as being slightly different (the notion of movement) – the key that fits, turning the lock.

The strategic therapist thus manipulates his relationship with the patient in order to achieve change in the patient's relationships with others. One of the most important tasks of a strategic therapist is thus to 'join' with whatever system presents itself. 'Joining' (Minuchin, 1974) can be described as a changing of communication style on the part of the therapist, to 'fit' with the communication patterns with which he is working.

The notion of the therapist as a participant-observer, who can strategically alter his way of communicating to 'join' or 'fit' with the patient, is thus the starting point for further thinking about the therapeutic relationship. As mentioned above, Fairbairn's notion of psychopathology as an 'attachment to bad objects' forms the theoretical basis for the conceptualization of psychopathology. The proposed mode of intervention in this chapter is based on my training as described above, as well as relational psychoanalytic conceptualizations of intervention, which will be discussed below.

The attachment to bad objects

In his first theoretical chapter in 1940, Fairbairn (1952) hypothesized that the child's reaction to the experience of being rejected by its object is an increased attachment to the object that failed to meet its needs. Unsatisfying relationships are experienced as intolerable and are internalized as both 'rejecting internal objects' and 'exciting internal objects'. Also internalized are aspects of the ego identified with the 'rejecting' and 'exciting' internal objects and the affective or libidinal link between them. These internal object relations units (the patient's internal world or intra-psychic structure) influence all further interpersonal relations and alter the way in which they are perceived. Fairbairn describes that the patient's internal world is maintained as a 'closed system'. He says that: *'it becomes still another aim of psychoanalytic treatment to effect breaches of the closed system which constitutes the patient's inner world, and thus to make this world accessible to the influence of outer reality'* (Fairbairn, 1958, p. 380; emphasis in the original).

There is thus a reversal of the expected movement of going towards 'good objects' and away from 'bad' ones. Fairbairn states that the release of bad objects from the unconscious is one of the chief aims of psychotherapy. He emphasizes though that the *bad objects can only be released if the analyst has become established as a sufficiently good object for the patient* (italics mine).

Although Fairbairn has written little on technique, it seems that he maintained a standard classical psychoanalytic technique, focusing on the therapist's use of interpretations.

Interpretation

Interpretation is the chief form of intervention from a classical and from an object relations psychoanalytic perspective – although there is some debate about what an interpretation actually is. For instance Ogden (1994) uses a definition of interpretation provided by Laplanche and Pontalis, where interpretation is described as a procedure that brings out the latent meaning in what the subject says and does.

In contrast to more traditional approaches to technique, Ogden (1994) extends conceptualizations of interpretation, by including in his notion of interpretation the idea of 'interpretative action'. By 'interpretative action', Ogden (1994) is referring to the analyst's communication of his understanding of an aspect of the transference/countertransference by an activity other than verbal symbolization. Ogden cautions that an important aspect of interpretative action is the analyst's consistent formulation for himself of the evolving interpretation in words. He states that in the absence of such efforts, the idea of interpretative action can degenerate into the analyst's rationalization for impulsive non-self-reflective acting out.

Further, Ogden (1994) pays attention to the manner of the patient's verbal communications, which he calls the 'matrix of the transference'. According to Ogden (1994), the analyst should interpret the interplay between the context (matrix) and content of the analytic interaction. Furthermore, Ogden describes how he often deliberately matches his verbal interpretations, and his interpretations-in-action to the patient's communication style.

A relational approach

It seems that Ogden (1994), with his acknowledgement of 'interpretative action', recognizes the first axiom of communications theory as expounded by Watzlawick, Beavin and Jackson in 1967, i.e. behaviour has no opposite. In other words, there is no such thing as non-behaviour – one cannot not behave.

Relational analyst Aron (1996) concurs with this. He states that the classical model of psychoanalysis distinguishes between 'words' and 'acts'. He agrees that we are always communicating verbally and non-verbally. According to this line of thinking, words are also acts, and acts also have meaning. It follows then that everything is an 'act'. To do nothing is an act as much as doing something. The emphasis is thus not only on what we say, but also how we say it and indeed whether we say it at all, as well as on what we do, how we do it and again whether we do it at all. Aron sees an interpretation as a creative expression of the analyst's conception of some aspect of the patient. He refers to relational writers who prefer the word 'intervention' to 'interpretation'.

From a relational perspective, the psychoanalytic process can thus be seen as one of negotiation (Aron, 1996). From this perspective, re-enactment of the patient's relational constellations is seen as inevitable, valuable and therapeutic. The emphasis, however, is that this time, it is important that the patient has a new experience of relating based on new meanings that have been generated via verbal and non-verbal communication.

Building on the new openness to pluralism and diversity advocated by relational psychoanalysis, this chapter aims to explore the possibility of incorporating techniques used by the strategic therapists (Minuchin, 1974) into psychoanalytic possibilities for intervention. Based on the relational notions of the therapeutic process as a process of negotiation, and accepting that modification of technique is required when working with some patients, this chapter endorses the inevitability and usefulness of enactment. However it takes relational theorizing one step further. It advocates the *deliberate and strategic re-enactment* of countertransference by the therapist, an intervention very different from the usual psychoanalytic technique of interpretation and also from the relational technique of inevitable enactment and interpretation described above.

A 'strategic/relational approach'

My hypothesized approach is based on the strategic approaches to psychotherapy. The strategic approaches advocate the importance of the therapist as 'participant/observer' and suggest that the therapist utilize an armamentarium of deliberate and well-thought-out strategies to facilitate change in families. This chapter suggests that the psychoanalytic therapist use the strategic technique of 'joining' (Minuchin, 1974) to focus on the 'family' inside the individual. It is suggested here that the therapist utilize his countertransference responding (i.e. his/her own reactions) to identify the 'family' within the individual. According to my strategic/relational model the therapist is required to deliberately enact the 'bad' relational constellations that he has been able to identify via his countertransference responding, in order to enter the 'closed system' of internalized object relations units described by Fairbairn. This means that the therapist initially has to be 'bad' from a traditional psychoanalytic perspective (deliberate enactment), in order to become 'good' (use verbal symbolic communication – interpretation).

According to Minuchin's theory of family therapy (1974), in order to 'join' with the family or different parts of the family, the therapist may emphasize the aspects of his personality that synchronize with that of the family. Correspondingly, according to the hypothesized approach, the therapist alters his or her style of communication to 'fit' with that of the 'family' he or she has identified *within* the individual via his or her countertransference responding.

Joining

Minuchin states that like an anthropologist, the family therapist joins the culture of the family with which he is dealing. He experiences the pressures of the family. According to Minuchin (1974), the family's impact on the therapist is what makes the family known to him (i.e. his countertransference responses from a psychoanalytic perspective). At the same time, he observes the family from the outside. In an oscillating rhythm he engages and disengages with the family. To understand and know a family in this way is a vital component of family therapy.

According to this line of thinking about therapy, the family moves only if the therapist has been able to enter the family in ways that are syntonic to it. He must accommodate the family and intervene in a manner that the particular family can accept. Unlike the anthropologist, the family therapist (acknowledging that he cannot not influence) is intent on changing the culture he joins. Change, however, is dependent on the process of joining. According to Minuchin joining techniques may not always advance the family toward the therapeutic goals, but they are successful when they ensure that the family return for the next session. He states that joining a family requires a therapist to adapt.

Minuchin says that to join the family, the therapist must accept the family's organization and style and blend with them. He must experience the family's interactional patterns and the power of the patterns. Minuchin says that the therapist must recognize the predominance of certain family themes and participate with family members in their exploration.

According to this therapeutic modality, the therapist thus adapts his or her style of communication to that of the family. Minuchin (1974) details three types of joining techniques: maintenance, tracking and mimesis. *Maintenance* refers to the technique of providing planned support of the family structure, as the therapist perceives it and analyses it. The therapist elects to maintain specific interactional patterns. Maintenance operations often involve the active confirmation and support of family patterns. Minuchin (1974) describes *tracking* as a technique where the therapist follows the content of the family's communication and behaviour and encourages them to continue. Minuchin describes *mimesis* as a universal human operation. A therapist uses mimesis to accommodate to a family's style and affective range. He or she adopts the family's tempo of communication, slowing the pace, for example, in a family that is accustomed to long pauses and slow responses. In a jovial family the therapist becomes jovial and expansive. In a family with a restricted style, communications become sparse.

Regarding the technique of joining, it is Minuchin's view (1974) that when used deliberately, joining can speed up the early phase of treatment.

It is suggested here that this technique should be included with psychoanalytic techniques when working with individuals who are attached to both internal and external 'bad objects' (Fairbairn, 1952).

After the task of joining has been achieved Minuchin (1974) describes the next type of intervention required as 'restructuring'. From the perspective of my suggested 'strategic/relational approach' however, the initial joining procedure is aimed at establishing a therapeutic relationship in which the patient is gradually able to internalize the therapist as a 'good object' and in time to tolerate verbal interpretations.

A clinical example

The therapist is L, a clinical psychologist in private practice. She and her patient Thandi were part of a study into the hypothesized approach (Webster, 2004). Thandi is described by L as an attractive, friendly 11-year-old girl. Her presenting problem was that of stealing, usually food, from her adopted mother, teacher, friends, and the school tuck-shop. She attended therapy for six months on a weekly basis, with some disruptions because of holiday breaks. The therapy ended because Thandi's family relocated to another city.

Background information

Thandi is the child of a homeless street woman. Her mother was a poverty-stricken alcoholic, and Thandi was neglected and uncared for until taken into a children's home at the age of five months. The rules in the children's home were rigid and strict. Thandi's adoptive mother C is a political activist and journalist and started to visit the baby when she was six months old. She describes her as being a really sweet baby – 'as good as gold'. C adopted Thandi and took her home for about six months, but then due to administrative issues regarding cross-racial adoptions, Thandi was removed to the children's home for a further six months. When she was 18 months old, Thandi was taken to live with C full-time. C subsequently married M, as a result of which Thandi found herself with an adopted sister aged five years and an adopted brother aged 18 months. The stealing started when she was six. The therapist, L, describes her impression of Thandi's home life as being chaotic. The mother is described as being very controlling and aggressive and the father as being withdrawn.

Progression of therapy

Thandi entered the therapy with some ambivalence. On the one hand, she said she needed 'more time to play'; on the other, she seemed extremely threatened by the unstructured nature of the psychoanalytic play situation. She seemed desperate to please the therapist, but evoked anxiety in the therapist, L, who increasingly felt pressurized to be pleasing herself, and also pressurized into telling Thandi what to do. The trauma of Thandi's past is replayed in the therapy situation by her extreme anxiety in response to the therapeutic situation, which she seemed to experience as being chaotic and unstructured, like her life was with her alcoholic mother when she was an infant, or as her current home situation is described by the therapist. However, as will be seen, when the therapist provides guidelines and structure, it is possible that she is re-enacting the rigid and strict children's home or the controlling mother. In response to this enactment Thandi initially becomes compliant, but the anxiety decreases and there is a possible shift in the therapy.

The main self and object representations evident in the therapy transcripts provided by L can be described in Fairbairn's (1952) terms discussed above, and are those of a split self (anxious and helpless, or pleasing – as good as gold), seen in relation to three different types of 'bad object': two types of rejecting objects (chaotic and punitive) and an exciting object (structured, but possibly rigid and strict). Examples are evident in the following interactions.

Therapy transcript 1

Thandi: (Looks around the room.) I don't know what to do.
L: Are you maybe wishing that I would tell you what to do?
Thandi: Yes (says this with great enthusiasm). At school I know what to do, and at home if I tell my mother that I'm bored she tells me to do my homework or go and play.
L: So you're used to being told what to do, or you just know, so being here with me and me not telling you feels different.
Thandi: Yes, at home I play with my beads (shows L the bracelets she made) or I read a bit or play outside.
L: Maybe also because you know school and home and what is expected of you. This place and me are new to you, it is all unfamiliar, so you're unsure of what to expect.
Thandi: I feel clueless.
L: The nervous feeling is uncomfortable and if I told you what to do then it would go away.

Thandi:	Yes.
L:	(I feel terrible pressure to help her out of her discomfort and am beginning to feel as if I'm being punitive.)

The therapy session continues in this manner with Thandi becoming increasingly anxious and requesting structure. She states repeatedly that she does not want to choose anything to play with in case L becomes upset.

L:	What do you think could happen if I got upset? Because it's like you're worried something bad could then happen.
Thandi:	If you got upset then you'd tell my mother and it would be a big 'gemors' (mess).
L:	You'd get into trouble.

It seems evident here that one part of the self is represented as helpless and scared in relation to a chaotic, disordered and unstructured (rejecting) object (her alcoholic mother or her current chaotic home environment). Another self/object relationship that is evident in the above, is a pleasing, compliant and very anxious self in relation to a rejecting object that is angry and punitive – the mother or therapist as experienced in the counter-transference (L experienced herself as being punitive) and in terms of Thandi's expectations of the therapist's responses.

Further on during the therapy, the self and object representations appear to change and reverse. Thandi enacts the object representations, seeming angry and punitive. The therapist, L, experiences corresponding self-representations that evoke feelings of being unsure, helpless and scared of punishment. An example follows.

Therapy transcript 2

Thandi:	Don't stare at me.
L:	You don't want me to even look at you.
Thandi:	You're staring and it's rude. Callie (her sister) stares and I hate it.
L:	I have become like your little sister who irritates you.
Thandi:	Look over there (she points to a place in the office opposite to her).
L:	(At this point I have already begun to feel disempowered and also helpless, like I cannot even think.) If I don't even look at you, but look over there then we feel as if we are far away from each other. Like we could be in different rooms even.
Thandi:	Get out!

During a follow-up interview in the study (Webster, 2004) the therapist L described a subsequent session where she felt that the anxiety related to the lack of structure became too overwhelming for herself and Thandi. She therefore decided to provide Thandi with directions (e.g. 'You can draw or paint'). L stated that this is not her usual style of therapy, and she experienced it as an enactment of the strict children's home environment. However, Thandi complied with the instructions. L stated that both she and Thandi had experienced extreme relief after this enactment. At the time she realized that this was a re-enactment of a strict or controlling object but she decided to go ahead with it anyway. She was also aware when she enacted that this may have been motivated by her own anxiety and by her own wish to be an ideal mother/therapist (as good as gold), an issue that she has become increasingly aware of during her own therapy and supervision. However she said that she felt strongly that Thandi's anxiety about her interpretative stance was related to the fact that from Thandi's perspective this was experienced as withholding (i.e. an enactment of the chaotic and potentially punitive object).

When asked during the interview whether she felt the enactment in the previous sessions facilitated therapy, L stated that she liked to think that Thandi had felt very understood and contained by her enactment of the exciting object, that is: by the actual provision of structure and guidelines for behaviour. Subsequent transcribed material shows a possible shift in the type of communication between the therapist and Thandi. An example of this different type of communication follows.

Therapy transcript 3

(Thandi had been caught stealing food. Thandi tells L that she took food on three occasions, and lied to cover it up, but was discovered eating it. She says that her mother had been screaming and swearing at her all the way to the session.)

Thandi: I know it was wrong, I know I shouldn't have taken the food and lied, but I can't help myself. (This is said in a truly desperate way, and L's heart goes out to her.)
L: It's something you can't control, and that's so hard to understand.
Thandi: I don't know why, and I don't know how this (therapy) has helped. I thought it would but I'm still doing it.
L: Like a confusion and a big disappointment.
Thandi: Well, I still don't know why I'm doing it and it's still there.
L: Yes.
Thandi: (cries quietly and talks more about therapy. She also talks about her mother) My Mom makes me unhappy. (Silence.)
Thandi: I hate her and wish I could have another Mom. I would keep my Father, but I know that it will never happen, that we are going to have to stay together. (Silence.)

Thandi: She shouts all the time, and when I try and talk to her and tell her not to shout, she says that she shouts because of me.

L: Like it's your fault.

Thandi: That if I didn't do these things then she would be nicer. I know that she doesn't want another daughter but I wish I could have another Mom.

When comparing the sessions it seems that there may be a change in the type of communication from one that is dominated by anxiety and enactments, evident in transcripts 1 and 2, and the communication that is evident in transcript 3. In transcript 3, it seems that the pressure to enact is absent. It seems that Thandi and L work together to create meaning out of events that have occurred outside of the therapeutic context. There are also comments that relate more directly to the therapeutic relationship where Thandi and L attempt to make sense of what they are working on together within the therapeutic context.

Discussion

The clinical material presented above illustrates the intentional use of countertransference enactment rather than interpretation. It seems that the therapist, L, was aware of the pressure to enact and was able to reflect on the pressure both in terms of her own psychological functioning and in terms of Thandi's self and object representations. None the less, L made the conscious decision to enact. It was her experience that this enactment provided considerable relief to the patient and that failure to enact would have been seen by Thandi as an enactment of a chaotic or punitive self/ object relationship and therefore more traumatic for her. L therefore decided to enact the exciting object representation. The enactment may be seen in terms of the 'joining' strategy described above. That is, L maintained Thandi's familiar interaction patterns by providing a strict structure; she confirmed Thandi's experience by asking questions and responding to her requests to tell her what to do; and she matched her hesitant tempo of communication – maintenance, tracking and mimesis (Minuchin, 1974). It is possible that the enactment, which can be seen in the light of 'joining', facilitated the treatment and provided a therapeutic climate where the patient was more easily able to articulate what was on her mind and was able to be receptive to a broader range of interpretation. Although this enactment may be seen as an enactment of an 'exciting object representation', i.e. the strict children's home or the strict mother, it also seems that L was very aware of the enactment and offered Thandi 'options' rather than a strict structure. She was also sensitive to Thandi's responses. Thus, although 'enacting a bad object', she was also a 'good object', joining with Thandi and understanding the meaning of her experiences.

Concluding remarks

The chapter proposes the deliberate and strategic use of countertransference responses as a therapeutic strategy. Traditional approaches emphasize 'thought about' verbal interpretations, and Ogden (1994) endorses 'thought about interpretative action'. Contemporary object relations approaches and relational psychoanalysis acknowledge that enactments are inevitable and should be 'thought about', possibly interpreted and at times disclosed, but it seems that both may have difficulty with deliberate and 'thought about' (strategic) enactment proposed here. For instance, Aron (1996) cautions that although in relational psychoanalysis the emphasis is on the fact that the analyst is a participant-observer, this should not be taken to mean that the analyst makes active or artificial attempts to participate or to influence the patient through the self-conscious or purposeful adoption of a role. Contemporary views of the use of countertransference enactment involve what Renik (1993, p. 410) calls: 'the skillful recovery of an error'; however this chapter calls for the skilful *re-enactment* of countertransference enactment, which may, initially be inadvertent. The suggested alteration in technique is designed to attach the patient to the therapist in the beginning stages of therapy, because as stated by Minuchin (1974) at least this ensures that the patient returns for the next session. In Fairbairn's terms: the bad objects can only be released if the analyst has become established as a sufficiently good object for the patient (Fairbairn, 1952).

To re-iterate the primary point: this chapter holds that for some patients when the past *is not* in the present, then *it is* traumatic. The emphasis is on the therapist's structure being the same as the patient's structure (fit), as well as being slightly different (the notion of movement) – the key that fits (the intervention), turning the lock (the patient) (Dell, 1985).

To paraphrase Winnicott (1965) quoted at the beginning of the chapter: in the end we succeed by failing . . . but failing the patient's way.

References

Alexander, F. & French, T. M. (1946) *Psychoanalytic Psychotherapy: Principles and Application*. New York: Ronald Press.
Aron, L. (1996) *A Meeting of Minds: Mutuality in Psychoanalysis*. London: The Analytic Press.
Dell, P. (1982) Homeostasis and family therapy: a brief history. *Family Process*, 21: 21–44.
Dell, P. (1985) Understanding Bateson and Maturana: toward a biological foundation for the natural sciences. *Journal of Marital & Family Therapy*, 11(1): 1–20.
Fairbairn, W. R. D. (1952) *Psychoanalytic Studies of the Personality*. London: Routledge & Kegan Paul.
Fairbairn, W. R. D. (1958) On the nature and aims of psychoanalytic treatment. *International Journal of Psychoanalysis*, 39: 374–385.

Minuchin, S. (1974) *Families and Family Therapy*. London: Tavistock Publications.

Ogden, T.H. (1994) *Subjects of Analysis*. London: Karnac Books.

Sullivan, H. S. (1953) *The Interpersonal Theory of Psychiatry*. New York: Norton.

Watzlawick, P., Beavin, J. B. & Jackson, D. D. (1967) *Pragmatics of Human Communication*. New York: Norton.

Webster, P. (2004) The therapist as 'bad object': The use of countertransfence enactment to facilitate communication in therapy. Unpublished doctoral dissertation, Rhodes University, Grahamstown, South Africa.

Winnicott, D. W. (1965) The capacity to be alone. In D. W. Winnicott *The Maturational Processes and the Facilitating Environment* (pp. 29–37). New York: International University Press.

11 Working with refugees

An enactment of trauma and guilt

Janet McDermott

When I first heard that my city was signing up to a policy of forcible detention and relocation of refugees, I was ashamed and angry. When I heard that people fleeing persecution and torture were to be labelled 'asylum seekers', not refugees, and were to be assumed to be lying until they could prove the truth of their tragic stories, I vowed never to use the term myself. I sought to distance myself from the new agencies springing up to manage the influx of bewildered souls shunted up the M1 by the coachload on a weekly basis.

But I could not keep away. In doing nothing I experienced the collusion and abdication of the 'bystander'. For reasons I describe later, I felt implicated and compelled to involve myself, and to demonstrate some solidarity. So now I find myself in my fourth year of working as a counsellor in a primary medical service established for so-called 'asylum seekers' forcibly dispersed by the Home Office to Sheffield from London and the South East. In the counselling room I grapple with the minute-by-minute impact of my deeply emotional response to this situation on my therapeutic practice. I ask myself all the time whether I am responding out of my own guilt or anger or grief, and check constantly the appropriateness of my responses because I am in this maelstrom too. I am not separate from it, though I have a different location within it from my clients.

In this chapter I explore the enactment of trauma in therapy with refugee clients, and consider an example from my work as a person-centred therapist with clients who have recently arrived in Britain as refugees and are seeking asylum here.

Enactment as co-creation

Enactment to me means the bringing into being, and setting in motion, of structures, events and processes that have particular and powerful meaning for the context in which they occur. An enactment in therapy involves the bringing into being of a process or events that replay earlier processes or events, or recreate earlier structures, in the lives of the client and the therapist. Particular earlier material from the lives of both people interacts in complex ways to bring about a unique and co-created drama in the therapeutic relationship. The replaying is not intentional but arises out of the collision of material in both the client and the therapist that is not in the awareness of either person at the start of the enactment process. In examining the example I explore in this chapter, I identify the elements of it that were known, and those that were initially out of my awareness, in order to understand the dynamic that produced the enactment.

As a person-centred therapist, I understand the vast range of responses, sensations and feelings through which I move each day to be available to my awareness to differing degrees, dependent on whether they fit with or threaten my concept of self. If they fit with my concept of self I will be open to receiving them and will be able to name and integrate them into the flow of my ongoing experiencing. If they threaten my concept of self they may remain hidden from me and will not be susceptible to integration.

In his theory of personality and behaviour, Rogers describes integration as being a state when

> all the sensory and visceral experiences [of the organism] are admissible to awareness through accurate symbolization, and organizable into one system which is internally consistent and which is, or is related to, the structure of self.
>
> (Rogers 1951, p. 513)

An enactment occurs in a therapeutic relationship because the emotional material at its source is sufficiently hidden, or out of the awareness of both parties, for the enactment to evolve within the relationship over some time before becoming apparent to either the client or the therapist. If the material is identified too early the enactment is effectively thwarted. It needs adequate 'cover' to come to fruition. It is arguable whether it is always better if the therapist is attuned enough and astute enough to spot a potential enactment and nip it in the bud, or whether the 'acting out' of previously unprocessed motivation and experience from client and therapist in the dynamic arena of a co-created enactment can be productive in itself.

Value is placed in the person-centred approach on the openness of the therapist to the emerging flow of experiencing in herself and within the relationship, and on the surfacing of unanticipated material for both client and therapist. There is no assumption that she will know before she starts, or at any point in the journey with a client, all that will surface next. This is particularly the case for British-born therapists like myself, working with clients whose experiences in other parts of the world of turbulence, communal violence and state terror are beyond our own experiences. Andrew Cooper and Sue Rendall writing about their experiences of therapeutic work with survivors of trauma in Kosovo, observe that often we do not know that we do not know how to begin to listen to their experience. Actually, to do so is merely to enact the first principle of all sound therapeutic work. To achieve this entails abandoning the known and familiar and becoming, in some measure, strangers to ourselves.

(Cooper and Rendall, 2002, p. 252)

In the description that follows of an enactment in therapy, I start by focusing on what was known to me initially, and what was hidden from me, of my own motivations in undertaking the work. I move on to examine what became known to me during the therapy of the client's process, and then consider aspects of my own motivation and the client's inner relationship to his trauma that came to light in the dynamic process of the enactment. I consider the danger for the client in my missing the evolving enactment at a crucial point, and the value of the experience for him in the reconnection with his own agency that resulted from my missing it.

The therapist's motivations

I am a person-centred therapist of Asian heritage. In the context of a primary care health team I offer short and medium term counselling to refugees suffering the effects of trauma. I refer to my clients as 'refugees', although current government policy dictates that they be termed 'asylum seekers' until their asylum applications are accepted and they are granted refugee status in law. I use the term 'refugee' in the sense it has always been used across the world to refer to people forcibly displaced from their homes by violent and traumatic events.

I work with people who have experienced recent trauma of a personal, collective and global nature. On arrival in Britain this trauma is usually compounded by re-traumatisation in the asylum-seeking process itself, with its threat of imminent return to the site of the trauma and associated oppressive processes of protracted legal applications, enforced inactivity, evictions, destitution, regular signings at police stations, subsistence by vouchers, and forced removals. As a therapist engaged with clients in making sense of accumulations of terrifying, annihilating and bewildering experiences, I face dilemmas about where to place myself in the work without being overwhelmed by the global power struggles and colonial legacies embodied in the lived experiences I am sitting with every day. I struggle to feel clear about my own responses to the contested political context in which the therapeutic work is located, and I am sometimes in danger of getting lost in the resonances of my own history and inheritance. There is much potential for both the client and myself to replay, or enact from, our personal, family and community histories in the arena of the counselling room.

When I started working with refugees I felt motivated to show my solidarity as a black woman with a group of other black people I perceived to be totally excluded from the society I lived in. This was a conscious, but somewhat abstract, political rationalisation; I was less aware of the layers of feeling below the surface of inherited survivor guilt, my need to atone for privilege, and my own search for acceptance, community and sanctuary. This left me in a state of some incongruence in relation to my work, as there was strong emotional material being touched by the work, but this was out of my awareness and not being articulated, at least initially.

Dick Blackwell suggests that therapists' motivation to get involved in work with refugees is often connected to a need to engage with areas of the self that are deeply hidden and have escaped previous examination. He says of counsellors working at the Medical Foundation for the Care of Victims of Torture:

> Very few counsellors . . . have very much idea of what, at a deep intrapsychic level, motivates them to engage in work with survivors of torture and organized violence. This suggests that such motivation exists in areas of the psyche barely touched on in training analysis . . . It further suggests that undertaking this sort of work is a way of engaging with some of these outstanding issues.
>
> (Blackwell, 2005, p. 81)

In my own development, unresolved childhood experiences of feeling excluded for being different produced a yearning for belonging and acceptance that could not be satisfied purely within the family and was unavailable to me in the white community. This yearning, combined with early conditions of worth of social responsibility and the duty to give something back to society, created a strong pull in adulthood towards helping roles in black community settings. The source and power of this pull and its role in resolving and integrating painful childhood experiences were not fully apparent to me when I began practising as a counsellor. As a trainee black counsellor I had limited access to forums in which I could explore freely the complexity of my feelings about my own racial identity or anticipate the consequences of such feelings in my work.

In outlining the conditions he felt were necessary and sufficient for therapeutic change, Rogers identified that the client and therapist must be in psychological contact, that the therapist must experience unconditional positive regard and empathy for the client and must be able to communicate these to the client, and that the therapist shall be congruent and integrated in the relationship (Rogers, 1957). He describes congruence as a state when 'the feelings the therapist is experiencing are available to him, available to his awareness, and he is able to live these feelings, be them, and be able to communicate them if appropriate' (Rogers, 1967). If I describe briefly the factors in my personal history that link directly to some of the experiences of my clients, it will become apparent how these factors both contributed to my ability to be empathic and offer unconditional positive regard to my clients, while their unacknowledged nature compromised my self-awareness and my congruence.

Born in Britain, I am the child of Anglo-Indian migrants who left India in the uncertainty and fear following the massacres of Partition. My parents came from a minority community whose mixed Indian and European roots went back generations and had isolated them from both Indian and British communities throughout the colonial period in India. The departure of many of my relatives from India was a hurried and fearful one, and for my mother involved being persuaded by family members to leave her own mother behind, without having the information that her mother was dying or knowing that would be their final parting. My mother's experience of bereavement across continents, robbed of any opportunity for ending or leave-taking, was mirrored for me in a sudden bereavement across continents that occurred in my own life decades later. It is also mirrored many times over in the countless unresolved losses and separations I hear about in my work with refugee clients whose relatives have been killed in unexpected and traumatic circumstances, or are missing in violent conflicts and may never be found.

The arrival of refugees in Sheffield, the city where I had grown up and still lived and worked, triggered feelings in me that had not been fully articulated up to that point. The shame and complicity I felt with the government's 'dispersal' policy, of scooping up disorientated refugees newly arrived in the country and tossing them northwards indiscriminately, was both an intellectual rebellion and the intensely personal guilt of knowing there was no superior merit or desert to distinguish my family from today's refugees other than timing and luck. My family had made the passage to England before the first immigration laws pulled up the drawbridge against the peoples of Asia and Africa. Comparing the treatment of newly arriving refugees today with the alacrity with which members of my family disembarked at Tilbury Docks and walked straight into their new lives 50 or more years before I had a sense of, 'there but for the grace of God . . .' My first instinct was to have nothing to do with the Asylum Law and its implementation, but I also could not turn my gaze away. Petruska Clarkson talks of a fourth role of the 'bystander' in the victim-persecutor-rescuer drama triangle originally developed by Stephen Karpman (Clarkson, 1996). I felt a rebellion against occupying the 'bystander' role. I felt compelled to find out more, to bear witness and to face a pain I later realised I felt implicated in causing, and felt guilty for not experiencing directly myself. This unacknowledged guilt was combined with a connected search as an Asian woman with a complicated mixed heritage background, for acceptance and validation from other black people, which had been in my awareness for a long time and had motivated most of my life and career choices.

Embarking on therapeutic relationships with this complex legacy of known, partially known and largely unacknowledged feelings in relation to my own and collective family experiences of migration, dislocation and bereavement, I was likely to become caught up with my clients in revisiting their experiences and my own in disorganised ways and through processes that might remain out of my awareness for some time. I was indeed a 'stranger to myself' and vulnerable to the occurrence of processes containing strongly evocative material, that were not amenable to prediction or prevention. Enactments of trauma are precisely such powerful and covert processes.

Refugee trauma and re-traumatisation

Having examined some of the material I was bringing into the work in my person as the therapist, I will say something about the general context of the work and will then describe a therapeutic relationship with a client I shall call Albert, which illustrates the interaction of the client's traumatic experience and my own unresolved feelings about the work to produce a powerful enactment of the client's original trauma.

The medical team I am located in was established to work with asylum-seeking patients dispersed by the Home Office to Sheffield. Most of our patients have fled to the UK from areas of the world where communities and whole countries have been profoundly traumatised for centuries by colonial oppression, war and entrenched political and communal conflicts – places like Afghanistan, Iran, Iraq, Palestine, Congo, Burundi, Sierra Leone. Some people have grown up in an environment of constant fear and serious daily threat to life; others have had childhood assumptions of security and peace shattered by sudden violent events. Recent trauma experienced by refugees is likely to have involved witnessing or experiencing violent assault, rape, murder or torture, including witnessing the violent deaths of close family members, and experiencing life-threatening situations in attempting to flee. Most of my clients are at some stage of applying for asylum on political or humanitarian grounds, but a significant number have exhausted all avenues of appeal and are homeless, destitute and vulnerable to deportation at any moment. Most clients want me to know something of the past trauma they have experienced; not all want to work directly on it. Many choose to focus on the present trauma they are experiencing in the asylum system, as the current insecurity, fear, grief and sense of betrayal they experience in their lives is too overwhelming to allow space for processing past material. Whatever the focus, the past trauma is present in some way in the current therapeutic relationship, and it encounters, and evokes, powerful emotional material from my own history.

Whether working with past or present material, we need to understand the ways in which refugee clients feel overwhelmed by huge political and historical forces over which they have no control. As Embleton Tudor and Tudor discuss in their chapter on a person-centred theory of trauma and enactment, the individual self is a construct located within a whole organism, which exists in constant relationship to its environment. Human beings in different contexts differentiate to differing degrees their individual selves from the family and social groups into which they're born. In Western countries the individual self is strongly differentiated from other selves and from the environment, and much emphasis is placed on individual autonomy and agency. In other parts of the world the self is experienced in more merged family and community identities and is also rooted strongly in the immediate physical environment in which the individual, and possibly generations of her ancestors, have lived. In advocating a 'revisioning' of the highly autonomous and separate concept of self put forward in traditional person-centred theory, Len Holdstock says of concepts of the self found outside the West:

> a common factor would appear to underlie the approach to self in most of the world's cultures. This common factor seems to be the socio-centric or embedded self, not the bounded masterful self.
>
> (Holdstock, 1993, p. 242)

When the organism is subjected to trauma it is overwhelmed by the environment, and the sense of self is seriously damaged or temporarily lost. The trauma cannot be explored without being placed in its context and without the environment in which it has happened being acknowledged. This is as much the case with a road accident as with war trauma and genocide. It is even more crucial when the individual's identity is already closely enmeshed with the community identity of a persecuted group.

Trauma suffered as the intentional outcome of human action in large and violent political movements undermines the individual's sense of self in a particularly profound way. There is a merging of the individual self into the mass political identity of the persecuted:

> in situations of mass violence and persecution, individuality is rendered totally insignificant. The erstwhile individual person disappears into a merged persecutory context. He or she ceases to exist.
>
> (Blackwell, 2005, p. 50)

I bring to my work a feminist perspective and an awareness of the continuing impact of colonialism and racism on individuals' lives and relationships across the globe. Understanding the oppressive social forces that interact with and determine personal histories can reduce shame and release feelings such as anger and grief, enhancing rather than detracting from exploration of the client's complex relational and intrapsychic issues.

Some refugee clients seek counselling for specific personal issues in their interpersonal relationships, their past histories, or their feelings about themselves, much as other clients. But the vast majority are struggling with the pain of traumatic experiences that are inseparable from the social and political contexts in which they occurred. This pain continues on their arrival in the UK, as their initial wave of relief at being in a place of safety is replaced by the realisation that real sanctuary is rarely granted. The continuing insecurity, powerlessness and vulnerability to assault and violation by others they feel as a result of the protracted asylum application process and their interim status as non-citizens in any country, is expressed in physical and somatic symptoms as well as intellectually. The impersonal external forces of the state take on a concrete physical reality for them and are often perceived and related to as actual individual persecutors. Experiences of being disbelieved and having their stories rejected by immigration judges and tribunals are experienced as personal insults and betrayals. The potential for ordinary police officers and civil servants to become at any moment effectively their jailers and executioners is a live and ever-present reality for the hundreds of asylum seekers who have to sign at police stations every month in order for the Immigration Service to keep track of them and be able to move to detain and deport them at any chosen moment.

In working with people inhabiting this state of suspended animation, in which they are unable to work, unable to participate in society, unable to contemplate a future beyond the chilling sight of the next Home Office letter lying on the mat, I have to be mindful at all times of this context and have to position it at the core of the work. Many of my clients feel they have no place in the world; in a profound and pervasive way at all levels of their being they are homeless and stateless. Renos Papadopoulos of the Tavistock Clinic explains this sense of homelessness in the following way:

> loss of home is not just about the conscious loss of the family home with all its material, sentimental and psychological values, but it is of a much more fundamental and primary kind and it creates a disturbance (called here 'nostalgic disorientation') which is closer to 'ontological insecurity', 'existential anxiety'. . . The shared themes of these conditions are a deep sense of a gap, a fissure, a hole, an absence, a lack of confidence in one's own existence and consequently in 'reading life' which leads to a particular kind of frozenness.
>
> (Papadopoulos, 2002, p. 18)

The client's journey

I will now describe the case of a client who came to me in an acute state of alienation, existential angst, and what Papadopoulos has called 'frozenness', or what Embleton Tudor and Tudor refer to in this volume as 'constriction'. In my work with this client I was unaware of the impact of some of my own feelings and motivations in the work, and I also misread at a particular point certain aspects of the client's traumatised state, leading to a dangerous enactment of his original trauma.

Albert fled to Britain from a central African country following attacks on his family and a period of detention without trial. He had seen his father killed by soldiers in front of him, and had been captured himself and subjected to abusive and degrading torture in detention. He was virtually catatonic when I first encountered him. In a profound state of shock, his organism and sense of self had been so profoundly violated, he said of himself, 'I feel like an animal, not a human being'. The truth of his story was not denied by the Home Office, but he was refused asylum on the grounds that, firstly, he was too insignificant a player to fear further political persecution if returned to his country; secondly, his country was judged to be currently safe and at peace despite serious internal security problems and widespread human rights violations; and, thirdly, although he was severely depressed, he was not entitled to asylum on humanitarian grounds because there were deemed to be adequate mental health services in his country of origin.

Our work together was very slow, as Albert was only able to speak very little and very slowly at first and had difficulty taking in anything that was said to him. This was not to do with any difficulty with the English language, as he was fluent in English, the official language of his country of origin. It was to do with his traumatised and constricted mental state. The descriptions given by Embleton Tudor and Tudor of the hyperarousal, constriction, dissociation and helplessness present in the traumatised person capture exactly my experience of Albert. Perceptual constriction, designed to focus on the threat at a time of extreme danger and shut out other awareness, can persist in someone suffering the effects of repeated or prolonged trauma and can make it difficult for them to hear others clearly or attend to ordinary social interactions. In time I learnt that I didn't need to repeat my questions to Albert; he had usually heard the first time but needed a long interval in which to digest the material and formulate a response. I tried to tune into his speech and adapt my own. I worked at silencing all my assumptions and expectations and becoming very still in my body and mind in order to receive his bewilderment and pain, articulated in sparse, compelling sentences. He often took time to arrive and to 'meet' me, but I always felt in psychological contact with him, both when he communicated directly, through a look or a volunteered comment, and when he was lost in his own thoughts but indicating, through the posture and turn of his body towards me, that he was aware of my presence.

Both his GP and I experienced Albert's slow-motion process as a little like someone slowly coming back to life. He had an equally trusting relationship with both of us. Much of my work with refugees is in a therapeutic partnership, sometimes with a GP, sometimes an interpreter, or sometimes with a mental health worker from a secondary care team specialising in transcultural work. Working in this way involves careful negotiation of boundaries and requires a shared and very explicit understanding of confidentiality between all parties. Blackwell observes that therapists working with refugees often transgress the usual confidentiality boundaries they hold with other clients. In doing so we collude with and replay the intrusion of the state, both the country of origin and the UK, into the individual's private space. Because their private trauma and humiliation has been told in Home office interviews, tribunals, health screenings and advice surgeries, many times over, it is in danger of becoming public property, perpetuating the violated boundaries of the original trauma (Blackwell, 2005, p. 78).

As Albert began to speak more fluently of his experiences, he started to contact the terror and grief he felt in relation to his father's death in front of him, and the loss of his mother and siblings, whom he believed to have been killed in the raid when he was captured. He talked about having terrible nightmares in which he was back in the place of his torture and incarceration again. He lived in constant terror of being deported to the site of his original trauma and falling into the hands of the security forces of his country again. He spoke of suicidal feelings and of a plan to drown himself, imagining drowning would be like falling asleep, sinking into a peace he could not find in his present life. This evoked strongly conflicting feelings in me: anxiety for his safety, a desire to rescue and instil hope, alongside a collusive identification with his search for a release from the unbearable pain of his memories and flashbacks. One day he told me that he had bought a rope to hang himself with, and he kept looking at it in his room. He was both frightened of it and reassured by it, as a kind of insurance policy giving him a quick way out if he needed it. I reflected with him on what his telling me might mean about his need to share the burden of his despair and asked him how he would feel if I looked after the rope for him for a while, on the understanding that it was still his. He said he would like this a lot and went straight home and brought the rope into the clinic for me the same day.

Although calm in the session, I was very shaken by these events and arranged to speak to my supervisor the next day. We explored what it meant for me to have taken such an active custodial role in relation to my client's suicide plan and what it meant for me to be doing this in the context of a multidisciplinary team, where the ultimate responsibility for patient welfare remains with the doctors. At that point my focus was very much on the immediate sense I had of needing to establish some safety for Albert. I think we recognised that he could have got another piece of rope at any time, and this was a symbolic step for him towards being held. As we talked it through I realised I had a duty to share with Albert's GP both that he had had a suicide plan and means to carry it out, and the action I had taken in relation to this. I decided that the initial confidentiality agreement I had made with Albert allowed me to do this, as it included a provision for talking to others to prevent him from harm. I was not sure he had taken in this agreement at the time we made it, because of his traumatised state in our initial meetings, but in agreeing to give me the rope, he had clearly been asking for help in keeping himself safe and alive, and I could not provide that alone. I knew he had a sense of his GP and me holding him jointly, so I shared with her what had happened. The next time I saw him I explained what I had done, and he confirmed that his own understanding of confidentiality was that his doctor and I carried a shared responsibility for supporting him through his bleakest moments. It seemed to my supervisor and me that Albert's choice to bring the rope to me, and my act of receiving the rope and subsequent 'holding' of it for him, represented in a concrete way for Albert the symbolic protection and containment which both his GP and I had been offering.

Over subsequent weeks he talked less of killing himself, and whenever we mentioned the rope he was reassured that it was with me. Although my taking the rope at that moment averted a crisis, I later became uneasy about having custody of it; it felt sinister and dangerous, as if I had a gun in my drawer, although I kept telling myself it was no different from a length of rope I might take camping or use as a skipping rope for children. As Albert improved in his functioning, became more fluent and articulate in his speech, and began to engage a little with the world, I began to feel uncomfortably powerful holding the rope, like a teacher who had confiscated something for a child's own good. He was feeling more positive, had started going to college, was safe and comfortable in his accommodation, and had a new solicitor who was exploring the possibility of putting together a fresh asylum claim for him. All these were changes facilitated by me, but as Albert took them on, I began to experience them as signs of Albert extending himself into the world, and I lost sight of his persisting 'intension', or internal constriction. I began to attribute to him more agency than in reality he had, and I wanted to give him back some control. My unease was linked to my guilt at having so much power in the relationship and so much power in the world in relation to his extreme powerlessness. But it was an unarticulated guilt that was blocking some of my ability to perceive him accurately. In wanting to support his independence from me, I may have lost sight too early of the parental holding he had chosen in entrusting the rope to me.

We had been working together for some months in a primary care setting, where the average contract I offered clients was around 12 weeks, agreed as a benchmark because much of the work is with interpreters and considered generous for primary care. We negotiated an ending, and in our penultimate session discussed the rope. I asked him if he wanted it back as it was his, or if he wanted me to throw it away. He asked for it back as he said he wanted to get rid of it himself.

Some weeks later I met him in the surgery waiting room and he asked if he could see me. I was very busy and about to go on holiday so I could only give him an appointment for a time after my return from holiday. As we were in a crowded public place with other patients and staff milling around us, I didn't ask him if he still had the rope. He didn't argue with the appointment time. This was not surprising, as the trauma he had experienced had produced in him a sense of helplessness and extreme passivity in the face of new threats or crises. When I tried to check if he could manage to wait that long, he said it was fine. As we appeared to have met only by chance, I did not think his need was urgent. If I had reflected on this I might have reconnected with what I knew of his passivity, his lack of confidence and his frozenness, and noticed that even to ask for an appointment was extraordinarily proactive on his part. In fact it was a sign of desperation.

When I returned from holiday and we eventually met, he told me that the day he came in to ask for an appointment with me he had gone home and set up the rope to hang himself in his room, testing it on the light fixing and anchoring one end to something on the door. He had lain in his bed looking at it for a day and two nights trying to decide when to hang himself. Then, on the second morning, he had taken it all down and put the whole length of rope in the bin. I was deeply shocked, and my understanding of our relationship underwent an instant and profound shift. We talked about how easily I had overlooked his request for help and completely missed his desperation. I remembered then how he had talked before about waiting helplessly to be killed each day he was in detention, having seen others being killed in front of him, and how all he wanted was for the agony to be over, the decision made. I began to wonder if my missing the urgency of his request had been interpreted as the passing of the death sentence that gave permission for him to execute himself. He was not sure himself that this was what had happened. He was only clear that his failure to get an appointment to see me immediately had been followed by him rigging up the noose. He was unable to say what he had been thinking or feeling, only what he did, and I was left feeling that I had possibly slipped into the role of his judge and executioner.

What happened then, as he describes it, was a refusal that rose up inside him to carry out the sentence he felt had been passed, a refusal to be his own executioner. The extremity of what could be interpreted as my abandonment of responsibility seemed to have stimulated him to take control of his own fate and revoke the sentence, opting for life and refusing to collude with his oppressors, including me.

The enactment of guilt

I was profoundly shocked by the role I had unwittingly been playing in the enactment of this trauma in our relationship. By offering to look after the rope for him I had thought we were in a partnership, having made a deal together to protect him from killing himself. After discovering what he had been through while I was away, I started to feel that, in taking the rope originally, I had taken the keys to the jail and had assumed the power of his jailer, judge and executioner. At the point when I returned the rope to him I thought I was responding to my experience of him growing and changing, and I believed he could cope with the responsibility of disposing of it. But he ended up keeping it as an insurance policy against being overwhelmed again. When he did become overwhelmed it seemed that he had come back to see me to know if he was to live or should contemplate dying. When I was unable to see him or hold him, he understood that he was to die. I had no awareness that this was the process I might be in, not until afterwards. This was partly at least because I was unaware of the impact of my own motivations in my relationship with him. In our encounter there was a process for me of quite strong identification with the role of rescuer or saviour, as identified by Stephen Karpman in his concept of the Drama Triangle (Karpman, 1968). This was motivated by my need to atone for my privileged position by 'saving' another less privileged than myself. The powerful guilt I felt, both as a British citizen and as a child of immigrants who had 'made it' to statehood successfully where others were now failing daily in front of me, set me on a mission to rescue that I was only dimly aware of as being a mission. Renos Papadopoulos highlights such motivation in his reflections on therapeutic work with refugees:

> One of the most difficult dynamics in working with refugees is the closed system of victim-saviour that refugees and therapists can easily co-construct . . . However, this system is not limited to the dyad of victim-saviour because saviours do not save victims without an attempt to protect them from their violators. Thus, the triangle of victim-saviour-violator tends to keep perpetuating itself creating endless variations with different people in the same roles.
>
> (Papadopoulos, 2002)

My attachment to the rescuer role with Albert blocked me from seeing either the possibility that I might become the persecutor, or the extent to which, in taking the rescuer position, I had left Albert in a powerless and dependent victim place where he was vulnerable to further persecution. The enactment of trauma in therapy that arises out of experiences of torture and state persecution can invest the therapist with either the omnipotence of the guard or torturer, or the mantle of the rescuer. Both are seductive processes for the therapist and involve the adoption by the client of postures of extreme passivity and assiduous compliance, combined with hyper-vigilance.

What is interesting about this enactment is that in the end, when a rescuer was not forthcoming, Albert broke the triangle himself by becoming his own rescuer. We could equally see in my failure to see him immediately on that day a powerful communication that he was released from any potential involvement in the 'triangle'. It may be that at that point I stepped out of the role of rescuer and conveyed to him my instinctive trust in his actualising process, that 'forward-moving tendency of the human organism' that Rogers claims the therapist 'relies on most deeply and fundamentally' (Rogers, 1951, p. 489). In staying with what I had been experiencing of him as a survivor rather than a victim, it is possible that I conveyed to him that the choice was his: to contemplate hanging himself, or to choose to live. He went away and tested out these alternatives for himself and chose life. There is a fine line between the potential for damage and the potential for facilitation and growth in a therapist's 'not knowing', and a fine line between a mistake resulting from naivety or complacency, and an instance of therapist fallibility producing a deep shift in the client and the relationship. Given what followed in his life, there is also the question of whether for him to have killed himself would have been a mistake or the profoundest wisdom.

Postscript

In February 2007 Albert was detained in a police cell when, like hundreds of other people seeking asylum all over the country, he went to his monthly signing at a police station. He was not allowed to collect any of his belongings, but a police officer went to his bedsit to retrieve his medication. He was pronounced fit to travel by a police surgeon, and the next day he was driven to Heathrow and deported to his country of origin carrying only his packet of anti-psychotic medication.

References

Blackwell, D. (2005) *Counselling and Psychotherapy with Refugees*. London: Jessica Kingsley.

Clarkson, P. (1996) *The Bystander (An End to Innocence in Human Relationships?)*. London: Whurr.

Cooper, A. & Rendall, S. (2002) Strangers to ourselves. In R. K. Papadopoulos (ed.) *Therapeutic Care for Refugees: No Place Like Home* (pp. 239–252). London: Karnac.

Holdstock, L. (1993) Can we afford not to revision the person-centred concept of self? In D. Brazier (ed.) *Beyond Carl Rogers* (pp. 229–252). London: Constable.

Karpman, S. (1968) Fairy tales and script drama analysis. *Transactional Analysis Bulletin*, 7(26): 39–43.

Papadopoulos, R. K. (ed.) (2002) *Therapeutic Care for Refugees: No Place Like Home*. London: Karnac.

Rogers, C. R. (1951) *Client-Centred Therapy*. London: Constable.

Rogers, C. R. (1957) The necessary and sufficient conditions of therapeutic personality change. *Journal of Consulting Psychology*, 21: 95–103.

Rogers, C. R. (1967) *On Becoming a Person*. London: Constable.

12 Chronic and acute enactment

The passive therapist and the perverse transference

Christina Wieland

The term enactment refers to an acting-out (or acting-in) by both the therapist and the patient and is often referred to as a moment at which the therapist departs from his usual neutrality and his interpretative stance and resorts to some sort of action (verbal or otherwise) It often refers to some dramatic moment in the session when the analytic container bursts and the uncontained emotions are played out as if some kind of drama were taking place. Cassorla refers to this dramatic moment as 'acute enactment', in this way distinguishing it from 'chronic enactment' (Cassorla, 2001, 2005). Chronic enactments seem to be very common and go often unnoticed but they can be the main reason for a kind of stalemate in analysis.

The term began to be used with some frequency in the 1980s (McLaughlin, 1991) and is sometimes referred to as 'countertransference enactment' (Gabbard, 1995) or 'acting out in the countertransference'. Already in 1956 Roger Money-Kyrle talked about the ordinary ways that the analyst can act out his countertransference by abandoning his analytic stance and providing reassurance or expressing impatience (Money-Kyrle, 1956) and in 1976 Sandler talked about the way the analyst adopts a complementary position in the patient's internal world (Sandler, 1976).

In his paper 'Countertransference: the emerging common ground' Gabbard reviews the debate on enactments and concludes that a consensus is emerging that enactments are inevitable but that no agreement exists as to their usefulness. A general consensus, however, seems to exist that it is the analytic work and the working through that follows an enactment which leads to the re-introjection by the patient of the part projected into the analyst and therefore to psychic change (Gabbard, 1995).

In a similar vein Betty Joseph looked at ordinary enactments that go on all the time and constitute the main body of the analysis (Joseph, 1975, 1985). Joseph has explored in great detail the patient's attempts to seduce or recruit the therapist into his 'cause' and to draw her into his defensive system. Echoing Klein she describes transference as a 'total situation' in which acting-out, acting-in and enactments are part of the moment to moment unfolding of the transference and help elucidate what cannot be verbalized. In her various papers Joseph laid bare the workings of the clinical situation and described the attempts of the patient, often successful, to draw the analyst into a particular role. If the analyst/therapist does not become aware of this process a low level enactment can be set up which leads to a kind of stalemate. This seems to correspond to what Cassorla has called chronic enactment (Cassorla, 2001, 2005).

The pull to join the patient, and therefore to enact the patient's internal world, is probably constant, Joseph says, and the analyst may only realize it after he has listened to his own voice becoming sarcastic, or becoming particularly 'understanding'. At other times the analyst may become defensive and adopt a comfortable position, and in that sense he has allowed himself to be manipulated into a position that makes both patient and analyst comfortable. Many Kleinians, notably Michael Feldman and Elisabeth Spillius (1986, 1988), Irma Brenman Pick (1985), Edna O'Shaughnessy (1983) and John Steiner (1993) among others, used the term in a similar way.

This 'role responsiveness' had already been described by Sandler in his paper 'Counter-transference and role responsiveness' (1976). In this paper Sandler pointed out that patients cast themselves in a certain role and at the same time cast the analyst/therapist in a complementary role. 'The patient's transference would thus represent an attempt by him to impose an interaction, an interrelationship . . . with the analyst/therapist in a complementary role (Sandler, 1976, p. 44). Sandler also points out that, besides his free floating attention, the analyst uses 'free floating responsiveness'. This role responsiveness can go on unnoticed for a long time, and the analyst may only become aware of this after something has been acted out. Sandler does not use the term enactment but implies that role responsiveness is a normal everyday compromise which the analyst needs to become aware of.

Often the pull by the patient to draw the therapist into his defensive world is felt by the therapist as controlling and tyrannical. The therapist's freedom is felt to be restricted and he feels manipulated. Symington describes this state of affairs in his paper 'The analyst's act of Freedom as agent of therapeutic change' (Symington, 1983). In this paper Symington refers to Bion who was consulted once by an analyst who was worried that his patient felt that he thought of her as a whore. Bion's answer was 'Why shouldn't I be allowed to come to that conclusion?' As the analyst seemed quite shocked with Bion's answer Bion continued 'the point I want to show is that there is a wish to limit my freedom of thought' (quoted in Symington, 1983). This 'act of freedom' that Symington refers to in his paper is a mental shift that frees the analyst from the tyranny of the patient's projections and makes him capable of thinking freely. It need not be an enactment, but it often is discovered through an enactment that reveals the tyranny that dominated the transference up to that point. Symington himself does not call it enactment but calls it the x phenomenon, maybe in this way differentiating it from more pathological enactments in which the analyst is drawn into repeating something. In the case he gives, the analyst's action was not a repetition but an 'act of freedom' that ended the masochistic submission of the analyst to the patient's sadism.

Such masochistic attitude on the part of the analyst is described in a paper by Cassorla who maintains that the acute enactment he describes in the paper was the result of a long established 'chronic' enactment in which the analyst allowed himself to become the masochistic partner in a sado-masochistic relationship (Cassorla, 2005).

As I have already mentioned Cassorla has distinguished two types of enactment – chronic and acute enactment (Cassorla, 2001). He maintains that acute enactment often occurs because a chronic enactment that had been happening in a particular analysis for a long time has gone unnoticed, and the acute enactment occurs in order to bring this to the attention of the therapist/analyst. Cassorla gives the example of a collusive relationship between analyst and patient that had been allowed to continue because powerful feelings of oedipal exclusion were hidden behind an illusion that the patient was included in the analyst's family. In this sense the analyst was pulled into the patient's world and had adopted a position of blindness that was comfortable to both. This chronic enactment was followed by an acute enactment when the illusory nature of the patient's belief and the analyst's collusion were revealed.

In this chapter I would like to examine a type of role responsiveness that in fact constitutes chronic enactment and can easily go unnoticed for a long time because it mimics and exploits a normal therapeutic relationship with a neutral therapist. In the therapy with patients with borderline functioning the neutrality of the therapist can be easily exploited and the therapist can be rendered impotent and passive. In fact a sado-masochistic relationship with a passive therapist is established. Often intimidation is used by the patient to keep the therapist in this state. The intimidation can take the form of a fear in the therapist that to be an active, potent therapist and explore the patient's defences is equivalent to driving the patient towards a breakdown or some other catastrophe including open violence in the consulting room. In this way the therapist often colludes in a sado-masochistic relationship under the illusion that he is containing the patient's aggression, that he is not retaliating and that he remains neutral.

I think that in analysis and psychoanalytic psychotherapy the therapist's unobtrusiveness and purely interpretative stance can be easily exploited by the sadistic/mafia part of the patient so that the therapist may find himself in a passive, impotent place. In this case a sado-masochistic scenario is played out and goes unnoticed in the name of therapy and neutrality. This happens because it is often confused with Winnicott's 'use of the object' and an attitude of non-retaliation (Winnicott, 1971), or with Freud's neutral stance, or with Bion's containing function of the analyst (Bion, 1967, 1970). In fact this is a chronic enactment where the therapist allows himself to be used as a toilet for the excrement of the patient and often even acts as a laxative. (I shall expand on the difference between a genuine containment and a sado-masochistic relationship later on.)

To illustrate this I shall introduce a clinical example. The patient is a 35-year-old woman who had spent a great deal of the first two years of her therapy challenging the therapeutic setting and provoking confrontations. Alternatively she would spend whole sessions trying to pacify me, presenting herself as a victim who had a rough time in the hands of her parents, teachers, employers and the public in general. Everybody looked down on her, and if she did not stand up for herself people would tread on her. Needless to say that any attempt on my part to concentrate on what she was doing, saying or feeling and on the events in the consulting room, was met with extreme anger and indignation because it felt to her that I was not taking seriously her complaints that people had no respect for her.

My patient was what is usually called a 'replacement child', being born two years after her mother had lost her first child – a boy who died three days after he was born. Another boy followed 18 months after her birth. The combination of being 'special' (as the surviving child), not being recognized for who she was (as her mother identified her with her dead brother), and being superseded by the next brother very early in life seemed to have been quite traumatic for her, especially as the mother seemed to have been quite depressed during her childhood. The father seemed not to have been very containing either, as he was described as aggressive, bordering on violence, and 'a 'bully'. My patient seemed to have acted as mother for her younger hyperactive brother. There seems to have been a lack of containment within the family, and my patient adopted a false caring self towards her brother. The aggression involved in this kind of false self had not been evident until she entered therapy.

The fact that she had a difficult childhood with a bullying father, a masochistic mother, and a delinquent younger brother, was always brought up as the 'cause' of how she was feeling and acting. What she wanted from me was to be totally passive and listen with empathy to the most out-rageous accusations towards employers, members of the public, friends etc. and empathize with her as to how hard done by she was and how justified her explosions of rage were. Her status as a victim was not to be ques-tioned.[1] Needless to say that when I queried the extreme nature of what she was saying I not only became the object of her fury and derision but at times I felt as if I was going to drive her to some kind of disaster – self-harm or suicide as she often threatened.

She had been a heavy drinker and had used drugs in the past. Since she began a three times a week therapy she had cut down on the amount of alcohol she consumed and abstained from hard drugs, but it was always a precarious situation with her threatening to revert to heavy drinking 'to cope with therapy' and 'to deal with the amount of rage that therapy causes me'.

In the course of the first couple of years her external life improved. She drank less, left an abusive boyfriend, got herself permanent employment and bought her own flat. But the situation in therapy continued to be very precarious and I felt as if I was walking on eggshells. She found the setting very difficult to bear. Getting up and walking restlessly around the room, examining everything, picking up books were not unusual acts. It was as if she was impersonating at times her hyperactive brother, at times her bullying father and at times her masochistic/victim mother. But more than this any vulnerability was replaced by defiance, derision and provocation. Not that small changes in her relationship with me did not take place, but they were very quickly reversed and she returned to a stance of superior dismissal of me and of the setting.

Breaks were marked by more acting-out before and after the break, but the break itself was 'OK'. Coming late, missing sessions, bringing tea or coffee to the sessions and once a sandwich were all things she did with a kind of provocative triumph on her face. 'I didn't have time to eat', or 'you don't understand how hectic my life is'. 'You sit here and pontificate but I have to rush here after a full day's work' etc. Interpretations – that she was making it very clear that she did not want or need my food; that she could not accept any rules or limits; that she was contemptuous towards the setting and towards me; that she was triumphant in her defiance – were met with more derision.

I often felt paralysed and de-skilled, sure that somebody else would find the right interpretation to contain her rage or would be more containing which would act as a catalyst for change.

One day, the second session after the Easter break, she came in and headed straight for the chair rather than the couch. From previous experience I knew this meant an obvious defiant stance. She looked at me with a sarcastic smile and proceeded to tell me how everything was shit and that therapy was not helping at all and the situation at work was getting worse – people seemed to be thinking that she was a doormat to be walked on and ignored. I attempted a transference interpretation about how she felt I ignored her during the break and how she experienced this as humiliating. She screamed at me that this was not about me – what did I think, that everything was about me? And what did I care about the break? It was a respite actually as the sessions were utterly meaningless.

She was now in a state of mind that I knew quite well. She was out of reach, cold and superior, without any awareness of any needs or any wish to communicate with me, as if she really was under the influence of a mafia boss as Rosenfeld described (Rosenfeld, 1987).

She then proceeded to delve into her rucksack and got out a can of beer. She looked at it and sized it up as if undecided what to do with it, but in a way as if she was exhibiting a superior weapon against which I would have no power but which she had not yet decided whether she would use or not. For a while she did this in the utter silence of the room. I felt quite paralysed and a bit scared.[2] Then, giving me a triumphant stare, she made a movement as if she was going to open it.

I knew, and in a split second I knew that she knew, that this was a provocation too far as if she was saying that within our 'contract' she had the right to do anything she liked – and what would I do anyway? as she had said in previous sessions.

What followed came as an utter surprise to me. I looked at her straight in the eyes and said very quietly 'Can you please put it back into your rucksack, otherwise I shall ask you to leave the room.'

I had no idea I was going to say this. It seemed to have come out of me very naturally and without effort. I was calm and non-retaliating but I had a quiet authority that surprised me as prior to this I felt very uncertain and frightened.

To my utter amazement she put the can back into her rucksack very quickly and apologized. She now looked very embarrassed and proceeded to say that she was surprised I had not thrown her out. We were then able to look at the part of her who wanted to be thrown out and cause yet another situation where she was unwanted and hard done by and where she was treated in a retaliatory manner. There was also the part of her that wished to be punished for all her attacks on me.

The following sessions consolidated a new way of working in which she was more of a participant seeking my help and listening to what I had to say, tolerating much more my voice and my different way of looking at things. We looked at what had happened, her motivation for challenging the boundaries in this way and her relief that the therapy had not been destroyed. She also began to dream and to bring her dreams to the session.

At the beginning of this period I queried what was happening, as I thought that the patient became compliant and that this new way of working was the result of a kind of total projective identification where the patient denied her aggression and envy by taking over my personality (Klein, 1955). Eventually the aggression came back but, as with Cassorla's patient (Cassorla, 2005), there was a difference in the way the aggression, and the envy and the sado-masochistic ways she adopted, were allowed to be handled in the consulting room. In fact there was more aggression towards me as a depriving mother and less contempt. The aggression was more connected to loss and the fear of loss and less to sado-masochistic defences. She was more open to listen to my interventions and to attempt, even if that was quite difficult, to look at what she was saying and doing. It was as if a tiny, thinking space had opened which allowed her to find a place from which to view the rest of herself. The third position, however precariously, was emerging. It was not that from here on everything was smooth and without problems but the establishment of the setting as a frame helped her to accept me as a therapist with whom she could be furious but from whom she was asking for help.[3]

I shall stop here and attempt to give a theoretical understanding of what had happened.

Cassorla (2001, 2005) sees acute enactment following a long-standing chronic enactment that had gone unnoticed. He reports an enactment of this sort in a session in which he responded to a very frustrating situation in the consulting room by interrupting the patient who was shouting at him by shouting louder than her and hitting his arms on his chair and saying 'that's enough'. This seemed to be the culmination of a long, frustrating and apparently endless situation which had been established between him and the patient in which the patient would moan and shout at him and endlessly complain, and nothing seemed to be good enough to satisfy her.

Cassorla proceeds to describe what followed his explosion of temper:

> I complained that she was not allowing me to speak, and that she was not listening to me. At that moment K stopped shouting and said – quite calmly, and with an air of triumph and in an ironic tone of voice – that I had shouted at her. I replied that, yes, she was right, I had really got agitated; I am only human after all. I added, 'It's just as well I am able to get agitated, otherwise you'd just make me agree with everything you say and I'd be afraid of you, dominated, and you wouldn't have an analyst any longer.
>
> (p. 706)

In the following sessions, Cassorla goes on, the constant moaning was reduced and the patient appeared less disturbed. At the beginning he thought that the patient was just compliant and afraid that she would drive the analyst mad, and he blamed himself for not being containing enough. But this view did not tally with the patient's behaviour in the consulting room. The patient appeared more coherent, more able to observe what was happening to her. He realized that the patient was not trying to protect him. She was still attacking but now there was more scope for the analyst's interpretations to be heard and to have more effect.

Cassorla realized that the enactment was not just the moment of his explosion but that an enactment had been happening long before this moment. He realized with hindsight that what he thought of as containing the patient's aggression was actually taking part in her sado-masochistic scenario and becoming the victim part of a sado-masochistic relationship. 'My reaction at the M moment was a sort of warning cry, a shout of "Enough!" against identifying with K's masochistic parts. I also became aware of those elements of mine that had become involved' (p. 707).

Thinking of the enactment that took place in my consulting room I can identify a similar situation where I erroneously thought that I was containing the patient by 'surviving' her aggression, whereas I became a masochistic object to be used, abused and derided. However I think that what my patient was asking for in that session was punishment, with her provocation to be punished, to be thrown out in disgrace, or for me to submit to her violent mafia boss and humiliate me. The situation was such that, within the sado-masochistic logic, one of us had to be punished, degraded, their dignity abolished. I think however that, in contrast, what happened was an 'act of freedom', to use Symington's words (Symington, 1983). This amounted to a sudden abolition of the terms of this enslaved relationship. In other words at that moment the third term entered the relationship. At the moment of my intervention I think I became a different kind of therapist. I became the keeper of the setting – the parent who sets limits and boundaries. The setting represents for both therapist and patient the Law – the third term – which is outside the omnipotence of both patient and analyst.

Some patients, especially borderline ones, spend a great deal of their therapy attempting to destroy the setting, which includes the therapist's place and role within it. A punishing response to this provocation through punishing interpretations or merely through angry silence or an angry tone of voice establishes and maintains the sado-masochistic relationship. A conciliatory response also maintains the sado-masochistic situation. But more importantly than this, the patient in this session went further than a painful sado-masochistic situation where the pursuit of punishment and humiliation either for the self or for the object, are the main features. I think that the patient in this situation passed over into perversion.

What happened in the session was neither a punishing, angry response/interpretation, nor was it a masochistic, or negligent /tolerating of the situation. With the benefit of hindsight I think that my response was a quiet but confident laying down the Law and establishing a benign, protective authority against the mafia and the perverse authority, i.e. establishing a mental space within which thinking could take place. My patient seemed reassured by this response, which was not what she was expecting at all. Coming from a family where the Law was established by violence or the threat of it and where lawlessness reigned outside the immediate presence of parents and teachers she seemed surprised and embarrassed as if seeing herself and what she was doing for the first time.

The patient's reaction, not only in that session but in the long run, convinced me that trust in the therapist is not just a matter of interpretation or containment but the intactness of the setting is absolutely essential. I am aware that I am stating the obvious here but I have in mind not only the gross breaches of boundaries as in this patient but all the other small, unnoticed breaches that go on – and have to go on no doubt – but which must not go on unnoticed. I am saying 'have to go on' for I think that they constitute the very substance of the transference/countertransference, and often we only become aware of them when the therapy feels stuck or unproductive despite positive noises on the part of the patient.[4]

I would like here to make another diversion into theory and try to understand theoretically the difference between containment and a sado-masochistic relationship. Symington (1983) maintains that transference consists of a creation of a 'corporate personality' which is constituted by parts of the patient and parts of the analyst and that the therapeutic process proceeds by the analyst slowly becoming aware of this new beast and slowly detaching himself through interpretation and occasionally through 'an act of freedom'. In this sense the established sado-masochistic relationship with my patient was a corporate personality and my intervention in the session mentioned above was an 'act of freedom' that allowed the whole situation to enter into consciousness and be available for thinking.

Another model that can be used to understand what happened is Betty Joseph's idea of 'recruitment'. As already stated Joseph showed that patients constantly attempt, and often succeed, to 'recruit' the analyst into their defensive world. In this sense enactments are very common in analysis, and psychoanalytic psychotherapy and the therapeutic effects consist of understanding the enactments. John Steiner goes a step further, for he believes that enactments are not just about the therapist being drawn into some illusory belief of the patient but into a whole pathological organization, or a 'psychic retreat', and when this happens he 'becomes unable to stay aloof and uncorrupted by perverse seduction and intimidation' (Steiner, 1993, p. 104).

I think Steiner's drawing attention to the organized nature of the perverse system goes to the heart of the problem and to the impossibility of containment when dealing with pathological organizations or 'psychic retreats'. Steiner himself tries to address the problem of containment in his paper 'Analyst-centred and patient-centred interpretations'. He maintains that some patients cannot tolerate patient-centred interpretations and one way of getting around this problem is by offering an analyst-centred interpretation to the patient, i.e. describing to the patient how he perceives the analyst. The trouble is that for some patients, including the patient described in this paper, no interpretations seem possible. Britton found another way of working with patients who cannot tolerate interpretations by thinking his own thoughts in silence side by side with the patient's input. Britton thinks that in this way a third space is established and tolerated which eventually leads to changes in the relationship between analyst and patient and to changes in the patient's internal world (Britton, 1998).

Britton's discovery goes to the heart of containment which uses thinking to create a third term – a new object. It is important to note that the analyst does not get involved in a sado-masochistic relationship but allows himself to take in the patient's thoughts, feelings and impulses and to have his own thoughts about them. He also digests his own impulse and urge to make an interpretation. This refusal to be drawn into the patient's pathological organization may sound easy but in practice it is not, and it is with instances when the therapist becomes involved and enslaved in it that he discovers its power and seductiveness. Britton is clear here that for some patients this is the only possible containment.

Pathological organization is not like a raw impulse or emotion but an organized system which maintains a certain equilibrium for the patient, and because of this I think that containment is impossible. In this sense when a pathological organization is in operation containment is irrelevant because the organization itself acts as a container.

The concept of the container was developed by Bion (1962, 1963, 1970) and it is closely connected to his concepts of reverie and alpha-function. In fact when he introduces the idea of container/contained towards the end of his book *Learning from Experience* he uses the same example that he used in his paper 'Theory of thinking' (Bion, 1967) when he talked about the mother's reverie and alpha function. The example has to do with the baby's fears projected into the breast (or mother's mind) and, having been allowed to remain there for a while, are felt to be modified 'in such a way that the object that is re-introjected has become tolerable to the infant's psyche' (p. 90).

In this example it is clear that what is projected into the mother's mind is an unmanageable emotion which comes under what Bion called beta-elements. For Bion beta-elements are raw impulses or raw emotions which are felt to be unbearable for the baby until the mother digests them and gives them back to the baby. What is given back is something that now has meaning and can be stored in the mind. In this exchange between mother and baby a transformation takes place, of meaningless or unbearable beta-elements to meaningful and bearable alpha-elements. When the baby takes back his own emotions digested and de-toxified, so to speak, he also takes in mother's capacity to digest emotions – the mother's alpha function. In this way mental and emotional growth takes place in the baby, and the baby's alpha function eventually emerges.

But Bion made another distinction – one between beta-elements and beta-screen. About the beta-screen he says that it is 'coherent and purposive' and is to be distinguished from 'confused states resembling a dream' (1962, p. 22) although it has some resemblance with them. A bit later he expands on beta-screen:

> An interpretation that the patient was pouring out a stream of material intended to destroy the analyst's psycho-analytic potency would not seem out of place. Equally apt would be an interpretation that the patient was concerned to withhold rather than to impart information.
>
> (p. 23)

It is important to note here that when he refers to the beta-screen Bion does not refer to the baby but to the patient. This is an important distinction to make because a beta-screen is, as he explains, an organized structure which is created by the reversal of alpha function and it cannot exist in a very young baby. We can say that it has similarities with the concepts of pathological organization and psychic retreat (Steiner, 1993).

Bion goes on to describe the destructive nature of the beta-screen but also its durability. Its destructiveness refers to the destruction of alpha function and its durability is due to the appropriation of the properties of alpha function such as consistency and organization. But in the creation of the beta-screen the world is, so to speak, upside down. Instead of the normal direction of transformation of beta-elements into alpha-elements we now have a 'reversal of alpha function'. This reversal however is not back to beta-elements but into the beta-screen (p. 25).

This is an important difference that needs to be understood if we want to understand what Bion meant by containment. For Bion explains that the objects created by the reversal of alpha function are the same as the ones he described in an earlier paper as 'bizarre objects':

> Reversal of alpha-function means the dispersal of the contact-barrier and is quite compatible with the establishment of objects with the characteristics I once ascribed to bizarre objects . . . the reversal of alpha-function did in fact affect the ego and therefore did not produce a simple return to beta-elements, but objects which differ in important respects from the original beta-elements which had no tincture of the personality adhering to them. . . . The reversal of alpha-function does violence to the structure associated with alpha-function.
>
> (p. 25)

To speak of containment when the beta-screen and the bizarre objects are in operation does not make sense. The patient when functioning under the influence of the beta-screen does not seek understanding but rejoices in misunderstanding, in creating the circumstances under which no understanding or containment is possible. I think my patient's provocations can be understood as attempts to destroy understanding and therefore avoid pain.

It is important that when Bion talks about containment he refers to raw impulses such as fear of dying in the baby, i.e. a primary emotion (this refers to beta-elements not to beta-screen). In this sense containment is the medium by which beta-elements are transformed into alpha elements. Bion differentiates between different types of container/contained relationship. In fact when we talk of containment in the session we usually refer to what Bion called the 'commensal' relationship in which both container and contained are permeated with emotion and change takes place in the direction of growth. On the other hand Bion talked about the case in which container and contained are 'disjoined or denuded of emotion (and) they diminish in vitality' (p. 90). But Bion described also a highly pathological relationship between container and contained – one that is permeated by envy and characterized by the denudation of both container and contained. This is the case of a kind of negative universe. The interaction between a minus container and a minus contained results in 'an envious stripping or denudation of all good and is itself destined to continue the process of stripping . . . as existing, in its origin, between two personalities' (p. 97).

I think that this describes the interaction between my patient and myself before the session when the acute enactment took place. What I had taken as containing the patient's aggression was in fact a relationship between a minus container and a minus contained and had led to denuding the therapy of all goodness.

When my patient was in the grip of her cold, superior side she was absolutely denuded of emotion or was full of some kind of spurious, stale emotion – bitterness, contempt, a wish to destroy and a determination to be punished.[5] I think that she manufactured these emotions – or rather states of mind – as a way of avoiding her real emotions of helplessness and vulnerability on the one hand and her envy of me as a nourishing therapist on the other. They constituted in fact her psychic retreat. Under these circumstances to talk about containment makes no sense at all. I could not contain what in fact was a well-maintained pathological organization that acted as a perverse container itself. Or to put it another way – to contain her at those moments is tantamount to maintaining the pathological organization and perhaps giving it legitimacy. My belief that I was in fact containing the patient's aggression was not just wishful thinking but had the negative result of leading to the denudation of all goodness in the therapy because it led to the perversion of the transference. In this sense, under the illusion that I was containing the patient, I had colluded with the patient in perverting the setting.

I think that the patient's state of bitterness, contempt and humiliation was a beta-screen – an organized, enduring state that avoided direct relating to me and to others in a way that would be new, and therefore, unpredictable. She repeated again and again the same scenario which, if painful, was at least known and predictable.

The differentiation between beta-elements and beta-screen is, I think, also made by Steiner in a different way and a different language, when he differentiates between the paranoid-schizoid position and the psychic retreat (Steiner, 1993). Both Bion and Steiner make the same point, i.e. that the paranoid/schizoid position is an unorganized state whereas the psychic retreat and the beta-screen are organized states with the purpose of defying vulnerability, dependence and psychic pain.

With patients who spend most of their life in psychic retreats enactments, both chronic and acute, are inevitable. There are however acute enactments, which we can say, with hindsight, are in the service of growth because they abolish the terms of a perverse transference (like Cassorla's example and I believe my intervention), and there are those which can damage the patient and the therapy. Maybe we hear less about the latter because therapists are less likely to report them publicly. The differentiating feature between the two might be what Symington called 'the analyst's act of freedom' which I referred to above (Symington, 1983).

In the case of Cassorla's patient he reports that after the acute enactment when he shouted at the patient, she was still aggressive, she would still attack him, but her capacity to listen to his interpretations and take them in improved, i.e. containment took place. Cassorla sees his acute enactment as a 'resource', in the sense that it led to understanding the chronic enactment that had been happening for a long time and had been ignored by him.

In the case of my patient what I thought was containing was actually a participation in a perverse situation. I was like the parent who turns a blind eye to the perversion in the family and consoles herself that if she gives enough love and understanding to the child it will all turn out all right. By saying what I said, I became the parent who says that there are certain things that are not digestible and we should not try to swallow them. Like sexual abuse the perversion of the setting oversteps a boundary. The action itself has to stop before any change can happen.

I think that by acting as I did – and there is no doubt this was action – I reinstated, to the relief of the patient, the Law and the third space. Like Cassorla's patient she continued to be aggressive and challenge my ability to contain her to the limit, but the space that had opened remained a third space where thinking could take place. Other pieces of acting-out followed, and the oscillation between being in the retreat and enticing me to join her in the hopeless repetition of the sado-masochistic world on the one hand, and being out, vulnerable, sometimes gentle and sometimes aggressive in her needy state, was repeated many times. My ability to distinguish between the two also increased and it became less likely that I would confuse a participation in a sado-masochistic scenario with containment.

In this chapter I have attempted to describe a clinical situation where the therapist's passivity and neutrality can be exploited by the perverse elements of the patient, and the therapist can be drawn into a chronic sado-masochistic relationship which can culminate in a piece of perverse acting-out that seeks to denude the therapeutic setting of any dignity. I argued that organized sado-masochistic states and perverse situations are not open to containment and that in these situations the re-establishment of the setting is the primary task. In this sense the intact setting *is* the containing element. The differentiation by the therapist during the session and at any given moment between psychic retreats – perverse or otherwise – and primary emotions i.e. beta-elements is, I believe, of primary importance for the course of therapy.

Notes

1 One could say that what was repeated was the relation between her masochistic mother and her bullying mother, or between her as a helpless child and the bullying father. However I think that her helplessness was absent from the sessions and what was apparent was a whole sado-masochistic scenario through which she exerted control over me and of which I eventually became aware.

2 With hindsight I think that the fear was related to the challenge I was about to make – a challenge of the sado-masochistic organization and the fear of the violence that kept it in place. I also think that my fear was also my patient's fear of the tyrant inside and also the fear of challenging this part of herself. This would also explain that my anxiety subsided once I made my intervention.

3 We could say, of course, that the chronic enactment has helped us understand the type and the extent to which the pathological organization had a grip on her and how it could be described after it had been enacted and lived by both of us. My

own intimidation was, I believe, an accurate description of the terror that the mafia-like organization exerted on her. In this sense I do not believe that an enactment is a repetition of a trauma but it is the externalization of the *response* to a trauma. What is acted out and participated in by both actors in the consulting room is the pathological organization that is the response to the trauma of her childhood (not the trauma itself) and an attempt on the part of the patient to contain the trauma.

4 The moment at which the acute enactment took place is also very important. The patient's provocation was extreme and my response was outside the usual neutral/analytic stance. It is as if the patient wanted to provoke a showdown and ask the question of who is in charge of the setting, me or her. The answer was outside this sado-masochistic dichotomy for I opted, quite unconsciously, for the third term, the setting, the Law, thus putting an end to the rule of tyranny.

5 The difference between a genuine and a 'spurious' emotion is that the first enhances the link with the therapist (or with a part of the patient) and leads to more integration in the patient. A spurious emotion is churned up, so to speak, by the patient in isolation and has either a blaming or a seductive quality. It is also quite repetitive in nature and seeks to avoid either understanding or change in the relationship between the patient and the therapist.

References

Bion, W. R. (1962) *Second Thoughts*. London: Karnac.

Bion, W. R. (1963) *Elements of Psychoanalysis*. London: Karnac.

Bion, W. R. (1967). *Learning from Experience*. London: Karnac.

Bion, W. R. (1970) *Attention and Interpretation*. London: Karnac.

Brenman Pick, I. (1985) Working through in the countertransference. In *Melanie Klein Today*, vol. 2. London & New York: Routledge.

Britton, R. (1998) *Belief and Imagination*. London: Karnac.

Cassorla, R. M. S. (2001) Acute enactment as a resource in disclosing a collusion between the analytic dyad. *International Journal of Psychoanalysis*, 82: 1155–1170.

Cassorla, R. M. S. (2005) From bastion to enactment: the 'non-dream' in the theatre of analysis. *International Journal of Psychoanalysis*, 86: 699–719.

Gabbard, G. O. (1995) Countertransference: the emerging common ground. *International Journal of Psychoanalysis*, 76: 475–487.

Joseph, B. (1975) The patient who is difficult to reach. In *Psychic Equilibrium and Psychic Change*. London & New York: Routledge, 1989.

Joseph, B. (1985) Transference: the total situation. In *Psychic Equilibrium and Psychic Change*. London & New York: Routledge, 1989.

Joseph, B. (1989) *Psychic Equilibrium and Psychic Change*. London & New York: Routledge.

Klein, M. (1955) On identification. In *Envy and Gratitude and Other Works*. London: The Hogarth Press, 1975.

McLaughlin, J. T. (1991) Clinical and theoretical aspects of enactment. *Journal of the American Psychoanalytic Association*, 39: 595–614.

Money-Kyrle, R. (1956) Normal countertransference and some of its deviations. In *Melanie Klein Today*, vol. 2. London & New York: Routledge.

O'Shaugnessy, E. (1983) The invisible Oedipus complex. In *Melanie Klein Today*, vol. 2. London & New York: Routledge, 1988.

Rosenfeld, H. (1987) Destructive narcissism and the death instinct. In *Impasse and Interpretation*. London & New York: Routledge.

Sandler, J. (1976) Countertransference and role-responsiveness. *International Journal of Psychoanalysis*, 3: 43–47.

Steiner, J. (1993) *Psychic Retreats*. London & New York: Routledge.

Symington, N. (1983) The analyst's act of freedom as agent of therapeutic change. *International Journal of Psychoanalysis*, 10: 283–291.

Winnicott, D. W. (1971) The use of the object and relating through identifications. In *Playing and Reality*. Harmondsworth, UK: Pelican Books.

Author index

Subject index